Siborne's 1815 Campaign: Volume 1 The March to Waterloo

NAPOLEON RETURNS

Siborne's 1815 Campaign: Volume 1
The March to Waterloo
Gilly, Ligny & Quatre Bras

William Siborne

LEONAUR

Siborne's 1815 Campaign: Volume 1 The March to Waterloo
Gilly, Ligny & Quatre Bras
by William Siborne
Edited by the Leonaur Editors

FIRST EDITION

Leonaur is an imprint of Oakpast Ltd

Copyright in this form © 2015 Oakpast Ltd

ISBN: 978-1-78282-435-0 (hardcover)
ISBN: 978-1-78282-436-7 (softcover)

http://www.leonaur.com

Publisher's Notes

Contents

Introduction by the Leonaur Editors

There have been many books published concerning the Battle of Waterloo during the 200 years which have elapsed since the battle was fought. Leonaur publish a number of them and, inevitably, in this the bi-centenary year of these famous events even more volumes have appeared from 'new' perspectives to 'coffee-table' picture books to meet the demands of a contemporary readership interested in the subject to one degree or another.

It is fair to say that many modern readers gravitate towards these books. The 'new' has its attractions in familiarity of form, presentation and language. The understandable fact is that for many readers the mannered writing style of the early nineteenth century can be somewhat 'heavy going' despite its obvious authenticity. Most people naturally find it easier and preferable to read a narrative written in a more contemporary style.

Inevitably, modern writers have to entirely refer to earlier writers on this subject. Every now and again a personal memoir, long forgotten in a dusty attic, may miraculously be discovered, but the main facts of the Battle of Waterloo have been well established for some time. Those who fought and survived the Battle of Waterloo in 1815 have long ago passed away and so there is no fundamental new source material now likely to emerge.

That brings us fairly to the author of the book you are now holding. This is not the place for a biography of William Siborne—potted or otherwise. It is sufficient to state that this book—presented by Leonaur in a new three volume edition—was written by one who could be rightly termed, 'the godfather' of Waterloo battle histories.

Siborne knew that the conflict which brought about the downfall of Napoleon was a major landmark in world history and he made its study his life's work. Almost everyone interested in the subject is aware of his famous model and the renowned *Waterloo Letters*. Born at the close of the 18th century Siborne was ideally placed to research his subject and avail himself of the first-hand narratives of the battle's participants. This he did with a meticulous breath and depth which is now well known to most students of the period. In short—when it comes to histories the Campaign of 1815 one may justifiably claim, 'there is first Siborne and then there is everyone else!'

The reason Leonaur has elected to publish Siborne's famous work in three volumes is because—in its original single volume work—this can appear to be a tome of daunting proportions. By breaking the original text into three we have been able to add illustrations, diagrams and maps and increase the size of those present in the original work. Additionally, many people have narrowly seen the destruction of the First Empire of the French as a one-day event—the Battle of Waterloo itself. This new edition devotes one volume to the events leading to the fateful encounter from the time of the emperor's escape from Elba, one volume devoted to the battle of June 18th and a third volume to the final engagements of the campaign to the fall of Paris. So this Leonaur edition might be said to be the most comprehensive presentation of Siborne's *magnum opus* yet published because it contains material not to be found in the original edition which will significantly enhance the text. For those readers very familiar with the battle itself it offers an opportunity to separately access first rate information about the events that preceded and followed the battle proper which tends to be absent from many other works, but which here is subject to the same thoroughness of historical research for which Siborne is justifiably famous.

However, a few words of caution are in order. Siborne could, of course, be nothing other than a man of his time and that naturally reveals itself in the nature of his writings. He was a product of an age where verbosity in prose was the rule rather than the exception, but even so Siborne could excel at the verbose by almost any standard. It might be conservative to state he would not use one adjective when two would suffice. In fact, Siborne might not 'rein in' his enthusiasm after three, four or even five extraneous contributions. The Leonaur Editors have taken the liberty of 'trimming' the worse of these literary excesses in the interests of creating a more comfortable read for modern readers, but it would be impossible to eradicate every trace of the author's literary propensities without completely re-writing the original work. The rule applies in part to the use of excessively long sentences by modern standards. We trust readers will appreciate that this is, in measure, the price of authenticity and a one worth paying in the light of Siborne's intrinsic quality of historical factual content.

Siborne was not simply an author, but a military man serving in the British Army during a period when a good number of the principal participants in the events he describes were still living and holding positions of significant influence in the army, the government and in society generally.

It should be remembered that the influence these people could bring to bear in ways that could affect the lives of those who occupied a less lofty position in the social order was direct and considerably less constrained than it is today. So when reading the original text it can seem that Siborne was prone to sycophancy or it may be that he was, in the very least, treading 'carefully' when he makes reference to the activities of powerful members of the aristocracy. In the interests of a fluid narrative the Leonaur Editors have removed some of these kinds of references where they were considered to be contributing little to the historical record.

Finally, modern readers will note the absence (and probably for good reasons already stated) of comments or opinions of censure on events or individuals in the Siborne text. The Prince of Orange, for example, fairs rather better in the appraisal of his military abilities than he did in the hands of historical arbiters of later times. The famous charge of the Union Brigade, as another example, is not presented as another occasion of the British cavalry running out of control in the style that had continually exasperated the Duke of Wellington. In fact, Siborne emphasises the superiority of the Allied Cavalry performance over that of the French cavalry on the 18th June and though this is a narrow view of the entire subject of the management of the mounted arm (given the performance of the New Model was a matter of record) in this, at least, he has a relevant point.

Putting aside all these peculiarities of time and place, Siborne's remains a remarkable, unique work of history and one which is rightly very highly regarded in its field. There can be no doubt that stylistic issues aside, Siborne's text is *'meat taken closest to the bone'* because he thoroughly, directly researched and cross-referenced his facts in a way that no other author has been in a position to emulate. This book represents a huge repository of primary source material without equal on this subject.

That ultimately remains William Siborne's essential legacy. Without Siborne our knowledge of the Campaign of 1815 would be immeasurably the poorer and so we should acknowledge all subsequent historians and writers on this subject are forever in his debt.

The Leonaur Editors

CHAPTER 1

Napoleon Lands Back in France

The history of Europe records but few events so universally and so intimately involving the policy and interests of her component States, as the escape of Napoleon Buonaparte from the island of Elba, on the 26th of February 1815—his landing in France, and his again ascending, unopposed, that throne from which Louis XVIII. had fled with precipitation, upon learning the triumphal approach towards the capital of his successful and formidable rival. With the rapidity of lightning the intelligence spread itself over the whole Continent, and with all the suddenness and violence of an electric shock did it burst amidst the delegates from the different States, who were then assembled in Congress at Vienna.

This important Assembly, so unexpectedly interrupted, had been called together to deliberate upon measures of international security and prosperity. Its purpose was to attempt to solve those intricate questions of policy necessarily arising out of the various combinations, which, in the course of a general war, with but little intermission, for nearly a quarter of a century, had so fatally unhinged and dismembered and disrupted Europe.

With one accord, a fresh appeal to the sword was decided upon; the military resources of every nation were again called into requisition. From State to State the cry "To arms!" was responded to with cheerfulness and alacrity, and immense armies were put in motion towards the French frontier: all animated with the sole object and fixed determination of annihilating, for ever, the common foe whom they had already conquered; but whom, as it would then appear, they had but ineffectually humbled.

The openly declared project of the Allied sovereigns to employ all their means, and combine all their efforts, towards the accomplish-

BELGIUM
and
PART OF FRANCE
to illustrate the
CAMPAIGN OF 1815
English Miles

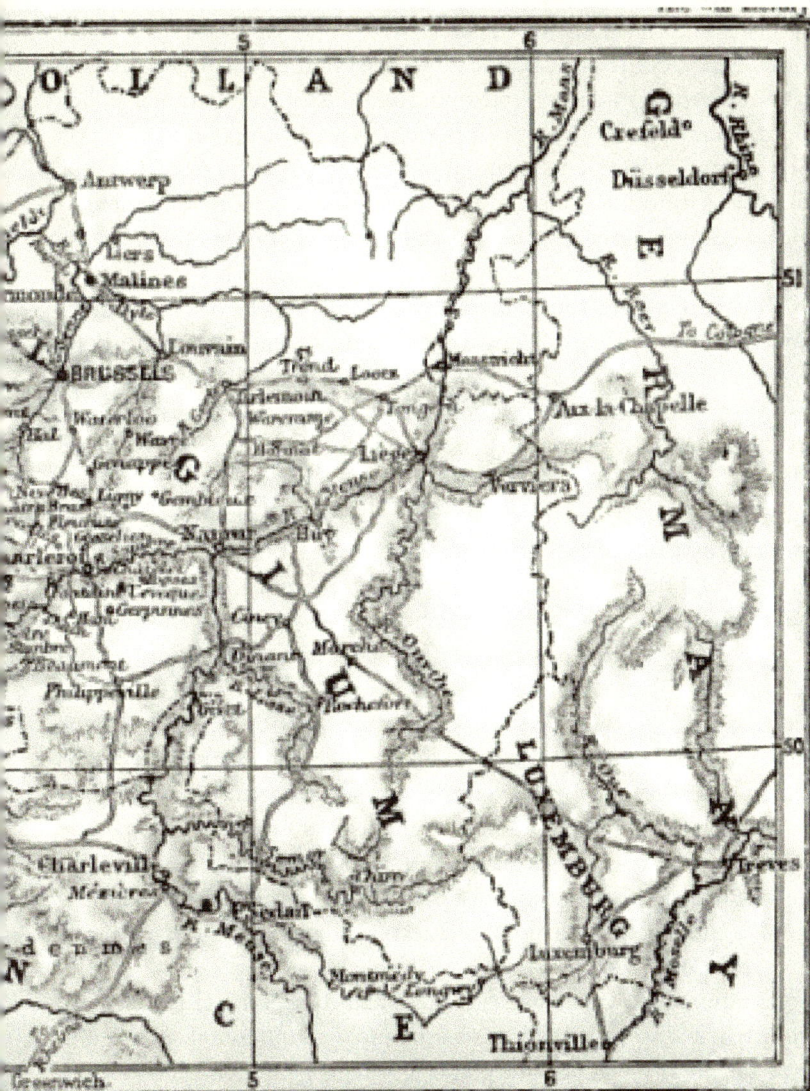

ment of the complete overthrow of the resuscitated power of Napoleon, with whom they had determined, thenceforth, to enter into neither truce nor treaty, was singularly favoured by the circumstance of their armies being still retained upon a war establishment.

The forces of the several Powers were continued on that scale, in consequence of the difficulties experienced in the Congress in dealing with and settling many perplexing questions of international policy, and moderating the warmth of the discussions that took place upon them. It was considered expedient to keep up powerful reserves, available both for home service, and for any contingencies that might arise out of combinations and revolts among those minor States, whose aversion to the new political arrangements was known.

Thus it had been found necessary to detach bodies of troops from the main bulk of the forces, in consequence of the state of the Poles placed under the protection of Russia, and of the Saxons inhabiting that portion of their country which had been ceded to Prussia. Also, in consequence of the powerful diversion, as regarded Austria, caused by the sudden irruption of Murat, King of Naples, into the north of Italy. Notwithstanding these necessary deductions it was possible to assemble, by the end of May, an efficient force of not less than 500,000 men, upon different points contiguous to the French frontier, with all the supplies necessary for the prosecution of a vigorous campaign.

The most important portion of this extensive line of frontier was undoubtedly that which fronted the Netherlands. Although it had been planned by the Allies that no advance was to be made by the troops in Belgium until the remainder of their forces had reached a line of connecting points along the French frontier, when all their armies were to march, in combined movement, upon the capital: still it was reasonably to be expected that Napoleon would not wait for the completion of this plan, but rather that he would endeavour, by a decisive effort, if not to frustrate its accomplishment, at least to diminish its efficacy.

It required no great exercise of military or political foresight to predict, that after having adopted a maturely considered disposition of force on the most important points along his general line of defence, and placed his frontier fortresses upon a respectable footing, Napoleon would open the tremendous game, upon which his crown, his political existence, and the fate of France, were now fairly staked,. He would order a bold, sudden, and resolute advance into Belgium—straining every nerve to vanquish, in detail, the Allied forces in that densely populated country; of which a vast portion was already prepared to declare in his favour.

His authority once established in Brussels, through the means of some signal triumph, the accession to his moral influence over the entire mass of the French nation would be immense. Flying to the succour of his nearest corps menaced from the banks of the Rhine by the approach of hostile forces (upon which his possession of Belgium would operate as a powerful check by the facilities thus afforded for a combined attack in front and flank), a series of successes, supported by fresh levies from the interior, might enable him even to dictate terms to the Allies.

Hence the importance of narrowly watching the Belgian frontier, and of making due preparations for meeting any attack in that quarter, was too obvious not to form a principal feature in the general plan of the Allies. Its defence was assigned to an army under the Duke of Wellington, comprising contingent forces from Great Britain, from Hanover, the Netherlands, Brunswick, and Nassau; and to a Prussian Army, under Field Marshal Prince Blücher von Wahlstadt.

At the moment of the landing of Napoleon on the French shore, the only force in the Netherlands consisted, in addition to the native troops, of a weak Anglo-Hanoverian Corps, under the command of His Royal Highness the Prince of Orange. The energy displayed by the Government of Great Britain, in engrafting upon this nucleus a powerful army, amounting at the commencement of hostilities, to about 100,000 combatants, notwithstanding the impediments and delays occasioned by the absence of a considerable portion of its troops in America, were truly surprising.

At the same time, the extraordinary supply of subsidies furnished by the British Parliament, without which not one of the armies of the Allied Sovereigns could have commenced operations, and by means of which England thus become the great lever whereby the whole of Europe was set in motion towards the attainment of the one common object, was admirably illustrative of the bold, decided, and straightforward policy of the most determined, the most indefatigable, and the most consistent, enemy of Napoleon.

Within the same period, the Prussian forces, originally limited to a corps of 30,000 men under General Count Kleist von Nollendorf, occupying the Prussian territories bounded by the Rhine, the Meuse, and the Moselle, were augmented to an effective army of 116,000 combatants.

IRELAND

WALES

ENGLAND

London

N O R T H

S E A

Ostend
Dunkirk
Lille

FLANDERS

Ghent
Brussels

R. Scheldt

Antwerp

Liège

Amiens

Sambre

Sedan

ENGLISH CHANNEL

River

Paris

Seine

River

Loire

F R A N C E

Saône

Lyons

BAY OF

BISCAY

R Garonne

R. Tarn

River Rhône

MAP OF
part of
EUROPE
showing boundaries of France
and adjoining Countries in
1815.

S P A I N

MEDI

ENGLISH MILES

50   0   100   200

H

DENMARK

River Elbe

PRUSSIA

Berlin

Hanover

POLAND

River Oder

Dresden

Elbe

LAND

River Rhine

Cologne

Aix la Chapelle

Coblenz

ARDENNES

Mayenne

P. Moselle

Thionville

Metz.

GERMANY

BAVARIA

River Danube

Vienna

Strasbourg

Munich

JURA MOUNTS

River Rhine

Bern

SWITZERLAND

BERNESE

RHÆTIC ALPS

AUSTRIA

Grenoble

NORIC ALPS

CARNIC ALPS

ADRIATIC SEA

I

Appenines

Nice

TUSCANY

Elba

CORSICA

Rome

TERRANEAN   SEA

SARDINIA

Great Britain and Prussia thus occupied the post of honour, and formed the vanguard of the mighty masses which Europe was pouring forth to seal the doom of the Napoleon dynasty.

A Russian Army, under Field Marshal Count Barclay de Tolly, amounting to 167,000 men, was rapidly traversing the whole of Germany, in three main columns. The right column, commanded by General Dochterow, advanced by Kalisch, Torgau, Leipzig, Erfurt, Hanau, Frankfort, and Hochheim, towards Mayence; the centre, commanded by General Baron Sacken, advanced by Breslau, Dresden, Zwickau, Baireuth, Nuremberg, Aschaffenburg, Dieburg, and Gross Gerau, towards Oppenheim; while the left column, commanded by General Count Langeron, took its direction along the line of Prague, Aube, Adelsheim, Neckar, and Heidelberg, towards Mannheim. The heads of the columns reached the Middle Rhine, when hostilities were on the point of breaking out upon the Belgian frontier. The intimation to these troops of another campaign in France, and of a probable in-occupation of Paris, had imparted new life and vigour to the spirit of inveterate hatred and insatiable revenge which they had so thoroughly imbibed against the French; and which had so invariably marked their career since the memorable burning of Moscow.

An Austrian Army of about 50,000 men, commanded by Field Marshal Prince Schwartzenburg, and the Army of Reserve under the Archduke Ferdinand, amounting to 40,000 men, were gradually occupying the most important points along the right bank of the Rhine, between Basle and Mannheim. In addition to this force, about 120,000 men were then assembling on the plains of Lombardy, upon the termination of the decisive Campaign against Murat; which secured the deposition of the latter, and the restoration of King Ferdinand to the throne of Naples.

Vigorous measures such as these on the part of Austria, indicated that her government, discarding alike the circumstance of a family alliance with Napoleon, and the views which had once induced it to enter into a league with him and with the Southern German States, as a security against its formidable northern neighbours, still adhered to its policy of entering into a general European compact.

The assembling also, on the Upper Rhine, of a Bavarian Army, commanded by Prince Wrede, of the Contingents of Baden and Würtemberg, under the hereditary Prince of Würtemberg, and of the troops of Hesse, amounting altogether to about 80,000 men, offered a sufficient guarantee for the line of policy espoused by the Confederated States of the Rhine.

Formidable as was the attitude assumed by the Allies towards France, and imposing as was their array of armies assembling upon her frontier; they nevertheless found their great antagonist prepared, on learning that they had determined on an irrevocable appeal to the sword, to throw away the scabbard. He assumed a bold and resolute posture of defence—armed at all points, and prepared at all hazards, either to ward off the blows of his adversaries, or to become, himself the assailant. The indefatigable exertions of Napoleon in restoring the Empire to its former strength and grandeur were really astonishing; and never, perhaps, in the whole course of the extraordinary career of that extraordinary man, did the powerful energies of his comprehensive mind shine forth with greater brilliancy and effect, than in his truly wonderful and incredibly rapid development of the national resources of France on this momentous occasion.

The truth of this assertion will be best confirmed by briefly enumerating some of the most important objects accomplished within the limited interval of three months—from his landing at Cannes, to his taking the field against the Allies.

Among them were—the complete overthrow of all obstacles in the way of his reascending the throne; the reconciliation of the several factions whose discordant views and interests had distracted the whole nation; the suppression of the insurrectionary movements in La Vendée, and the establishment of his authority over every part of the Empire; the projection of various public measures, laws, and ordinances; the remodelling of the civil and military administrations; the restoration of the army to its previous organisation under the Imperial Regime. Furthermore, the placing of the numerous fortresses of the kingdom in an efficient state; the erection of fortified works around Paris, Lyons, and other important points; the reorganisation of the National Guard *d'élite*, to the extent of 112,000 men, divided into 200 battalions, and destined principally for garrisoning the fortresses; the adoption of the most active operations in all the arsenals, and the employment of vast numbers of additional workmen in the manufacture of arms and ammunition.

Before all these we ought to place the raising, clothing, arming, drilling, and organising of 410,000 men (including the National *Guard d'élite*), which, in addition to the 149,000 men of which the Royal Army consisted on the 1st of March, formed, on the 1st of June, an effective force of 559,000 men, available for the national defence.

Chevau-Léger (*Français*) 1812

Of this number, the effective force of the troops of the Line amounted to 217,000 men, and the Regimental Depots to 146,000 men: the remainder, consisting of 200 battalions of the National *Guard d'élite*, of 20 regiments of marines, of 10 battalions of marine artillery, of coast guards, veterans, and organised pensioners, and amounting to 190,000 men, constituted the *Armée extraordinaire,* to be employed in the defence of the fortresses and of the coast.

Napoleon having calculated that an effective force of 800,000 men would be requisite to enable him to oppose the Allies with full confidence of success, had given orders for the formation, at the Regimental Depots, of the 3rd, 4th, and 5th Battalions of every regiment of infantry. and of the 4th and 5th Squadrons of every regiment of cavalry; also for the additional formation of 30 battalions of Artillery Train, of 20 regiments of the Young Guard, of battalions of Waggon Train, and of 2 regiments of marines. These and other measures he anticipated would furnish the force desired, but not until the 1st of October. The movements of the Allies, however, and his projected plan of active operations, precluded the possibility of his waiting for their full accomplishment. To augment the means of local defence, instructions were also issued for the reorganisation of the National Guard throughout the Empire, by which it was divided into 3130 battalions, and was to form, *when complete,* no less a force than 2,250,000 men!

Out of the disposable force of the troops of the Line, and partly also out of the National Guard *d'élite,* were formed seven *Corps d'Armée,* four corps of Reserve Cavalry, four corps of Observation, and an Army of the West or of La Vendée.

The Army of the North, generally designated the Grand Army, was to be considered as acting under the immediate orders of the emperor. It consisted of five *Corps d'Armée* (the First, Second, Third, Fourth, and Sixth), all the Reserve Cavalry, and the Imperial Guard. Its total force amounted to nearly 120,000 men; and its distribution, in the early part of June, was as follows:—

The First *Corps d'Armée* commanded by Count d'Erlon, had its headquarters at Lille; the Second, under the orders of Count Reille, was cantoned in the environs of Valenciennes; the Third, under Count Vandamme, was assembled in the environs of Mézières; the Fourth, under Count Gérard, in the environs of the Metz; and the Sixth Corps, commanded by Count Lobau, was stationed at Laon. The four corps of Reserve Cavalry under the chief command of Marshal Grouchy,

Chasseur à Cheval 1812

were in cantonments between the Aisne and the Sambre. The Imperial Guard was in Paris.

The Fifth *Corps d'Armée*, commanded by Count Rapp, formed the basis of an Army of the Rhine, and consisted of about 36,000 men. Its headquarters were at Strasburg, and it occupied the principal points along that part of the frontier between Landau and Hagenau; communicating with the Fourth *Corps d'Armée* on its left, as also with the First Corps of Observation on its right.

The Seventh *Corps d'Armée*, commanded by the Duke of Albufera, formed the basis of the Army of the Alps. It did not at that time amount to more than 15,000 men; but arrangements were made for its augmentation, by the end of June, to 40,000 men. It held the passes along the Italian frontier—was strongly posted at Grenoble, and at Chambery—communicating on its left with the First Corps of Observation; and covering the approach to Lyons, where very extensive works were carried on with the utmost vigour and activity.

The First Corps of Observation, called the Army of the Jura, commanded by Lieutenant General Lecourbe, guarded the passes along the Swiss frontier; had its headquarters at Altkirch, and occupied the line between Huningen and Belfort—communicating on its right with the Army of the Alps, and on its left with the Army of the Rhine. It did not, at that time, consist of a larger force than 4,500 men; which, however, was to be augmented to 18,000 on the arrival of additional battalions from the National Guard *d'élite* in course of active organisation.

The Second Corps of Observation, called the Army of the Var, commanded by Marshal Brune, had its headquarters at Marseilles; occupied Toulon and Antibes, and watched the frontier of the Maritime Alps. Its force, which then amounted to 5,300 men, was to be joined by sixteen battalions of the National Guard *d'élite*; and, in this way, increased to 17,000 men.

The Third Corps of Observation, called the Army of the Eastern Pyrenees, commanded by Lieutenant General Count Decaen, had its headquarters at Perpignan. It did not then consist of more than 3,000 men; but was to be augmented by thirty-two battalions of the National Guard *d'élite* to 23,000 men.

The Fourth Corps of Observation, called the Army of the Western Pyrenees, or of the Gironde, was commanded by Lieutenant General Clausel; had its headquarters in Bordeaux; consisted of the same force as that of the Third Corps; and was to be augmented in a similar manner.

The Army of La Vendée, commanded by General Lamarque, was occupied in restoring tranquillity to that part of the Empire. It consisted of about 17,000 men, including detachments supplied temporarily from the Third and Fourth Corps of Observation.

Arrangements had also been made for reinforcing, at the end of June, the two Armies of the Rhine and the Alps, with 50,000 men from the troops of the Line organised in the Regimental Depots, and with 100,000 men from the National Guard *d'élite;* and with a view to afford a Second Line and Support to the Grand Army, commanded by Napoleon in person, the latter was to be augmented by 100,000 men of the National Guard, and by 60,000 men of regular troops taken from the depots, where the additional battalions and squadrons of regiments were in course of daily organisation.

The general aspect of France at that moment was singularly warlike. It was that of a whole nation buckling on its armour; over the entire country armed bodies were to be seen in motion towards their several points of destination: every where the new levies for the Line, and the newly enrolled National Guards were in an unremitting course of drill and organisation: the greatest activity was maintained, day and night, in all the arsenals, and in all the manufactories of clothing and articles of equipment: crowds of workmen were constantly employed in the repair of the numerous fortresses, and in the erection of entrenched works. Everywhere appeared a continued transport of artillery, waggons, arms, ammunition, and all the material of war; whilst upon every road forming an approach to any of the main points of assembly in the vicinity of the frontiers, might be seen those well-formed veteran bands, Napoleon's followers through many a bloody field, moving forth with all the order, and with all the elasticity of spirit inspired by the full confidence of a renewed career of victory— rejoicing in the display of those standards which so proudly recalled the most glorious fields that France had ever won, and testifying by their acclamations, their enthusiastic devotion to the cause of the emperor, and their country.

The sentiments which so generally animated the troops of the Line, must not, however, be understood as having been equally imbibed by the remaining portion of the army, or indeed by the major part of the nation. There was one predominant cause, which, though its influence acted as an additional stimulus to the army, was the sole incentive to exertion with the civil portion of the community. It was the general prevalence of that aversion and contempt entertained by the French for their foreign invaders, whose former humiliation and subjection, the result of an almost uninterrupted course of victory and triumph to which the history of France presented no parallel, had served to flatter and to gratify the national vanity. It was this feeling, combined with a dread of that retributive justice which would inevitably follow in the train of a successful invasion, that operated so powerfully upon the mass of the nation, with whom the cry of "*Vive l'Empereur!*" merged into that of "*Vive la France!*"

To the above cause may also be traced the temporary reconciliation of the different factions which it was one of the main objects of Napoleon's celebrated *Champ de Mai* to establish. This convocation of the Popular Representatives, which had in a measure been forced upon the emperor by the political vantage ground the people had gained during even the short constitutional reign of Louis XVIII., and of which they had begun to feel the benefit, did not in any degree fulfil the expectations of its projector. The stern Republicans were dissatisfied with the retention of a Chamber of Peers, which, in the late reign, they had regarded as an English importation; and the Royalists were no less disgusted with the materials out of which such a Chamber had been constructed; while both parties felt it to be a mere semblance of a constitutional body, destined to be composed of the willing slaves of the despot, his ready instruments for counteracting and paralysing the effects of any violent ebullition of the popular will.

When it is considered that an overwhelming majority of the members of the new Chamber of Deputies were men of avowed Republican principles, and that in their very first sittings, they evinced by the tone of their debates, and by the tenor of their measures, a determination to uphold the authority vested in them by the people, and to make even the military power of the emperor subservient to their views of Popular Government; when, also, it is considered that the two predominant parties in the State, the Republicans and the Royalists, relied upon, and awaited but, the issue of events, for the ultimate success and realisation of their respective principles: it need not excite surprise that Napoleon, on quitting the capital to take the field, should have appeared to feel that he left behind him a power even more dangerous to the stability of his authority, and more destructive of his ambitious projects, than that which lie was going personally to confront.

He naturally calculated largely upon the enthusiasm of his troops and their devotion to his cause: but he must have entertained serious doubts as to whether this spirit was shared by the great majority of the nation; and must have foreseen that it would only be by means of a successful result of the approaching contest, that he could possibly avert the dangers to which his sovereignty was exposed, as much by the machinations of political opponents at home, as by the combinations of hostile forces abroad. He was now made painfully sensible of the vast change which the result of all his former wars, the restoration of the legitimate monarch, and the newly chartered Liberty of the Subject, had gradually wrought in the political feelings and sentiments of the nation.

In short, he found that he had to contend with a mighty, and an uncontrollable, power—the great moral power of Public Opinion—compared with which, the Military Power, centred in a single Individual, however brilliant the latter in genius can acquire no permanent stability, when not emanating from the broad and comprehensive moral energies of the nation. Even a succession of dazzling triumphs, when gained through the instrumentality of an arbitrary drain upon the national resources, and in opposition to the real interests and welfare of the State, tends but to hasten the downfall of the military dictator.

CHAPTER 2

The British Army

Belgium, the frequent battle-ground of Europe, whose every stream and every town is associated with the memory of bygone deeds of arms, was destined, in 1815, to witness another and a mighty struggle—a struggle in which were arrayed, on the one side, the two foremost of the confederated armies advancing towards the French frontiers; and, on the other, the renowned *Grande Armée* of Imperial France, resuscitated at the call of its original founder—the great Napoleon himself. During the months of April and May, troops of all arms continued to enter upon, and spread themselves over, the Belgian soil.

Here might be seen the British soldier, flushed with recent triumphs in the Peninsula over the same foe with whom he was now prepared once more to renew the combat; and here the Prussian, eager for the deadly strife, and impatiently rushing onward to encounter that enemy whose ravages and excesses in his Fatherland still rankled in his memory. The Englishman was not fired by the desire of retribution; for it had pleased Divine Providence to spare Great Britain from the scourge of domestic war, and to preserve her soil unstained by the footprint of a foreign enemy. The Prussian soldier looked forward with a sullen pleasure to the prospect of revenge: vengeance seemed to him a sacred duty, imposed upon him by all the ties of kindred, and by all those patriotic feelings, which, in the hour of Prussia's need, had roused her entire people from the abject state to which they had been so fatally subdued; which, when the whole country lay prostrate at the conqueror's feet, so successfully prompted her sons to throw off the yoke.

History will mark this deliverance as the brilliant point in Prussia's brightest era, affording as it does, a clear and parallel to that in which an equally forcible appeal to the energies of the nation was made with similar success by Frederick the Great, when opposed single-handed to the immense armies and powerful resources of surrounding States. France was about to expiate by her own sufferings the wrongs she had wrought upon his country and his kind, and the Prussian panted for an opportunity of satiating his revenge.

The Briton, if he had no such spur as that which urged the Prussian soldier forward, did not want a sufficiently exciting stimulus. He cherished that high feeling and proud bearing which a sense of the obligations imposed on him by his country and of her expectations of his prowess, could not fail to inspire; determined resolutely to discharge the former, and, if possible, to more than realise the latter.

These feelings and dispositions of the soldiery in the two most advanced of the Allied Armies were concentrated with intensity in the characters of their respective chiefs.

It may be said of Wellington, that he personified the pure ideal of the British soldier—the true character of his own followers. Resolute, yet cool, cautious and calculating in his proceedings; possessing a natural courage unshaken even under dangers and difficulties; placing reliance upon physical and moral strength, as opposed to the force of numbers;—it was not surprising that he should have inspired with confidence, soldiers who could see in his character and conduct the reflection of their own qualities. But besides these traits in his character there were others which peculiarly distinguished him as one of the greatest captains that his own or any other nation ever produced, and which would inspire confidence as to the result of the approaching contest, even opposed to Napoleon with whom he was now, for the first time, to measure swords.

It was naturally to be expected that Napoleon, from the moment he reascended the throne, would devote the utmost energies of his all-directing mind to the full development of whatever military means France, notwithstanding her recent reverses, yet retained; but the rapidity and the order with which so regular and so well organised a force as that which was now concentrating on the French side of the Sambre, had been collected and put in motion, were truly wonderful.

The speedy and almost sudden reappearance of the old army in all its *grandeur*, with its corps and divisions headed by men, who, by a series of daring and successful exploits, had proved their just titles to command, and endeared themselves to the old campaigners, was such that it seemed as if the French had realised the fable of the dragon's

THE DUKE OF WELLINGTON MEDALLION,
FRONT AND REVERSE

.

teeth, which it might be said they had sown as they crossed their frontiers in the previous year, when retreating upon the capital before the victorious Allies.

Never did any army contain within itself so much of that necessary essence in the composition of a military force,—unbounded enthusiasm, combined with the purest devotion to its leader. The oft-told tale of the veteran of so many a hard-fought field, indulging in the hope of aiding by his exertions, at any sacrifice, in again carrying the Eagles to the scenes of their former triumphs, excited the ardour of many a youthful aspirant to share with him the glory of wiping out the stain which had dimmed the lustre of his country's fame, and darkened a most eventful page in her annals.

Such being the nature of the elements ready to rush into collision, it was easy to foresee that the shock which that collision would produce, would be both violent and terrible; but no one could have anticipated that within the short space of four days from the commencement of hostilities, the die would be irrevocably cast, annihilating for ever the imperial sway of Napoleon, and securing to Europe one of the longest periods of peace recorded in her history.

CHAPTER 3

Anglo–Allied Army Under Wellington

By the middle of June, the Anglo-Allied Army which had been gradually assembling in Belgium, under the command of the Duke of Wellington, amounted to about 106,000 men, and was composed in the following manner:—

INFANTRY.

British	23,543
King's German Legion	3,301
Hanoverian	22,788
Brunswick	5,376
Nassau (1st Regiment)	2,880
Dutch and Belgian	24,174
	82,062

CAVALRY

British	5,913
King's German Legion	2,560
Hanoverian	1,682
Brunswick	922
Dutch and Belgian	3,405
	14,482

ARTILLERY

British	5,030	102 guns
King's German Legion	526	18 „

Hussars and Infantry of the Duke of Brunswick Oels's Corps

Hanoverian	465	12 „
Brunswick	510	16 „
Dutch and Belgian	1,635	56 „
	8,166	204 guns.

ENGINEERS, SAPPERS AND MINERS, WAGGON-TRAIN, AND STAFF CORPS.

British	1,240

TOTAL

Infantry	82,062
Cavalry	14,482
Artillery	8,166
Engineers, Waggon-Train, &c.	1,240

105,950 men and 204 guns.

The infantry was divided into two corps and a reserve. The First Corps, commanded by General His Royal Highness the Prince of Orange, was composed:

of the First Division, under Major General Cooke;

of the Third Division, under Lieutenant General Sir Charles Alten;

of the Second Dutch-Belgian Division, under Lieutenant General de Perponcher;

and of the Third Dutch-Belgian Division, under Lieutenant General Baron Chassé.

The left of this corps rested upon Genappe, Quatre Bras, and Frasne, on the high road leading from Brussels to Charleroi on the Sambre, and communicated with the right of the First *Corps d'Armée* of the Prussian Army, the headquarters of which corps were at Charleroi. De Perponcher's Dutch-Belgian Division formed the extreme left, having its headquarters at Nivelles, on the high road from Brussels to Binche. On its right was Chassé's Dutch-Belgian Division, more in advance, in the direction of Mons and Binche, and quartered principally in Roeulx, and in the villages between the latter place and Binche. The next division on the right was Alten's, having its headquarters at Soignies, on the high road from Brussels to Mons, and occupying villages between this town, Roeulx, Braine le Comte, and Enghien. The right division, Cooke's, had its headquarters at Enghien.

The Second Corps, commanded by Lieutenant General Lord Hill, consisted:

of the Second Division, under Lieutenant General Sir Henry
Clinton;

of the Fourth Division, under Lieutenant General the Hon.
Sir Charles Colville;

of the First Dutch–Belgian Division, under Lieutenant
General Stedmann;

and of a brigade raised for service in the Dutch Colonies,
called the Indian Brigade, under Lieutenant General
Baron Anthing.

The Second Division, which formed the left of this corps, communicated with Alten's right; its headquarters were at Ath, on the Dender, and upon the high road leading from Brussels to Tournai, and one brigade (the Third), occupied Lens, situated about midway between Ath and Mons.

The Fourth Division was the next on the right, having its headquarters at Audenarde on the Scheldt, and occupying also Renaix. One brigade of this division (the Sixth Hanoverian) garrisoned the fortress of Nieuport on the coast. The First Dutch–Belgian Division was cantoned in villages bordering upon the high road connecting Grammont with Ghent; and the so-called Indian Brigade occupied villages between this line and Alost.

The Reserve consisted:

of the Fifth Division, under Lieutenant General Sir Thomas
Picton;

of the Sixth Division, under Lieutenant General the Hon. Sir
Lowry Cole;

of the Brunswick Division, under the Duke of Brunswick;

of the Hanoverian Corps, under Lieutenant General Von der
Decken;

and of the contingent of the Duke of Nassau, which
comprised the 1st Regiment of Nassau Infantry,
containing three battalions, and forming a brigade under
the command of General von Kruse.

The Fifth and Sixth Divisions, and the Brunswick Division, were quartered principally in and around Brussels, excepting the Seventh Brigade, which together with Von der Decken's Corps, the 13th Veteran Battalion, the 1st Foreign Battalion, and the 2nd Garrison Battal-

A private of the XVth or King's Lt Drag. (Hussars)

ion, garrisoned Antwerp, Ostend, Nieuport, Ypres, Tournai, and Mons; and Von Kruse's Nassau Brigade was cantoned between Brussels and Louvain.

Of the fortresses already mentioned, those which had not been destroyed by the French when they gained possession of the country in 1794, namely, Antwerp, Ostend, and Nieuport, were strengthened, and each rendered capable of holding out a siege. By taking every possible advantage offered by the remains of the old fortifications, and by the continued employment of 20,000 labourers, through requisitions on the country, in addition to the military working parties, and by the accession of artillery and stores from England and Holland, the towns of Ypres, Tournai, Mons, Ath, and the Citadel of Ghent, were placed in a state of defence, and a redoubt was constructed at Audenarde to protect the Sluice Gates, which afforded the means of inundating that part of the country.

The cavalry of the Anglo-Allied Army, commanded by Lieutenant General the Earl of Uxbridge, consisted of seven brigades, comprising the British and the King's German Legion; of a Hanoverian Brigade: of five squadrons of Brunswick Cavalry; and of three brigades of Dutch-Belgian Cavalry.

The British and King's German Legion Cavalry, with the Hanoverian Brigade, were stationed at Grammont and Ninove, and in villages bordering upon the Dender. The Brunswick Cavalry was dispersed in the vicinity of Brussels. The First Brigade of Dutch-Belgian Cavalry was cantoned in the neighbourhood of Roeulx; the Second Brigade, in villages between Roeulx and Mons; and the Third Brigade, partly on the south side of Mons, in the direction of Maubeuge and Beaumont, and partly between Binche and Mons.

The wide dissemination of the Duke of Wellington's forces which the advanced line of cantonments presented—a line forming a considerable portion of a circle, of which Brussels was the centre, and the Tournai, Mons, and Charleroi roads were the marked radii—tended greatly to facilitate the means of subsisting the troops, and to render that subsistence less burthensome to the country; while, at the same time, it offered to the Duke, in conjunction with the interior points of concentration, and with the efficient Reserve stationed around the capital, full security for his being prepared to meet any emergency that might arise. The main points of interior concentration were (commencing from the right) Audenarde, Grammont, Ath, Enghien, Soignies, Nivelles, and Quatre Bras, from whatever point, therefore,

WELLINGTON IN THE FIELD
This was Wellington's favourite campaigning costume. The frock-coat was dark blue, the cloak grey lined with white. The telescope he carried all through Spain and Belgium and afterwards gave to Lord Stanhope.

offensive operations might be directed against that portion of the Belgian frontier occupied by the Army under Wellington—whether from Lille, by Courtrai, or by Tournai, between the Lys and the Scheldt; from Condé, Valenciennes, or Maubeuge, by Mons, between the Sambre and the Scheldt; or from Maubeuge, Beaumont, or Philippeville, by Charleroi, between the Sambre and the Meuse—the duke, by advancing to the threatened point with his Reserve, and placing the remainder of his troops in movement, had it in his power to concentrate at least two-thirds of his intended disposable force for the field, upon the line of the enemy's operations, within twenty-two hours after the receipt of intelligence of the actual direction and apparent object of those operations.

The Prussian Army, under the command of Prince Blücher von Wahlstadt, amounted to nearly 117,000 men, and was thus composed:—

Infantry	99,715
Cavalry	11,879
Artillery, Waggon-Train, and Engineers	5,303

116,897 men & 312 guns.

It was divided into four *corps d'armée.*

The First Corps, commanded by Lieutenant General Zieten,[1] consisted:—

of the First Brigade, under General Steinmetz;
of the Second Brigade, under General Pirch II.;[2]
of the Third Brigade, under General Jagow;
of the Fourth Brigade, under General Count Henkel;
of a Cavalry Reserve, under Lieutenant General Röder;
and of an Artillery Reserve, under Colonel Lehmann.

The right of this *corps d'armée,* the headquarters of which were at Charleroi, communicated with the left of the First Corps of the Duke of Wellington's Army. Its right brigade, the First, was cantoned in and

1. In order to avoid the constant repetition of the prefix "von" to the names of the German officers, I have omitted it altogether in the present edition; an omission, however, which I feel persuaded those officers will not consider as involving any breach of courtesy or respect.
2. Prussian general officers bearing the same family name, are usually distinguished by the addition of the Roman numerals. General Von Pirch I. is named on the next page.

A British Hussar

around Fontaine l'Evêque, which lies midway between Charleroi and Binche; the Second Brigade, in Marchienne au Pont, on the Sambre; the Third Brigade, in Fleurus; the Fourth Brigade, in Moustier sur Sambre; the Reserve Cavalry in Sombref, and the Reserve Artillery in Gembloux. The line of advanced posts of this corps extended from Bonne Esperance (two miles south-west of Binche) along the frontier of Lobbes, Thuin, and Gerpinnes, as far as Sossoye.

The Second *Corps d'Armée*, commanded by General Pirch I., consisted:

of the Fifth Brigade, under General Tippelskirchen;
of the Sixth Brigade, under General Krafft;
of the Seventh Brigade, under General Brause;
of the Eighth Brigade, under Colonel Langen;
of a Cavalry Reserve, under General Jürgass;
and of an Artillery Reserve, under Colonel Röhl.

The headquarters of this corps were at Namur, situated at the confluence of the Sambre and the Meuse, where also its first brigade (the Fifth) was stationed; the Sixth Brigade was cantoned in and around Thorembey les Beguignes; the Seventh Brigade in Heron; the Eighth Brigade in Huy; the Reserve Cavalry in Hannut; and the Reserve Artillery along the high road to Louvain. The line of advanced posts of this corps extended from Sossoye as far as Dinant on the Meuse, about midway between Namur and Givet.

The Third *Corps d'Armée*, commanded by Lieutenant General Thielemann, consisted:

of the Ninth Brigade, under General Borke;
of the Tenth Brigade, under Colonel Kämpfen;
of the Eleventh Brigade, under Colonel Luck;
of the Twelfth Brigade, under Colonel Stülpnagel;
of a Cavalry Reserve, under General Hobe;
and of an Artillery Reserve, under Colonel Mohnhaupt.

The headquarters of this corps were at Ciney: the Ninth Brigade was stationed at Asserre; the Tenth Brigade at Ciney; the Eleventh Brigade at Dinant; the Twelfth Brigade at Huy, on the Meuse; the Reserve Cavalry between Ciney and Dinant; and the Reserve Artillery at Ciney. The line of advanced posts of this corps extended from Dinant as far as Fabeline and Rochefort.

The Fourth *Corps d'Armée*, commanded by General Count Bülow von Dennewitz, consisted:

A PRIVATE OF THE 13TH LIGHT DRAGOONS

of the Thirteenth Brigade, under Lieutenant General Hacke;
of the Fourteenth Brigade, under General Ryssel;
of the Fifteenth Brigade, under General Losthin;
of the Sixteenth Brigade, under Colonel Hiller:
of a Cavalry Reserve, under General His Royal Highness
     Prince William of Prussia;
and of an Artillery Reserve, under Lieutenant Colonel
     Bardeleben.

The headquarters of this corps were at Liege, where was also stationed the Thirteenth Infantry Brigade; the Fourteenth Brigade was cantoned in and around Waremme; the Fifteenth Brigade at Hologne; the Sixteenth Brigade at Liers; the First Brigade of Reserve Cavalry at Tongern; the Second Brigade at Dalhem, and the Third Brigade at Lootz; the Reserve Artillery was cantoned in and about Gloms and Dalhem.

Prince Blücher's headquarters were at Namur.

The points of concentration for the respective corps were therefore Fleurus, Namur, Ciney, and Liege. The four corps were so disposed that each could be collected at its own headquarters within twelve hours; and it was fully practicable to form a junction of the whole army at any one of these points within twenty-four hours from the time of such collection. At Namur, the most central point, it would of course be accomplished in much less time.

Blücher had decided, in the event of an advance by the French across the line of the Sambre, by Charleroi, upon concentrating his army in a position in front of Sombref, a point upon the high road between Namur and Nivelles, above fourteen miles from the former place, and only seven miles and a half from Quatre Bras, the point of intersection of this road with the one leading directly from Charleroi to Brussels, and at which Wellington had agreed, in that case, to concentrate as large a force as time would admit, in order to check any advance in this direction, or to join Blücher's right flank, according to circumstances.

Should the enemy advance along the left bank of the Meuse towards Namur, this place would become the point of junction of the First, Second, and Fourth Corps of the Prussian Army, whilst the Third, collecting at Ciney, would, after presenting a stout resistance at Dinant, operate as effectively as circumstances would admit, against the right of the line of attack; and should he advance by the right bank of the Meuse towards Ciney, the army would concentrate at this point, with the exception of the Fourth Corps, which would assemble at Liege as a reserve, for the better security of the left flank and of the communications with the Rhine.

Such were the dispositions of the Allied commanders, who contemplated no change in their arrangements until the moment should arrive of the commencement of hostile demonstrations of a decided character, for which they were perfectly prepared, and for which a vigilant look-out was maintained along the general line of the advanced posts.

From the foregoing, however, it would appear that the concentration of Wellington's army on its own left, and that of Blücher's army on its own right, required longer time than that in which they could have been respectively accomplished on other points; and further that the distribution of the former was better calculated to meet the enemy's advance by Mons, and that of the latter to meet it by Namur, than to oppose a line of attack by Charleroi. This peculiar feature in the dispositions of the two commanders did not escape the vigilance of Napoleon, who, as will be seen in the sequel, made it subservient to his hopes of beating their armies in detail.

The French troops destined to constitute the Grand Army with which Napoleon had decided upon taking the field against the allied forces in Belgium, comprised the First, Second, Third, Fourth, and Sixth *Corps d'Armée;* four corps of cavalry; and the Imperial Guard: amounting altogether to 116,124 men:—

Infantry	83,753
Cavalry	20,959
Artillery, Waggon-Train, and Engineers	11,412

116,124 men & 350 guns

The First *Corps d'Armée*, commanded by Lieutenant General Count d'Erlon, consisted:

> of the First Infantry Division, under Lieutenant General Alix;
> of the Second Infantry Division, under Lieutenant General Baron Donzelot;
> of the Third Infantry Division, under Lieutenant General Baron Marcognet;
> of the Fourth Infantry Division, under Lieutenant General Count Durette;
> and of the First Light Cavalry Division, under Lieutenant General Jaquinot;

PRINCE BLÜCHER VON WAHLSTADT FROM A
MEDAL STRUCK IN HONOUR OF THE PRINCE
BY THE CITIZENS OF BERLIN

with 5 batteries of foot, and 1 of horse artillery.

In the beginning of June, this corps was stationed in and around Lille.

The Second *Corps d'Armée*, commanded by Lieutenant General Count Reille, consisted:

of the Fifth Infantry Division, under Lieutenant General Baron Bachelu;

of the Sixth Infantry Division, under Lieutenant General Prince Jerome Napoleon;

of the Seventh Infantry Division, under Lieutenant General Count Girard;

of the Ninth Infantry Division, under Lieutenant General Count Foy;

and of the Second Light Cavalry Division, under Lieutenant General Baron Piré;

with 5 batteries of foot, and 1 of horse artillery.

This corps was stationed in and around Valenciennes.

The Third *Corps d'Armée*, commanded by Lieutenant General Count Vandamme, consisted:

of the Eighth Infantry Division, under Lieutenant General Baron Le Fol;

of the Tenth Infantry Division under Lieutenant General Baron Habert;

of the Eleventh Infantry Division, under Lieutenant General Berthezene;

and of the Third Light Cavalry Division, under Lieutenant General Baron Domon;

with 4 batteries of foot, and 1 of horse artillery.

This corps was assembled in and around Mézières.

The Fourth *Corps d'Armée*, commanded by Lieutenant General Count Gérard, consisted:

of the Twelfth Infantry Division, under Lieutenant General Baron Pecheux;

of the Thirteenth Infantry Division, under Lieutenant General Baron Vichery;

of the Fourteenth Infantry Division, under Lieutenant General de Bourmont;

and of the Sixth Light Cavalry Division, under Lieutenant General Maurin;

with 4 batteries of foot, and 1 of horse artillery.

This corps occupied Metz, Longwy, and Thionville, and formed the basis of the Army of the Moselle; but it was now decided that it should approach the Sambre, and unite itself with the Grand Army.

The Sixth *Corps d'Armée*, commanded by Lieutenant General Count Lobau, consisted:

of the Nineteenth Infantry Division, under Lieutenant
General Baron Simmer;
of the Twentieth Infantry Division, under Lieutenant General
Baron Jeannin;
of the Twenty-First Infantry Division, under Lieutenant
General Baron Teste;
with 4 batteries of foot, and 1 of horse artillery.
This corps was assembled in and around Laon.

The four corps forming the Reserve Cavalry were placed under the command of Marshal Count Grouchy.

The First, commanded by Lieutenant General Count Pajol, consisted:

of the Fourth Cavalry Division (hussars), under Lieutenant
General Baron Soult;
and of the Fifth Division (lancers and *chasseurs*), under
Lieutenant General Baron Subervie;
with 2 batteries of horse artillery.

The Second Corps, commanded by Lieutenant General Count Excelmans, consisted:

of the Ninth Division (dragoons), under Lieutenant General
Strolz;
and of the Tenth Division (dragoons), under Lieutenant
General Baron Chastel;
with 2 batteries of horse artillery.

The Third Corps, commanded by Lieutenant General Count de Valmy (Kellermann), consisted:

of the Eleventh Division (dragoons and *cuirassiers*), under
Lieutenant General Baron L'Heritier;
and of the Twelfth Division (carabiniers and *cuirassiers*), under
Lieutenant General Roussel d'Hurbal;
with 2 batteries of horse artillery.

The Fourth Corps, commanded by Lieutenant General Count

GARDE IMPÉRIALE

Milhaud, consisted:

> of the Thirteenth Division (*cuirassiers*), under Lieutenant General Wathier;
>
> and of the Fourteenth Division (*cuirassiers*), under Lieutenant General Baron Delort;
>
> with 2 batteries of horse artillery.

The principal portion of the Reserve Cavalry lay in cantonments between the Aisne and the frontier.

The infantry of the Imperial Guard consisted:

> of the 1st and 2nd Regiments of Grenadiers, under Lieutenant General Count Friant;
>
> of the 3rd and 4th Regiments of Grenadiers, under Lieutenant General Count Roguet;
>
> of the 1st and 2nd Regiments of Chasseurs, under Lieutenant General Count Morand;
>
> of the 3rd and 4th Regiments of Chasseurs, under Lieutenant General Count Michel;
>
> of the 1st and 3rd Regiments of Tirailleurs, under Lieutenant General Count Duhesme;
>
> and of the 1st and 3rd Voltigeurs, under Lieutenant General Count Barrois;

The cavalry of the Guard consisted:

> of two regiments of Heavy Cavalry (*Grenadiers à Cheval* and dragoons), under Lieutenant General Count Guyot;
>
> and of three regiments of Light Cavalry (*Chasseurs à Cheval* and lancers), under Lieutenant General Lefèbvre-Desnouettes.

Attached to the Guard were 6 batteries of foot, and 4 batteries of horse artillery, with 3 batteries of reserve artillery; comprising altogether 96 pieces of cannon, under the command of Lieutenant General Desvaux de St. Maurice.

These troops were principally in Paris.

The French emperor having, upon the grounds explained in a former chapter, determined to take the field against the Allied Armies in Belgium, the commencement of active operations could no longer be deferred. When we reflect upon the disparity of force with which he was going to contend against two such generals as Wellington and Blücher, we are bound to acknowledge that it was an undertaking daring and perilous in the extreme, even for an individual of the dauntless and adventurous character of Napoleon.

A delay of only a few weeks would have secured for him, by means of the vast organisation which was in constant and rapid progress, a sufficient accession of disposable troops to have enabled him to effect a powerful diversion upon either Wellington's right, or Blücher's left, flank, and thus to impart an infinitely greater degree of weight and stability to his main operations; but then, on the other hand, this delay would also have brought the powerful armies of the confederated sovereigns across the whole line of his eastern frontier, and have led to the consummation of that combined movement upon the capital, the execution of which it was his great aim to frustrate.

But it was not the first time that Napoleon had advanced against such fearful superiority of numerical strength. In the previous year, when nearly surrounded by the victorious forces of Prussia, Austria, and Russia, when apparently overwhelmed by a succession of disasters, and when his army was daily diminishing by the desertion of newly raised conscripts, and presenting the mere wreck of its former self, he was at the very *acme* of his mental energy, and in the full possession of his determinate and all subduing will.

His great genius seemed to acquire additional vigour and elasticity, with the increasing desperation of his position; and darting with electric suddenness and rapidity, now upon one adversary and then upon another, maintaining with the renowned leaders of his detached forces, a combination of movements developing the highest order of strategy, he succeeded by his brilliant triumphs at Champaubert, Montmirail, and Monterau, not only in stemming the torrent of invasion, but in causing the resumption of the diplomatic preliminaries of a peace. This peace, however, these very triumphs induced him, as if by a fatality, to reject with scorn and indignation, although the terms were honourable in the highest degree under his then existing circumstances.

Hence, with such a retrospect, Napoleon might well indulge in hope and confidence as to the result of the approaching campaign, notwithstanding the want of sufficient time for a greater development of his resources. A finer or a more gallant army, or one more complete and efficient in every respect, than that which he was going to lead in person, never took the field.

He had selected for the line of his main operations the direct road to Brussels, by Charleroi, that being the road, as before remarked, on which Wellington's left, and Blücher's right respectively rested, and which he designed to maintain by first overcoming the Prussian Army, which was the most advanced on that line, and then attacking the An-

GARDE IMPÉRIALE

glo-Allied troops before they could be collected in sufficient strength to prevent his further progress; his grand object being to impede the junction of the two Armies; to vanquish them in detail; to establish himself in Brussels; to arouse the dense population in Belgium, of which a vast proportion secretly adhered to his cause; to reannex the country to the French Empire; to excite the desertion of the Belgian soldiery from the service of Holland; to prevent a check by these means to the operations of the invading armies crossing the Rhine; perhaps also to enter into negotiations; and, at all events, to gain, what was to him of vital importance, *time* for the advance and co-operation of further reinforcements from France.

The necessary orders were now despatched for the concentration of the Grand Army; and in order to mask its movements as much as possible, the whole line of the Belgian frontier was studded with numerous detachments of the National Guards furnished by the garrisons of the fortresses, more especially along that part of the frontier which passes in advance of Valenciennes, Condé, Lille, and even as far as Dunkirk; all the *debouchés* of which line were strongly occupied, the outposts tripled, and there was every apparent indication that either the principal attack, or at least a formidable diversion, was in course of preparation in that quarter.

These measures had the effect of strengthening the anticipations which Wellington had previously formed of offensive movements from the side of Lille and Valenciennes, and consequently of placing him still more upon his guard against any hasty and incautious junction of his forces with those of Blücher, until fully satisfied as to the true direction and object of Napoleon's main operations.

On the 12th of June, Lieutenant Colonel Wissell, whose regiment, the 1st Hussars of the King's German Legion, formed an extensive line of outposts in front of Tournai, reported to Major General Sir Hussey Vivian, to whose brigade the regiment belonged, that he had ascertained, from information on which he could rely, that the French Army had assembled on the frontier, and was prepared to attack. Vivian desired him to report upon the subject to Lord Hill, to whose corps his regiment was attached while employed on this particular service.

The next morning, Vivian repaired in person to the outposts, and found that a French cavalry picquet which had previously been posted opposite to Tournai, had a short time before marched to join the main army, and had been relieved by *Douaniers*. These, upon being spoken to by Vivian, did not hesitate to say that their army was concentrating,

GARDE IMPÉRIALE

and that if the Allies did not advance, their troops would attack. On returning to his quarters, Vivian communicated what he had seen and heard both to Lord Hill and the Earl of Uxbridge, by whom the circumstances were made known to the Duke of Wellington. His Grace, however, for reasons before stated, did not think the proper moment had arrived for making any alteration in the disposition of his forces.

Gérard's corps quitted Metz on the 6th of June, with orders to reach Philippeville by the 14th. The Imperial Guard began its march from Paris on the 8th, and reached Avesnes on the 13th, as did also Lobau's corps from Laon. D'Erlon's corps from Lille, Reille's corps from Valenciennes, and Vandamme's corps from Mézières, likewise arrived at Maubeuge and Avesnes on the 13th. The four corps of Reserve Cavalry concentrated upon the Upper Sambre.

The junction of the several corps on the same day, and almost at the same hour (with the exception of the Fourth, which joined the next day), displayed the usual skill of Napoleon in the combination of movements. Their leaders congratulated themselves upon these auspicious preparations, and upon finding the "Grand Army" once more assembled in "all the pomp and circumstance of glorious war:" the appearance of the troops, though fatigued, was all that could be desired; and their enthusiasm was at the highest on hearing that the emperor himself, who had quitted Paris at three o'clock on the morning of the 12th, and passed the night at Laon, had actually arrived amongst them.

Upon the following day, the French Army bivouacked on three different points.

The left, consisting of d'Erlon's and Reille's Corps, and amounting to about 44,000 men, was posted on the right bank of the Sambre at Solre sur Sambre.

The centre, consisting of Vandamme's and Lobau's corps, of the Imperial Guard, and of the Cavalry Reserves, amounting altogether to about 60,000 men, was at Beaumont, which was made the headquarters.

The right, composed of Gérard's corps and of a division of Heavy Cavalry, amounting altogether to about 16,000 men, was in front of Philippeville.

The bivouacs were established in rear of some slight eminences, with a view to conceal their fires from the observation of the enemy.

The army, while thus assembled, on the eve of opening the campaign, received through the medium of an *Ordre du Jour* the following spirit-stirring appeal from its chief:—

Napoleon, by the Grace of God, and the Constitutions of the Empire, Emperor of the French, etc., to the Grand Army,

At the Imperial headquarters,
Avesnes, June 14th, 1815.

Soldiers! this day is the anniversary of Marengo and of Friedland, which twice decided the destiny of Europe. Then, as after Austerlitz, as after Wagram, we were too generous! We believed in the protestations and in the oaths of Princes, whom we left on their thrones. Now, however, leagued together, they aim at the independence, and the most sacred rights of France. They have commenced the most unjust of aggressions. Let us, then, march to meet them. Are they and we no longer the same men?

Soldiers! at Jena, against these same Prussians, now so arrogant, you were one to three, and at Montmirail one to six!

Let those among you who have been captives to the English, describe the nature of their prison ships, and the frightful miseries they endured.

The Saxons, the Belgians, the Hanoverians, the soldiers of the Confederation of the Rhine, lament that they are compelled to use their arms in the cause of the princes, the enemies of justice and of the rights of all nations. They know that this coalition is insatiable! After having devoured twelve millions of Poles, twelve millions of Italians, one million of Saxons, and six millions of Belgians, it now wishes to devour the States of the second rank in Germany.

Madmen! one moment of prosperity has bewildered them. The oppression and the humiliation of the French people are beyond their power. If they enter France they will there find their grave.

Soldiers! we have forced marches to make, battles to fight, dangers to encounter; but, with firmness, victory will be ours. The rights, the honour, and the happiness of the country will be recovered!

To every Frenchman who has a heart, the moment is now arrived to conquer or to die!

Napoleon.
The Marshal Duke of Dalmatia,
Major General.

CHAPTER 4

Affair at Gilly

Napoleon, by his precautionary measures of strengthening his advanced posts, and of displaying along the whole line of the Belgian frontier an equal degree of vigilance and activity, had effectually concealed from his adversaries the combined movements of his several *corps d'armée*, and their concentration on the right bank of the Sambre.

During the night of the 13th, however, the light reflected upon the sky by the fires of the French bivouacs, did not escape the vigilant observation of Zieten's outposts, whence it was communicated to the rear that these fires appeared to be in the direction of Walcourt and of Beaumont, and also in the vicinity of Solre sur Sambre; further, that all reports received through spies and deserters concurred in representing that Napoleon was expected to join the French Army on that evening; that the Imperial Guard and the Second Corps had arrived at Avesnes and Maubeuge; also that, at one o'clock in the afternoon of that day, four French battalions had crossed the river at Solre sur Sambre, and occupied Merbes le Château; that late in the night the enemy had pushed forward a strong detachment as far as Sart la Bussière; and lastly, that an attack by the French would certainly take place on the 14th or 15th.

On the 14th of June, the Dutch-Belgian General van Merlen, who was stationed at St Symphorien, near Mons, and who commanded the outposts between the latter place and Binche which formed the extreme right of the Prussians, ascertained that the French troops had moved from Maubeuge and its vicinity by Beaumont towards Philippeville, that there was no longer any hostile force in his front, except a picquet at Bettignies, and some National Guards in other villages. He forwarded this important information to the Prussian General Steinmetz, on his left, with whom he was in constant communication, and by whom it was despatched to General Zieten at Charleroi.

The Prussian General Pirch II., who was posted on the left of Steinmetz, also sent word to Zieten that he had received information through his outposts that the French Army had concentrated in the vicinity of Beaumont and Merbes le Château; that their army consisted of 150,000 men, and was commanded by General Vandamme, Jerome Buonaparte, and some other distinguished officers; that since the previous day all crossing of the frontier had been forbidden by the French under pain of death; and that a patrol of the enemy had been observed that day near Biercée, not far from Thuin.

During the day, frequent accounts were brought to the troops of Zieten's corps, generally corroborative of the above, by the country people who were bringing away, and seeking some place of safety for, their cattle. Intelligence was also obtained of the arrival of Napoleon, and of his brother, Prince Jerome.

Zieten immediately transmitted the substance of this information to Prince Blücher and to the Duke of Wellington; and it was perfectly consistent with that which the latter had received from Major General Dörnberg, who had been posted in observation at Mons, and from General van Merlen (through the Prince of Orange) who, as already mentioned, commanded the outposts between that place and Binche. Nothing, however, was as yet positively known concerning the real point of concentration, the probable strength of the enemy, or his intended offensive movements, and the Allied commanders therefore refrained from making any alteration in their dispositions, and calmly awaited the arrival of reports of a more definite character concerning the enemy's designs.

Zieten's troops were kept under arms during the night, and were collected by battalions at their respective points of assembly.

Later in the day Zieten ascertained, through his outposts, that strong French columns, composed of all arms, were assembling in his front, and that every thing portended an attack on the following morning.

Zieten's communication of this intelligence reached Blücher between nine and ten o'clock on the night of the 14th.

Simultaneous orders were consequently despatched by eleven o'clock for the march of Pirch's corps from Namur upon Sombref, and of Thielemann's corps from Ciney to Namur. An order had already, in the course of the day, been forwarded to Bülow at Liege, desiring him to make such a disposition of his *corps d'armée* as should

GARDE IMPÉRIALE

admit of its concentration at Hannut in one march; and at midnight a further order was despatched, requiring him to concentrate his troops in cantonment about Hannut.

Zieten was directed to await the advance of the enemy in his position upon the Sambre; and, in the event of his being attacked by superior numbers, and compelled to retire, to effect his retreat as slowly as circumstances would permit, in the direction of Fleurus, so as to afford sufficient time for the concentration of the other three corps in rear of the latter point.

The vigilance which was thus exercised along both the Anglo-Allied and Prussian line of outposts, obtained for Wellington and Blücher the fullest extent of information which they could reasonably have calculated on receiving respecting the dispositions of the Enemy immediately previous to an attack. They had been put in possession of the fact that considerable masses of French troops had moved by their right, and assembled in front of Charleroi. Still, this baring of the frontier beyond Tournai, Mons, and Binche, of the troops which had previously occupied that line, and their concentration in front of Charleroi, might be designed to mask the real line of operation, to draw the Anglo-Allied troops towards Charleroi, upon which a feigned attack would be made, while the real attack was intended to be by Mons. Hence no alteration was made by the duke in the disposition of his forces; but the Prussian field marshal immediately ordered the concentration of his own troops at a point where they would be at hand in case Charleroi should be the real line of attack, and whence they could far more readily move to the support of Wellington, should that attack be made by the Mons road.

Zieten's position, and his line of advanced posts, have already been described. His right brigade (the First), having its headquarters at Fontaine l'Evêque, held the ground between Binche and the Sambre; his centre brigade (the Second) lay along the Sambre, occupying Marchienne au Pont, Dampremy, La Roux, Charleroi, Châtelet, and Gilly; a portion of his Third Brigade occupied Farciennes and Tamines on the Sambre, while the remainder was posted in reserve between Fleurus and the Sambre; and his left brigade (the Fourth) was extended along this river nearly as far as Namur. The Reserve Cavalry of the First Corps had been brought more in advance, and was now cantoned in the vicinity of the Piéton, having Gosselies for its point of concentration.

In this position, Zieten, without making the slightest alteration,

GENERAL BLÜCHER

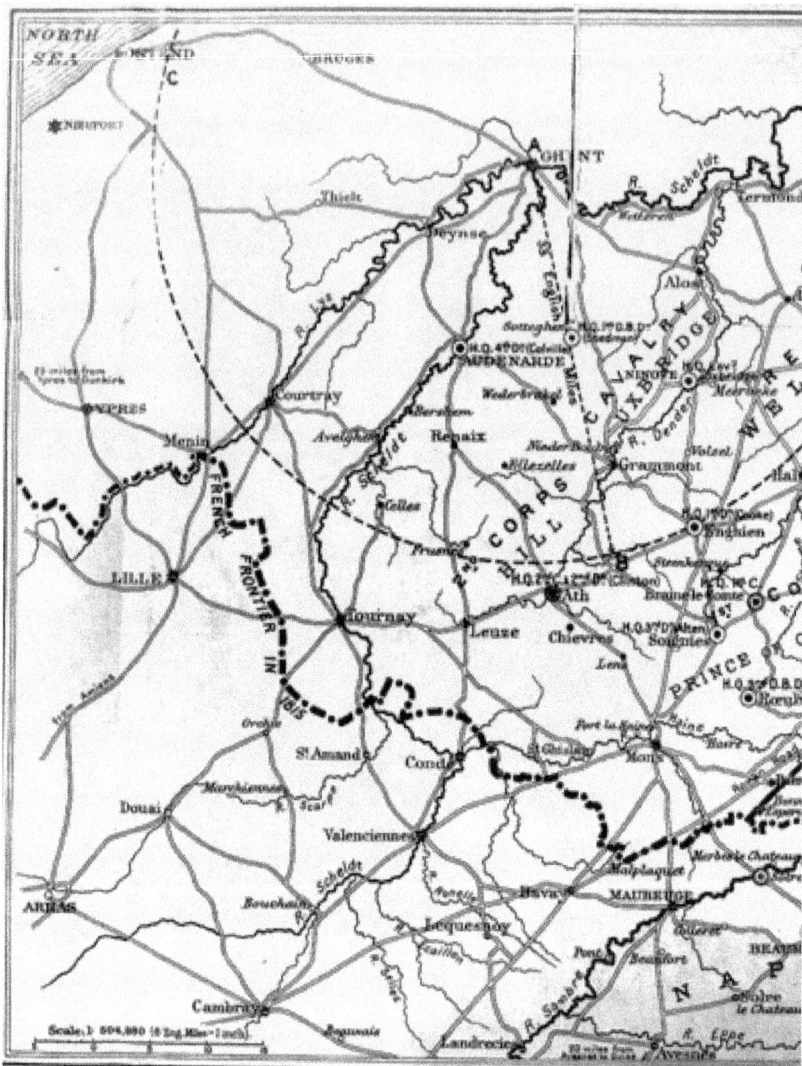

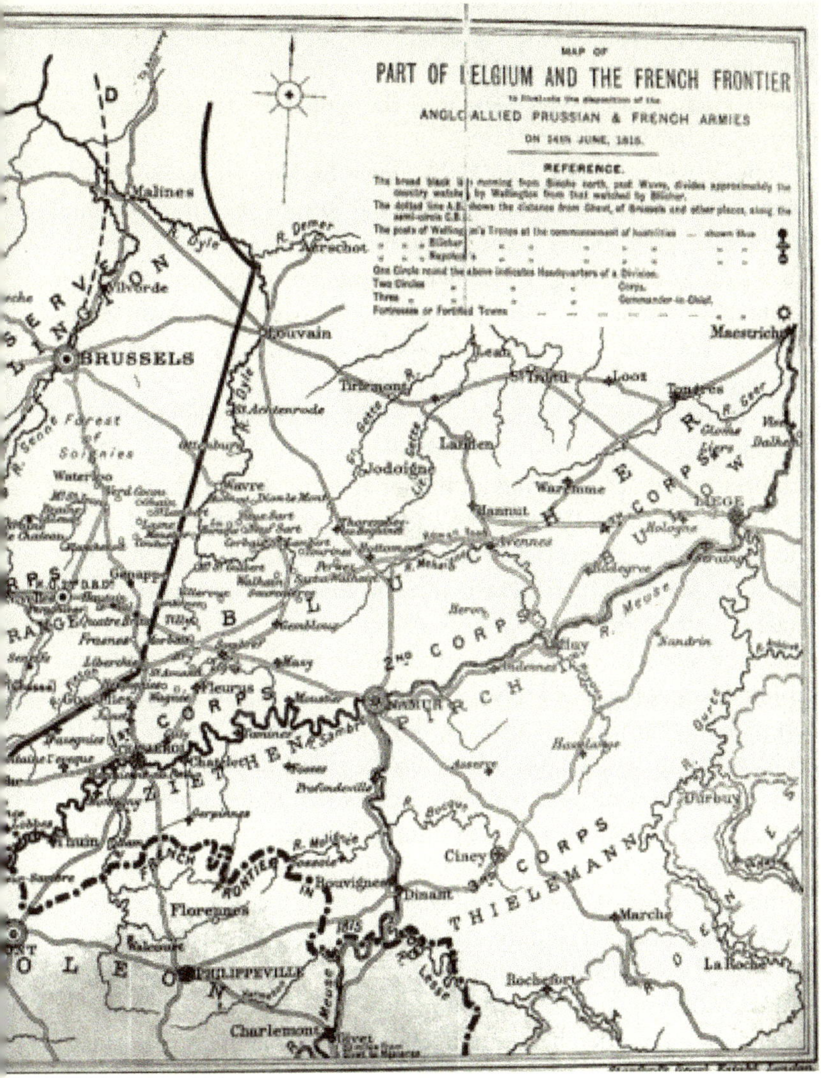

MAP OF

PART OF BELGIUM AND THE FRENCH FRONTIER

to illustrate the disposition of the

ANGLO-ALLIED PRUSSIAN & FRENCH ARMIES

ON 14th JUNE, 1815.

REFERENCE.

The broad black belt running from Binche north, past Wavre, divides approximately the country watched by Wellington from that watched by Blücher.

The dotted line A.B. shows the distance from Ghent, of Brussels and other places, along the semi-circle C.B.

The posts of Wellington's Troops at the commencement of hostilities ... shown thus
           "   "   Blücher   "   "
           "   "   Napoleon "   "

One Circle round the above indicates Headquarters of a Division.

Two Circles   "   "   "   "   Corps.

Three   "   "   "   "   Commander-in-Chief.

Fortresses or Fortified Towns

remained fully prepared for the expected attack on the morrow.

While Napoleon was occupied in prescribing his intended order of attack, he received a despatch from Count Gérard announcing that Lieutenant General de Bourmont, and Colonels Clouet and Villoutreys, attached to the Fourth Corps, had deserted to the enemy—a circumstance which induced the emperor to make some alteration in his dispositions.

The morning of the 15th had scarcely broken, when the French Army commenced its march towards the Sambre, in three columns, from the three bivouacs already mentioned as having been taken up during the previous night. The left column advanced from Solre sur Sambre, by Thuin, upon Marchienne au Pont; the centre from Beaumont, by Ham sur Heure, upon Charleroi; and the right column from Philippeville, by Gerpinnes, upon Châtelet.

As early as half past three o'clock in the morning, the head of the left column came in contact with the Prussian troops in front of Lobbes, firing upon, and driving in, the picquets of the 2nd Battalion of the 1st Regiment of Westphalian Landwehr, commanded by Captain Gillhausen. This officer who was well aware that the French troops that had assembled, the night before, in great force in his front, intended to attack him in the morning, had posted his Battalion so as to afford it every advantage to be derived from the hilly and intersected ground it occupied. The French, however, inclined more to their right, and joined other troops advancing along the road to Thuin, which lay on his left. Shortly after, they drove back an advanced cavalry picquet; and, at half past four, commenced a fire from four guns upon the outpost of Maladrie, about a mile in front of Thuin.

This cannonade, which announced the opening of the campaign by the French, was heard by the Prussian troops forming the left wing of Steinmetz's brigade; but the atmosphere, which was extremely thick and heavy, was most unfavourable for the conveyance of sound; so much so, that the greater portion of the right wing of the brigade remained for a considerable time in ignorance of the enemy's advance.

The firing, however, was distinctly heard at Charleroi; and Zieten, who, by the reports which he forwarded on the 14th to Wellington and Blücher, had fully prepared these commanders to expect an attack, lost no time in communicating to them the important fact, that hostilities had actually commenced.

Shortly before five o'clock, he despatched *courier jägers* to their respective headquarters, Brussels and Namur, with letters containing the information that since half past four o'clock, he had heard several cannon shots fired in his front, and at the time he was writing, the fire of musketry also, but that he had not yet received any report from his outposts. To Blücher he at the same time intimated that he should direct the whole corps to fall back into position; and, should it become absolutely necessary, to concentrate at Fleurus. His report to the Duke of Wellington arrived in Brussels at nine o'clock in the morning; that to Prince Blücher reached Namur between eight and nine o'clock. The former, while it placed the British commander on the *qui vive*, did not induce him to adopt any particular measure—he awaited further and more definite information; but the latter satisfied the Prussian field marshal that he had taken a wise precaution in having already ordered the concentration of his several corps in the position of Sombref.

The Prussian troops at Maladrie checked, for a time, the advance of the French upon Thuin, and maintained their ground for more than an hour, with the greatest bravery. They were overpowered, and driven back upon Thuin. This place was occupied by the 3rd Battalion of the 2nd Westphalian Landwehr, under Major Monsterberg, who, after an obstinate and gallant resistance, during which the battalion suffered an immense loss, was forced to retire, about seven o'clock, upon Montigny, where he found Lieutenant Colonel Woisky, with two squadrons of the 1st West Prussian Dragoons.

The French succeeded in taking this village, and the retreat was then continued in good order, under the protection of Woisky's dragoons, towards Marchienne au Pont; but before reaching this place, the latter were attacked, and completely overthrown by the French cavalry; and the infantry getting into disorder at the same moment were partly cut down, and many were taken prisoners. Indeed so severe was the loss which the 3rd Battalion of the 2nd Westphalian Landwehr suffered in this retreat, that the mere handful of men which remained could not possibly be looked upon as constituting a battalion in the proper meaning of the term. It was reduced to a mere skeleton. Lieutenant Colonel Woisky was wounded on this occasion; but continued, nevertheless, at the head of his dragoons.

Captain Gillhausen, who, as before stated, commanded the Prussian battalion posted at Lobbes, as soon as he had satisfied himself that Thuin was taken, saw the necessity of effecting his own retreat, which he did, after the lapse of half an hour, drawing in his picquets, and occupying the bridge over the Sambre with one company. He then fell

FRENCH HUSSARS BID FAREWELL

back, and occupied the Wood of Sar de Lobbes, where he received an order, as soon as the post of Hoarbes was also taken by the enemy, to continue his retreat, taking a direction between Fontaine l'Evéque and Anderlues.

The post at Abbaye d'Alnes, occupied by the 3rd Battalion of the 1st Westphalian Landwehr, under the temporary command of Captain Grollmann, also fell into the hands of the French, between eight and nine o'clock.

As soon as the commander of the First Prussian Brigade—General Steinmetz—was made acquainted with the attack upon his most advanced posts along the Sambre, he despatched an officer of his staff—Major Arnauld—to the Dutch-Belgian General van Merlen at St Symphorien, situated on the road between Binche and Mons, to make him fully acquainted with what had taken place, and with the fact that his brigade was falling back into position. On his way, Major Arnauld directed Major Engelhardt, who commanded the outposts on the right, to lose not a moment in withdrawing the chain of picquets; and on arriving at Binche, he spread the alarm that the French had attacked, and that the left of the brigade was warmly engaged, which rendered it necessary that the right should retire with the utmost expedition. Until this officer's arrival, the Prussian troops in this quarter were wholly ignorant of the attack; the state of the atmosphere, to which allusion has already been made, having prevented their hearing the slightest sound of any firing. They had a much greater extent of ground to pass over in retreat than the rest of the brigade, and yet, by the above unfortunate circumstance, they were the last to retire.

Zieten, having ascertained, about eight o'clock, that the whole French Army appeared to be in motion, and that the direction of the advance of its columns seemed to indicate the probability of Charleroi and its vicinity being the main object of the attack, sent out the necessary orders to his brigades. The First was to retire by Courcelles to the position in rear of Gosselies; the Second was to defend the three bridges over the Sambre, at Marchienne au Pont, Charleroi, and Châtelet, for a time sufficient to enable the First Brigade to effect its retreat towards Gosselies, and thus to prevent its being cut off by the enemy, after which it was to retire behind Gilly; the Third and Fourth Brigades, as also the Reserve Cavalry and Artillery, were to concentrate as rapidly as possible, and to take up a position in rear of Fleurus.

The three points by which the First Brigade was to fall back, were

Artillerie Ostpreuß. Westpreuß. Artillerie- Schlesische Pommersche Landwehr-Offizier Landwehr- Märkische Lützowscher
zu Fuß. Landwehr. Landwehr. Offizier. Landwehr. Landwehr. (Ostpreußischer). Kavallerie. Landwehr Jäger.
(Hornist).

Mont St Aldegonde, for the troops on the right, Anderlues for those in the centre, and Fontaine l'Evêque for the left. In order that they might reach these three points about the same time, Zieten ordered that those in front of Fontaine l'Evêque should yield their ground as slowly as the enemy's attack would admit. Having reached the line of these three points, about ten o'clock, the brigade commenced its further retreat towards Courcelles, having its proper left protected by a separate column consisting of the 1st Regiment of Westphalian Land-wehr and two companies of Silesian Rifles, led by Colonel Hoffmann, in the direction of Roux and Jumet, towards Gosselies.

At Marchienne au Pont stood the 2nd Battalion of the 6th Prussian Regiment, belonging to the Second Brigade of Zieten's corps. The bridge was barricaded, and with the aid of two guns, resolutely maintained against several attacks; after which these troops commenced their retreat upon Gilly, by Dampremy. In the latter place were three companies of the 1st Battalion of the 2nd Regiment of Westphalian Landwehr, with four guns. These also retired about the same time towards Gilly, the guns protecting the retreat by their fire from the churchyard; after which they moved off as rapidly as possible towards Gilly, while the battalion marched upon Fleurus; but the 4th Company, which defended the bridge of La Roux until Charleroi was taken, was too late to rejoin the latter, and therefore attached itself to the First Brigade, which was retreating by its right flank.

Lieutenant General Count Pajol's corps of Light Cavalry formed the Advanced Guard of the centre column of the French Army: it was to have been supported by Vandamme's corps of infantry, but by some mistake, this general had not received his orders, and at six o'clock in the morning had not quitted his bivouac. Napoleon, perceiving the error, led forward the Imperial Guards in immediate support of Pajol. As the latter advanced, the Prussian outposts, though hard pressed, retired, skirmishing in good order. At Couillet, on the Sambre, about a mile and a half below Charleroi, the French cavalry fell upon a company of the 3rd Battalion of the 28th Prussian Regiment, surrounded it, and forced it to surrender.

Immediately afterwards, the French gained possession of Marcinelles, a village quite close to Charleroi, and connected with this town by a dike 300 paces in length, terminating at a bridge, the head of which was palisaded. Along this dike the French cavalry ventured to advance, but was suddenly driven back by the Prussian Skirmishers, who lined the hedges and ditches intersecting the opposite slope of the embankment; a part of the village was retaken, and an attempt made to destroy the bridge. The French, however, having renewed the attack with increased force, succeeded in finally carrying both the dike and the bridge, and by this means effected their entrance into Charleroi. Major Rohr, who commanded this post, now felt himself under the necessity of effecting his retreat with the 1st Battalion of the 6th Prussian Regiment, towards the preconcerted position in rear of Gilly, which he did in good order, though hotly pursued by detachments of Pajol's dragoons.

By eleven o'clock, the French were in full possession of Charleroi, as also of both banks of the Sambre above the town, and Reille's corps was effecting its passage over the river at Marchienne au Pont.

The right column of the French Army, commanded by Count Gérard, having a longer distance to traverse, had not yet reached its destined point, Châtelet on the Sambre.

The Fourth Brigade of Zieten's corps, as also the advanced portion of the Third, continued their retreat towards Fleurus; General Jagow, who commanded the latter, having left the two Silesian Rifle Companies and the Fusilier battalion[1] of the 7th Prussian Regiment at Farciennes and Tamines, for the purpose of watching the points of passage across the Sambre, and of protecting the left flank of the position at Gilly. But, from the moment the French made themselves masters of Charleroi, and of the left bank of the Sambre above that town, the situation of the First Brigade under General Steinmetz became extremely critical. Zieten immediately ordered General Jagow, whose brigade was in reserve, to detach Colonel Rüchel with the 29th Regiment of Infantry to Gosselies, for the purpose of facilitating General Steinmetz's retreat. The colonel found that General Röder (commanding the Reserve Cavalry of the corps) had posted there the 6th Regiment of Prussian *Uhlans* (lancers) under Lieutenant Colonel Lützow, to whom he confided the defence of Gosselies, which he occupied with the 2nd Battalion of the 29th Regiment, while he placed himself in reserve with the other two battalions.

As soon as the French had assembled in sufficient force at Charleroi, Napoleon ordered Count Pajol to detach General Clary's Brigade towards Gosselies, and to advance with the remainder of the First Corps of Reserve Cavalry towards Gilly. General Clary, with the 1st French Hussars, reached Jumet, on the left of the Brussels road, and

---

1. The Prussian regiments of infantry generally consisted of three battalions, of which the Third was the Fusilier battalion.

only but little more than a mile from Gosselies, before the First Prussian Brigade had crossed the Piéton. He now advanced to attack Gosselies, but was met by Lieutenant Colonel Lützow and his dragoons, who defeated and repulsed him, and thus secured for General Steinmetz time to pass the Piéton; and as soon as the latter had turned the defile of Gosselies, Colonel Rüchel with the 29th Regiment moved off to rejoin the Third Brigade.

The check thus experienced by General Clary led to his being supported by Lieutenant General Lefèbvre-Desnouettes, with the Light Cavalry of the Guard and the two batteries attached to this force; and a regiment from Lieutenant General Duhesme's division of the Young Guard was advanced midway between Charleroi and Gosselies as a reserve to Lefèbvre-Desnouettes. The Advanced Guard of Reille's corps, which had crossed the Sambre at Marchienne au Pont, was also moving directly upon Gosselies, with the design both of cutting off the retreat of Zieten's troops along the Brussels road, and of separating the Prussians from the Anglo-Allied Army. D'Erlon's corps, which was considerably in the rear, received orders to follow and support Reille.

General Steinmetz, upon approaching Gosselies, and perceiving the strength of the enemy and the consequent danger of being completely cut off, with the utmost promptitude and decision directed the 2nd Battalion of the 1st Westphalian Landwehr to march against the enemy's left flank, with a view to divert his attention and to check his advance, while, protected by the 6th Lancers and the 1st Silesian Hussars, he continued his retreat towards Heppignies. This plan was attended with complete success; and Steinmetz reached Heppignies with scarcely any loss, followed by General Girard at the head of the Seventh Division of the Second French *Corps d'Armée*, with the remainder of which Reille continued his advance along the Brussels road. Heppignies was already occupied by the 2nd and 3rd Battalions of the 12th Prussian Regiment, and with this increase of strength Steinmetz drew up in order of battle, and upon Girard's attempting to force the place, after having previously occupied Ransart, he advanced against him, and drove him back in the direction of Gosselies. A brisk cannonade ensued, which was maintained on the part of the Prussians, only so long as it was deemed necessary for covering their retreat upon Fleurus.

In conformity with Zieten's Orders, General Pirch II., when forced to abandon Charleroi, retired to Gilly, where, having concentrated the Second Brigade, about two o'clock, he took up a favourable position

Garde Impériale

along a ridge in rear of a rivulet; his right resting upon the abbey of Soleilmont, his left extending towards Châtelineau, which flank was also protected by a detachment occupying the bridge of Châtelet, Gérard's corps not having as yet arrived at that point.

He posted the Fusilier battalion of the 6th Regiment in a small wood which lay in advance on the exterior slope of the ridge; four guns on the right, upon an eminence commanding the valley in front; two guns between this point and the Fleurus road, as also two guns on the right of the road, to impede as much as possible the advance of any columns towards Gilly. The sharpshooters of the Fusilier battalion of the 6th Regiment, by lining some adjacent hedges, afforded protection to the artillery. The 2nd Battalion of the 28th Regiment was stationed beyond the Fleurus road, near the abbey of Soleilmont, in such a manner as to be concealed from the enemy.

The 1st Battalion of this regiment stood across the road leading to Lambusart; and its Fusilier battalion was posted more to the left, towards Châtelet. The 2nd Battalion of the 2nd Westphalian Landwehr was posted in support of the battery in rear of Gilly. The 1st Battalion of this regiment, previously mentioned as on the march from Damp-remy to Fleurus, passed through Lodelinsart and Soleilmont, and re-joined the brigade in rear of Gilly, before the affair had terminated. The 1st and 2nd Battalions of the 6th Regiment formed the reserve. The 1st West Prussian Dragoons were posted on the declivity of the ridge towards Châtelet: they furnished the advanced posts, and pa-trolled the valley of the Sambre, maintaining the communication with the detachment at Farciennes, belonging to the Third Brigade.

General Pirch, foreseeing that in the event of the enemy succeed-ing in turning his right, a rapid advance along the Fleurus road would be the means of greatly molesting, if not of seriously endangering, his retreat upon Lambusart, took the precaution of having this road blocked up by an abatis in the wood through which it led.

Vandamme did not reach Charleroi until three o'clock in the af-ternoon, when he received orders to pursue the Prussians, in con-junction with Grouchy, along the Fleurus road. It was, however, a considerable time before any advance was made. In the first place, the whole of Vandamme's corps had to cross the Sambre by a single bridge; secondly, both generals were deceived by exaggerated reports concerning the strength of the Prussians in rear of the Fleurus woods; and Grouchy who had gone forward to reconnoitre, returned to the emperor with a request for further instructions. Upon this, Napoleon undertook a reconnaissance in person, accompanied by the four *squadrons de se*rvice; and having formed an opinion that the amount of force in question did not exceed 18,000 or 20,000 men, he gave his orders for the attack of General Pirch's brigade.

The French generals having directed their preparatory dispositions from the windmill near the farm of Grand Drieu, opened the engagement about six o'clock in the evening, with a fire from two batteries. Three columns of infantry advanced in echelon from the right, the first directing its course towards the little wood occupied by the Fusilier battalion of the 6th Prussian Regiment; the second passing to the right of Gilly; and the third winding round the left of this village. The attack was supported by two brigades of General Excelmans' cavalry corps, namely, those of Generals Bourthe and Bonnemain; of which one was directed towards Châtelet, thus menacing the Prussian left flank, and the other advanced along the Fleurus road.

The battery attached to the Second Prussian Brigade was in the act of replying with great spirit to the superior fire from the French artillery, and the Light Troops were already engaged, when General Pirch received Zieten's orders to avoid an action against superior numbers, and to retire by Lambusart upon Fleurus.

Perceiving the formidable advance and overwhelming force of the enemy, he did not hesitate a moment in carrying those orders into effect, and made his dispositions accordingly; but the retreat had scarcely commenced when his battalions were vigorously assailed by the French cavalry. Napoleon, in the hope of profiting by this retrograde movement, sent against the retreating columns the four *squadrons de service* of the Guard, under General Letort, a distinguished cavalry officer attached to his staff. The Prussian infantry withstood the repeated attacks of the French cavalry with undaunted bravery, and aided by the gallant exertions of Lieutenant Colonel Woisky, who boldly met the enemy with the 1st West Prussian Dragoons, and checked his progress, the greater part of it succeeded in gaining the wood of Fleurus.

The Fusilier Battalion of the 28th Regiment (of which it will be recollected, one company had previously been captured on the right bank of the Sambre) was the only column broken on this occasion. It had been ordered to retire into the wood by Rondchamp, but before it could complete the movement, it was overtaken by the enemy's cavalry, by which it was furiously assailed, and suffered a loss of two thirds of its number.

The Fusilier battalion of the 6th Regiment was more fortunate.

When about five hundred paces from the wood, it was attacked by the enemy's cavalry on the plain, but forming square, and reserving its fire until the French horsemen had approached within twenty or thirty paces, it gallantly repelled several charges. As the vigour with which these attacks were made began to slacken, the battalion cleared its way with the bayonet through the cavalry that continued hovering round it. One of its companies immediately extended itself along the edge of the wood, and kept the French cavalry at bay. The latter suffered severely on this occasion, and General Letort who led the attacks was mortally wounded.

The Brandenburg Dragoons had been detached by Zieten in support of Pirch's brigade, and opportunely reaching the field of action, made several charges against the French cavalry, which they repulsed and compelled to relinquish its pursuit.

Pirch's brigade now took up a position in front of Lambusart, which was occupied by some battalions of the Third Brigade, and General Röder joined it with his remaining three regiments of cavalry and a battery of horse artillery. At this moment, the French cavalry, which was formed up in position, opened a fire from three batteries of horse artillery, and thus brought on a cannonade, with which, however, the affair terminated.

The First Prussian Brigade having safely executed its retreat from Heppignies, towards Fleurus, reached St Amand about eleven o'clock at night.

The detachments left by the Third Brigade at Farciennes and Tamines, had been previously called in, and effected their retreat without any molestation, as did also, subsequently, the Second Brigade from Lambusart, by Boulet, towards Fleurus, protected by the Reserve Cavalry.

Zieten's corps, at three o'clock in the morning had possessed a line of advanced posts, from Dinant on the Meuse, crossing the Sambre at Thuin, and extending as far as Bonne Esperance, in advance of Binche; thus stretching alone a space of from forty to fifty miles in length: its main force occupied the Sambre from Thuin as far as its confluence with the Meuse, an extent of, at least, thirty six miles, exclusive of the numerous windings throughout the whole course of the river between those two points. The men had, since daybreak, been constantly under arms, in motion, and almost as constantly engaged, pursued, and assailed upon all points by an overwhelming superiority of force, headed by the *élite* of the French cavalry; and it was not until

GARDE IMPÉRIALE

about eleven o'clock at night that the corps effected its concentration in position between Ligny and St Amand, at a distance varying from fourteen to twenty miles in rear of its original extended line of outposts; after having successfully fulfilled the arduous task imposed upon it of gaining sufficient time for the concentration, on the following day, of all the Prussian corps, by stemming, as well as its scattered force would admit, the imposing advance of the whole French Army.

The loss of the First Prussian *Corps d'Armée* on the 15th of June, amounted to 1200 men. The fusilier battalions of the 28th Regiment and of the 2nd Westphalian Landwehr, reduced to mere skeletons, were united, and formed into one battalion.

Before ten o'clock on the morning of the 15th, a further order was despatched from the Prussian headquarters to the Third *Corps d'Armée*, to the effect that after resting during the night at Namur, it was to continue its march upon the morning of the 16th, towards Sombref.

At half past eleven o'clock in the forenoon a despatch was forwarded to Bülow, announcing the advance of the French, and requesting that the corps after having rested at Hannut, should commence its march upon Gembloux by daybreak of the 16th, at the latest.

By three o'clock in the afternoon of the 15th, the Second *Corps d'Armée* had taken up the position assigned to it between Onoz and Mazy in the immediate vicinity of Sombref, with the exception, however, of the Seventh Brigade, which, having been stationed in the most remote of the quarters occupied by the corps, did not reach Namur until midnight. Here the latter found an order for its continuance in Namur until the arrival of the Third *Corps d'Armée*; but as this had already taken place, the Brigade, after a few hours' rest, resumed its march, and joined its corps at Sombref about ten o'clock in the morning of the 16th June. Thielemann passed the night at Namur, which he occupied with the Tenth Brigade; the Ninth Brigade bivouacked on the right, and the Eleventh on the left, of Belgrade, a village at a short distance from the town, on the road to Sombref; the Twelfth Brigade in rear of the Ninth; the Reserve Cavalry at Flavinne, between that road and the Sambre; and the Reserve Artillery on the left of the road.

It has already been explained that on the 14th, Blücher sent off a despatch to Bülow desiring him to make such a disposition of his corps as should enable his troops to reach Hannut in one march; and that at midnight of the 14th, a second despatch was forwarded, requiring him to concentrate the Fourth Corps at Hannut. The first of these despatches reached Bülow, at Liege, at five o'clock on the morning of the 15th; when he issued the necessary orders with an instruction that they should be acted upon as soon as the troops had dined, and forwarded a report of this arrangement to headquarters. These orders to his troops had been despatched some hours, and the consequent movements were for the most part in operation, when, towards noon, the second despatch arrived.

Bülow, considering the effect which the change required by this new order would have upon the troops, inasmuch as their reception was prepared in quarters to which, in this case they would no longer proceed, and they would have nothing provided for them in the destined bivouac near Hannut, also as a great proportion of them could not receive the orders for the change in the direction of their march until evening, decided upon deferring the new movement until daybreak of the 16th. The despatch, moreover, did not require him to establish his headquarters at Hannut, but merely suggested that the latter appeared the most suitable for the purpose. The general was, besides, perfectly unconscious of the commencement of hostilities, which, indeed, he had expected would be preceded by a Declaration of War; and he had also good grounds for an opinion which he had formed that it was in contemplation to assemble the whole army at Hannut.

He made a report to headquarters of his reasons for deferring the execution of the order, with the intimation that he would be at Hannut by midday of the 16th. Captain Below, on Bülow's Staff, who carried this despatch, arrived at nine o'clock in the evening of the 15th at Namur, where he discovered that the headquarters of the Army had been transferred to Sombref.

At half past eleven o'clock in the forenoon of the 15th, another despatch was forwarded to Bülow from Namur, announcing the advance of the French, and requesting that the Fourth Corps, after having rested at Hannut, should commence its march upon Gembloux, by daybreak of the 16th at latest. The orderly who carried it was directed to proceed to Hannut, the presumed headquarters of Bülow's corps on that day. On reaching that place, the orderly found the previous despatch lying in readiness for the general, and, mounting a fresh horse, he then went on with both despatches to Liege, where he arrived at sunrise. The orders which they contained had now, however, become impracticable, in consequence of Bülow's not having immediately carried into effect the *first* order to collect at Hannut;

GARDE IMPÉRIALE

and thus by one of those mischances, which, in war, occasionally mar the best planned operations, the opportune arrival of the Fourth Prussian Corps at the Battle of Ligny, which would, in all probability, have changed the aspect of affairs, was rendered a matter of impossibility.

Late in the evening, and after Prince Blücher had established his headquarters at Sombref, Captain Below arrived with the before mentioned report from Count Bülow; on receiving which His Highness was made sensible that he could no longer calculate with certainty upon being joined by the Fourth Corps on the following day.

It was seven o'clock in the evening of the 15th, when Marshal Ney, who had just arrived, joined the emperor near Charleroi, at the point where the road to Fleurus branches off from the one to Brussels. Having expressed the pleasure he felt at seeing him, Napoleon gave him the command of the First and Second *Corps d'Armée*; explaining at the same time that Reille was advancing with three divisions upon Gosselies; that d'Erlon would pass the night at Marchienne au Font; that he would find under his orders Piré's Light Cavalry Division; as also the two regiments of *chasseurs* and lancers of the Guard, of which, however, he was not to make use except as a Reserve. The emperor added:

> Tomorrow, you will be joined by the Reserve Corps of Heavy Cavalry under Kellermann. Go and drive back the enemy.

It has already been shown in the preceding chapter, that the extreme left of the Duke of Wellington's army, composed of de Perponcher's Second Dutch-Belgian Division, rested upon the Charleroi road to Brussels. The Second Brigade of this Division, under Colonel Gödecke, was thus located:—1st Battalion of the 2nd Regiment of Nassau, at Hautain le Val; the 2nd Battalion, at Frasne and Villers Peruin; the 3rd Battalion, at Bézy, Sart à Mavelines, and Quatre Bras; both battalions of the regiment of Orange-Nassau, at Genappe. There was also at Frasne a Dutch battery of horse artillery, under Captain Byleveld.

Early on the morning of the 15th, these troops were lying quietly in their cantonments, perfectly unconscious of the advance of the French Army, when they heard a brisk cannonade at a distance in the direction of Charleroi; but not having received the slightest intimation of the enemy's approach, they concluded that the firing proceeded from the Prussian artillery practice, which they had frequently heard before, and to which they had therefore become accustomed. Gradually towards noon, however, the cannonade became more distinctly audible; and, in the afternoon, the arrival of a wounded Prussian soldier completely set at rest all doubt as to the advance of the French. An orderly was immediately despatched with the intelligence to the regimental headquarters, whence it was also communicated to General de Perponcher's headquarters at Nivelles.

In the meantime, Major Normann, who commanded the 2nd Battalion of the 2nd Regiment of Nassau, drew up the latter with the battery in position in rear of Frasne, and upon the road to Quatre Bras, after having posted a picquet of observation in advance of the village.

Perponcher lost not a moment in ordering both brigades of his division to hasten towards their respective points of assembly; the 1st Brigade, under General Bylandt, to Nivelles, and the 2nd, under Colonel Gödecke, to Quatre Bras.

Before this order, however, could possibly reach these troops, Prince Bernhard of Saxe Weimar, who commanded the regiment of Orange-Nassau, at Genappe, having been informed by the officer of the Dutch-Belgian *Maréchaussées*, who had been compelled to quit his post at Charleroi, that the French were advancing from that place, took upon himself to move forward with the above regiment from Genappe to Quatre Bras, and despatched a report of such movement to the headquarters of the brigade at Hautain le Val, as also, subsequently, to General de Perponcher at Nivelles, by Captain Gagern, of the Dutch-Belgian Staff, who happened to be just then at Genappe, for the purpose of collecting information.

About six o'clock in the evening, parties of lancers belonging to Piré's Light Cavalry Division of Reille's corps appeared in front of Frasne, and soon drove in Major Normann's picquet.

This officer placed a company on the south or French side of Frasne, for the purpose of preventing as long as possible the entrance of the French into the village. Byleveld's battery took post on the north side of the village, and the remaining companies of the 2nd Battalion of the 2nd Regiment of Nassau drew up in its support. Two guns were upon the road, and three on each side of it. After some time, the lancers, having been reinforced, compelled the company before mentioned to retire through the village and fall back upon the main body, which then opened a vigorous fire, by which this front attack by the French cavalry was defeated. The latter then made a disposition to turn the left flank of these troops; on perceiving which Major Normann and Captain Byleveld resolved upon falling back to within a short distance in front of Quatre Bras. The retreat was conducted in excellent order, the battery continuing to fire along the high road.

Quatre Bras was the rendezvous of the Second Brigade; and the 3rd Battalion of the 2nd Regiment of Nassau, which was cantoned in its immediate vicinity, had already, without waiting for the receipt of superior orders, assembled at that point. Prince Bernhard, on arriving there with the regiment of Orange-Nassau, and learning the particulars of the engagement at Frasne, assumed the command as senior officer, and being fully impressed with the importance of securing the point of junction of the high road from Charleroi to Brussels, with that from Namur to Nivelles, came to the resolution of making a firm stand at Quatre Bras. This decision accorded entirely with the spirit of the orders which had in the meantime been despatched from Braine le Comte, the Dutch-Belgian headquarters, on the receipt of intelligence of the French having crossed the Sambre. General de Perponcher, who commanded the division, had also approved of the prince's determination, and Colonel Gödecke who was at Hautain le Val, and who had hitherto commanded the Second Brigade, now tendered his command to His Serene Highness, who immediately accepted it.

The prince pushed forward the 3rd Battalion of the 2nd Regiment of Nassau, in Column, upon the high road towards Frasne, detached two companies of the 1st Battalion, and the Volunteer *Jägers*, to the defence of the wood of Bossu, and the remaining companies on the high road towards Hautain le Val; and posted the remainder of the brigade at Quatre Bras, along the Namur road. Of Byleveld's horse battery, four guns were posted in advance in the direction of Frasne, two on the road to Namur, and two in rear of the main body.

By the determined show of resistance which His Serene Highness displayed, as well as by the vigorous cannonade which he maintained, Piré's Advanced Guard, the left flank of which became endangered by the Dutch occupying the wood of Bossu, was forced to retire in its turn, which it did unmolested, and brought back intelligence that Quatre Bras was occupied by ten battalions with artillery, and that Wellington's troops were moving to concentrate at this important point.

At ten o'clock at night, Ney's forces were thus disposed:—Piré's Light Cavalry Division and Bachelu's infantry division occupied Frasne, a village situated upon the Brussels road, about two miles and a half on the French side of Quatre Bras; the two regiments of *chasseurs* and lancers of the Guard were in reserve in rear of Frasne; Reille was with two divisions, and the artillery attached to them, at Gosselies: these divisions ensured the communication until the arrival of d'Erlon's corps, which was to remain that night at Marchienne au Pont. The remaining division of Reille's corps (Girard's) was at Heppignies, and thus served to maintain the communication with the main column under Napoleon. The troops were greatly fatigued by having been kept constantly on the march since three o'clock in the morning; the strength of the different regiments, the names of their colonels, and even of the generals, were unknown to the marshal, as also the number of men that had been able to keep up with the heads of the columns at the end of this long march.

These circumstances, combined with the information brought in from Quatre Bras, induced Ney to decline risking a night attack upon that point; and he contented himself with taking up a position in advance of Frasne. Having issued such orders as he deemed essential, and enjoined the most vigilant look out, he returned to Charleroi, where he arrived about midnight; partook of supper with Napoleon (who had just arrived from the right wing of the army), and conferred with the emperor upon the state of affairs until two o'clock in the morning.

The first intimation which the Duke of Wellington received on the 15th, of hostilities having commenced, was conveyed in the report already alluded to, as having been forwarded by General Zieten, shortly before five o'clock in the morning, and as having reached Brussels at nine o'clock. It was not, however, of a nature to enable the duke to form an opinion as to any real attack being contemplated by the enemy in that quarter. It simply announced that the Prussian outposts in front of Charleroi were engaged. It might be the commencement of a real attack in this direction, but it might also be a diversion in favour of an attack in some other direction, such as Mons. In fact, until further information was received, it could only be considered in the light of an affair of outposts.

Not long after three o'clock in the afternoon, the Prince of Orange arrived in Brussels, and informed the duke that the Prussian outposts had been attacked and forced to fall back. His Royal Highness had ridden to the front at five o'clock in the morning, from Braine le Comte, and had a personal interview at St Symphorien, with General van Merlen, whose troops were on the immediate right of the Prussians, who had retired. After having given to this general verbal orders respecting his brigade, the prince left the outposts between nine and ten o'clock, and repaired to Brussels to communicate to the duke all the information he had obtained respecting the enemy's attack upon the Prussian advanced posts.

This, however, was not sufficiently conclusive to induce His Grace to resolve upon any immediate step; but, in about an hour afterwards, that is, about half past four, General von Muffling, the Prussian officer attached to the British headquarters, waited upon the duke with a communication which had been despatched from Namur by Prince Blücher at noon, conveying the intelligence that the French had attacked the Prussian posts at Thuin and Lobbes on the Sambre, and that they appeared to be advancing in the direction of Charleroi. The duke was fully prepared for this intelligence, though uncertain how soon it might arrive. The reports which had been made to him from the outposts, especially from those of the 1st Hussars of the King's German Legion, stationed in the vicinity of Mons and Tournai, gave sufficient indication that the enemy was concentrating his forces. But, as observed in the preceding chapter, His Grace was determined to make no movement until the real line of attack should become manifest; and hence it was, that if the attack had been made even at a later period, his dispositions would have remained precisely the same.

The duke at once gave orders for the whole of his troops to assemble at the headquarters of their respective divisions and to hold themselves in immediate readiness to march. At the same time an express was despatched to Major General Dörnberg, requiring information concerning any movement that might have been made on the part of the enemy in the direction of Mons.

The following were the movements ordered by the duke. Upon the left of the army, which was nearest to the presumed point of attack—Perponcher's and Chassé's Dutch-Belgian divisions were to be assembled that night at Nivelles, on which point Alten's British division (the Third) was to march as soon as collected at Braine le Comte; but this movement was not to be made until the enemy's attack upon the right of the Prussian Army and the left of the Allied Army had become a matter of certainty. Cooke's British division (the First) was to be collected that night at Enghien, and to be in readiness to move at a moment's notice.

Along the central portion of the army—Clinton's British division (the Second) was to be assembled that night at Ath, and to be in readiness also to move at a moment's notice. Colville's British division (the Fourth) was to be collected that night at Grammont, with the exception of the troops beyond the Scheldt, which were to be moved to Audenarde.

Upon the right of the army—Stedmann's Dutch-Belgian division, and Anthing's Dutch-Belgian (Indian) Brigade were, after occupying Audenarde with 500 men, to be assembled at Sotteghem, so as to be ready to march in the morning.

The cavalry were to be collected that night at Ninhove, with the exception of the 2nd Hussars of the King's German Legion, who were to remain on the look out between the Scheldt and the Lys; and of Dörnberg's brigade, with the Cumberland Hussars, which were to march that night upon Vilvorde, and to bivouac on the high road near to that town.

The Reserve was thus disposed—Picton's British Division (the Fifth), the 81st British Regiment, and Best's Hanoverian brigade (of Cole's division), were to be in readiness to march from Brussels at a moment's notice. Vincke's Hanoverian brigade (of Picton's division) was to be collected that night at Hal, and to be in readiness at daylight on the following morning to move towards Brussels, and to halt on the road between Alost and Assche for further orders. The Duke of Brunswick's corps was to be collected that night on the high road between Brussels and Vilvorde. Kruse's Nassau brigade was to be collected at daylight on the following morning upon the Louvain road, and to be in readiness to move at a moment's notice. The Reserve Artillery was to be in readiness to move at daylight.

It was ten o'clock at night when the first intelligence of the attack made by the French in the direction of Frasne, was received at the Prince of Orange's headquarters, at Braine le Comte. It was carried by Captain Gagern, who, as previously mentioned, had been despatched by Prince Bernhard of Saxe Weimar, with His Serene Highness's report of the affair, to General Perponcher at Nivelles, and who was subsequently sent on by the general, with this information to the above headquarters. Lieutenant Webster, *aide de camp* to the Prince of Orange, started soon afterwards for Brussels, with a report from the Dutch-Belgian Quartermaster General, de Constant Rebecque, stating what had taken place, and detailing the measures which he had thought proper to adopt. These measures did not entirely coincide with the instructions above given, as issued by the duke, because they were consequent upon the affair at Frasne, with which His Grace at that time was unacquainted; but they were perfectly consistent with the spirit of those instructions, inasmuch as they were not adopted "until the enemy's attack upon the right of the Prussian Army, and the left of the Allied Army had become a matter of certainty." The enemy's advance along the Charleroi road had already been successfully checked at Quatre Bras, and the necessity of immediately collecting at this important point, the troops ordered by the duke "to be assembled that night at Nivelles" was too obvious to be mistaken.

A little before ten o'clock on the same evening, a further communication reached the duke from Prince Blücher, announcing the crossing of the Sambre by the French Army, headed by Napoleon in person; and the required intelligence from other quarters having arrived almost at the same moment, and confirmed him in the opinion "that the enemy's movement upon Charleroi was the real attack," he issued, at ten o'clock p.m., the following Orders for the march of his troops to their Left :—Alten's division to continue its movement from Braine le Comte upon Nivelles. Cooke's division to move from Enghien upon Braine le Comte. Clinton's and Colville's divisions to move from Ath, Grammont, and Audenarde, upon Enghien. The cavalry to continue its movement from Ninhove upon Enghien.

The disposition of the French left column, under Ney, during the night of the 15th, has already been shown. The centre column of the French Army was thus located—Vandamme's corps bivouacked in the wood of Fleurus; Pajol's corps of Light Cavalry at Lambusart; the Third Light Cavalry Division, under Domon, on the left, at the outlet of the wood, and the Heavy Cavalry Corps of Excelmans between the Light Cavalry and Vandamme; the Guards bivouacked between Charleroi and Gilly; and Lobau's corps, together with Milhaud's Heavy Cavalry corps, lay in rear of Charleroi. The Eight Column, consisting of Gérard's corps, bivouacked in front of the bridge of Châtelet, which point it had reached during the evening.

The result of the proceedings on the 15th was highly favourable to Napoleon. He had completely effected the passage of the Sambre; he was operating with the main portion of his forces directly upon the preconcerted point of concentration of Blücher's Army, and was already in the immediate front of the chosen position, before that concentration could be accomplished; he was also operating with another portion upon the high road to Brussels, and had come in contact with the left of Wellington's troops; he had also placed himself so far in advance upon this line, that even a partial junction of the forces of the Allied commanders was already rendered a hazardous operation, without a previous retrograde movement; and he thus had it in his power to bring the principal weight of his arms against the one, whilst, with the remainder of his force, he held the other at bay. This formed the grand object of his operations on the morrow.

But however excellent, or even perfect, this plan of operation may appear in theory, still there were other circumstances, which, if taken into consideration, would scarcely seem to warrant a well grounded anticipation of a successful issue. Napoleon's troops had been constantly under arms, marching, and fighting, since two o'clock in the morning, the hour at which they broke up from their position at Solre sur Sambre, Beaumont, and Philippeville, within the French frontier: they required time for rest and refreshment; they lay widely scattered between their advanced posts and the Sambre; Ney's forces were in detached bodies from Frasne as far as Marchienne an Pont. the halting place of d'Erlon's corps; and although Vandamme's corps was in the wood of Fleurus, Lobau's corps and the Guards were halted at Charleroi, and Gérard's corps at Châtelet. Hence, instead of an imposing advance, with the first glimmering of the dawn of the 16th, the whole morning would necessarily be employed by the French in effecting a closer junction of their forces, and in making their preparatory dispositions for attack; an interval of time invaluable to the Allies, by the greater facility which it afforded them for the concentration of a sufficient force to hold their enemy in check, and to frustrate his design of defeating them in detail.

In taking a calm retrospect of the dispositions made by Napoleon on the night of the 15th of June, we become strongly impressed with a conviction, that to the laxity of those dispositions, to the absence which they indicated of that energetic perseverance and restless activity which characterised the most critical of his operations in former Wars, may, in a very great degree, be attributed the failure of the Campaign on the part of the French. The great advantages derived by Napoleon from the result of his operations during the 15th, have been already set forth; but of what avail were those advantages to him, if he neglected the requisite measures for effectually retaining them within his grasp; or if, having secured them, he hesitated in following them up with the promptitude and energy which their complete development demanded of him? His position, if judged by that of his most advanced forces, was all that could be desired; but, by fatally neglecting to concentrate the remainder of his troops in the immediate support of that advance, the important advantages which such a position held forth were completely neutralised. Doubtless the troops required rest; but, if one portion required it more than another, it was that which now lay most in advance: they had performed the longest march, and had withstood, in addition, the whole brunt of the action; so there was no reason whatever why the remainder of the French Army should not have been so far advanced as to afford direct support to the important position taken up by the leading divisions: that which had been so successfully effected by the heads of the columns, might have been attained with infinitely greater ease and security by the masses which followed.

And even supposing that serious impediments stood in the way of the full accomplishment of this concentration, such as the usual delays occasioned by the lengthening out of the columns of march, to what did they amount in comparison with so many brilliant instances of what had been overcome by the noble and heroic efforts of a French Army headed by Napoleon? Had it even required some sacrifice, which at the most could only have consisted in the temporary diminution of strength, by the loss of stragglers on the march, what was this when placed in the balance with the fulfilment of the grand design of Napoleon's invasion of Belgium—preventing the junction of the Allied Armies, and overthrowing them in detail?

The commencement of this design, in which the essential requisite was rapidity of movement, had been eminently successful: a vantage ground had been gained which offered the most encouraging prospect of success: of Blücher's four corps, only one, Zieten's, had assembled in the chosen position of Ligny, on the night of the 15th; Pirch's, which had arrived from Namur, was in bivouac between Onoz and Mazy, about six miles from Ligny; Thielemann's corps, which had quitted its cantonments around Ciney at half past seven o'clock in the morning, passed the night at Namur, about fifteen miles from Ligny; Bülow's corps, supposed by Blücher to be then at Hannut, was still at Liege, about sixty miles distant from Ligny.

Between this position of Ligny and that occupied by the leading divisions of Napoleon's main army, namely the villages of Lambusart, Wagnée, and the wood of Fleurus, there was an interval of not more than from two to three miles! Hence every thing was favourable to the French emperor's plan, which only required to be carried on with the same vigour and activity that had marked its commencement; the fate of Napoleon, of France, and of Europe, hung upon its issue; not an hour, not a moment should have been suffered to pass unheeded;

and had the French right been concentrated during the night in this position, as also the left under Ney, between Gosselies and Frasne, and had an impetuous attack, with overwhelming force, been made not later than five o'clock on the following morning, upon both Zieten's and Pirch's corps, not at that time united, it is very possible that these troops would have been beaten in detail, that Thielemann's corps, advancing from Namur, would either have shared the same fate, or have moved off in the direction of Hannut or Liege to effect a junction with Bülow, whilst Ney would either have been enabled to secure the important point of Quatre Bras before the arrival of any considerable portion of the Anglo-Allied troops, or would have held his own force advantageously disposed for a junction with that of Napoleon, on the latter moving to the left, by the Namur road, for the purpose of bringing the great mass of his army against Wellington.

Instead of this, what happened? Of the French right, its main force remained the whole night at Charleroi and Châtelet, on the Sambre, whilst between the advance of Ney's forces at Frasne and his rear at Marchienne au Pont, there was an interval of about twelve miles. Napoleon did not advance towards Fleurus until between eleven and twelve o'clock on the 16th, by which time Zieten's, Pirch's, and Thielemann's corps were all concentrated and in position, and he did not commence the Battle of Ligny until nearly three o'clock in the afternoon; while Ney, on his side, in consequence of his operations having been rendered subordinate to those of the emperor, delayed to advance with any degree of vigour until between two and three o'clock, about which time Wellington's Reserve reached Quatre Bras, from Brussels, and joined the forces then engaged in front of that point!

EMPEROR NAPOLEON

CHAPTER 5

Nivelles and Quatre Bras

With the early dawn of the 16th of June, the whole of the Duke of Wellington's forces were in movement towards Nivelles and Quatre Bras. Previously to starting from Brussels for the latter point, His Grace despatched an order for the movement of the cavalry and of Clinton's British division upon Braine le Comte, as also of the troops under Prince Frederick of the Netherlands, consisting of Stedmann's Dutch Belgian division, and of Anthing's Dutch Belgian (Indian) Brigade, from Sotteghem to Enghien, after leaving 500 men, as before directed, in Audenarde.

Picton's division quitted Brussels by the Charleroi road about two o'clock in the morning; and the Duke of Brunswick's corps somewhat later. Kruse's Nassau Brigade received orders to follow along the same road, but having been dispersed in extended cantonments between Brussels and Louvain, it required some considerable time to collect together, and did not therefore reach Quatre Bras sufficiently early to take part in the action.

The disposition made by Colonel the Prince Bernhard of Saxe Weimar at this point, on the night of the 15th, with the Second Brigade of Perponcher's Dutch-Belgian division, has already been described. Soon after ten o'clock on that evening, Major Count Limburg Stirum, Dutch *aide de camp* to the Prince of Orange, left Braine le Comte for Nivelles, with a verbal order from the Dutch-Belgian quartermaster general, enjoining General Perponcher to hold his ground to the last extremity, to support his Second Brigade by the First, and even to ask for aid from the Third Anglo-Allied Division, and from the Dutch-Belgian cavalry division; and, at all events, to send an officer to acquaint the commanders of these divisions with the state of affairs. This message appears to have reached Nivelles about midnight.

Previously to this, that is, between nine and ten o'clock in the evening, Captain Crassier's company of the 27th Battalion of *Chasseurs* moved out from Nivelles towards Quatre Bras *en reconnaissance*. About two o'clock in the morning, Perponcher himself followed with the remainder of the *chasseurs*, which body reached Quatre Bras at four o'clock. General Bylandt, who commanded the First Brigade, ordered the remaining battalions of the latter, and his artillery, to commence their march from Nivelles at five o'clock. The 7th Dutch Line Battalion was directed to remain at Nivelles until relieved by Alten's division.

At three o'clock in the morning, Perponcher arrived at Quatre Bras, and after having reconnoitred the position, immediately commenced operations for recovering the ground lost on the previous evening. Just at this time a detachment of about fifty Prussian Hussars of the 2nd Silesian Regiment, under Lieutenant Zehelin, who, on the previous day, had been driven back from near Gosselies, and had retreated towards Hautain le Val, gallantly advanced to the front, attacked the enemy's outposts, forced them to retire, and then formed a chain of vedettes. As soon as the Dutch-Belgian troops had advanced to within a short distance of these Prussian Hussars, the latter moved off by their left towards Sombref.

Prince Bernhard of Saxe Weimar's Brigade penetrated deeper into the wood of Bossu, and secured the entrances into it from the French side.

Perponcher directed the 2nd Battalion of the 2nd Regiment of Nassau to take post on an eminence in advance towards Frasne, and stationed the 3rd Battalion of this regiment more to the left. The latter, however, was soon relieved by the 27th Chasseurs, which battalion, on reaching Quatre Bras, at four o'clock in the morning, had detached two companies to the left. These moved steadily forward in extended order towards the wood of Delhutte, outside of which the enemy showed his Light Troops. They succeeded in forcing back the French into a hollow way bordering the wood, where the latter maintained themselves for some little time, and then retired into the wood itself. Taking advantage of the cover afforded by the edge of the wood, the French now poured a deadly fire upon their assailants, who retreated to some favourable ground a little in advance of their battalion.

The Prince of Orange arrived at Quatre Bras about six o'clock, and immediately reconnoitred the position of the enemy, and that occupied by his own troops. Having expressed his perfect satisfaction

PRINCE OF ORANGE LEADING THE ATTACK AT QUATRE BRAS

with all the arrangements and dispositions which had been made, both on the previous evening and on that morning, he ordered the troops then present to take up a position more in advance, for the purpose of imposing upon the enemy; enjoining at the same time, all unnecessary firing, it being desirable under then existing circumstances, to avoid bringing on prematurely an attack by the enemy.

Ney, having quitted Charleroi at a very early hour in the morning, returned to Gosselies, where he communicated with Reille, whom he ordered to assemble the force then with him, consisting of two infantry divisions and their artillery, and to advance upon Frasne: to which point the marshal repaired in person. Here he collected all the information which the generals and other officers had been able to obtain respecting the enemy; and being naturally anxious to make himself acquainted with the details of the force placed so suddenly under his orders, he desired Colonel Heymès, his first *aide de camp*, to repair to every regiment, and note down their strength and the names of the commanding officers; after the performance of which duty, Colonel Heymès laid before the marshal a return of the troops in the field.

The uncertainty in which Ney was placed as to the amount of force concentrated by the Allies during the night in rear of Quatre Bras, and the conviction which he had reason to entertain that the Prussians were in strong force at no very great distance on his right, and that therefore any check experienced by the main column under Napoleon, would endanger his right flank and even his line of communication, rendered him cautious in attacking a point so considerably in advance of the emperor's left, without ample means at hand to enable him, in case of disaster, to maintain that line, or, in the event of success, to effectually establish himself at Quatre Bras, and derive every possible advantage from its possession, by checking, if not defeating in detail, any body of troops that might be approaching it as a point of concentration from either Nivelles or Brussels.

Hence he became extremely anxious for the arrival of d'Erlon's corps and the promised Third Corps of Heavy Cavalry under Kellermann; the more so, as although Lefèbvre-Desnouette's Light Cavalry of the Guard was nearer at hand, he had been desired by Napoleon not to make use of it. Officers of the *chasseurs* and lancers of the Guard (in consequence of the deficiency of staff officers) were sent to the rear in the direction of Marchienne au Pont, with orders to hasten the march of the First Corps upon Frasne; while Ney himself was busily occupied in reconnoitring the enemy's position and movements.

Whilst so employed, a despatch reached him from the emperor, acquainting him that he had just ordered Kellermann's Dragoons to march to Gosselies, where they would be at his disposal; stating, at the same time, his intention to withdraw Lefèbvre-Desnouette's Light Cavalry of the Guard from the force under his command; and expressing a wish to be informed of the exact disposition of the First and Second Corps, and of the cavalry divisions attached to them, as also of the probable strength of the enemy, and of the particulars which had been obtained concerning him.

The 5th Battalion of Dutch Militia, which arrived at Quatre Bras about seven o'clock, was ordered, some time afterwards, to occupy the farm of Gemioncourt. The other battalions of Bylandt's Brigade, as they arrived in succession, formed a reserve, extending itself from the point of intersection of the two high roads along the Nivelles road, and in rear of the wood of Bossu. About nine o'clock, Captain Stievenaar's Foot Battery attached to Bylandt's brigade also arrived at Quatre Bras.

Aided by these reinforcements, the Prince of Orange made his dispositions for impeding as much as possible the expected French attack, and maintaining his ground in front of Quatre Bras until the arrival of the Allied troops, which he knew were rapidly approaching from Brussels and Nivelles. The arrival of the First Brigade induced him to make a further advance, and extension to the right, of the Second Brigade; retaining a firm hold of the wood of Bossu. He disposed of his artillery in the following manner: upon the high road, in advance of his centre and in front of Frasne, he placed two guns of Perponcher's divisional Horse Artillery; three guns a little in left rear of these, and three guns towards the left, so as to keep the road to Namur in view. He also placed six guns of the divisional Foot Artillery a little to the right of, and in line with, the advanced guns of the Horse Battery, and the remaining two guns on the right wing of his First Line.

His Royal Highness had unfortunately no cavalry in the field; yet such was the firm countenance which he displayed in the arrangement of his nine battalions and sixteen guns that the enemy, unaware of this circumstance, and probably misled by the appearance, at an early hour, of the chain of vedettes formed by the Prussian detachment of Hussars, to which allusion has previously been made, and also conceiving that a considerable force had already assembled at Quatre Bras, made no vigorous attempt, until the afternoon, to dislodge him from his position.

Between ten and eleven o'clock, the Duke of Wellington arrived in person at Quatre Bras, where he joined the Prince of Orange, of whose dispositions he fully approved. He reconnoitred the ground; observed only a few of the enemy in front, who occasionally fired a shot; saw that there was a little popping musketry, but that nothing more serious was at that time threatened in this quarter.

Conceiving that the enemy was not in any great force at Frasne, while at the same time, accounts reached him that Prince Blücher, in his position at Ligny. was menaced by the advance of considerable masses; the duke, accompanied by his staff and a small escort of cavalry, shortly afterwards rode off to hold a conference with the Prussian commander, whom he found at the windmill of Bussy, between Ligny and Bry; whence he had an opportunity of observing the French preparatory dispositions for attack.

These having led the duke to conclude that Napoleon was bringing the main force of his army to bear against Blücher, he at once proposed to assist the prince by first advancing straight upon Frasne and Gosselies, as soon as he should have concentrated sufficient force, and then operating upon the enemy's left and rear, which would afford a powerful diversion in favour of the Prussians, from the circumstance that their right wing was the weakest and most exposed, and considering the object of Napoleon's movement, the one most likely to be attacked.

Upon a calculation being made, however, of the time which would elapse ere the duke would be able to collect the requisite force for undertaking this operation, and of the possibility of Blücher being defeated before it could be carried into effect, it was considered preferable that Wellington should, if practicable, move to the support of the Prussian right by the Namur road. But a direct support of this kind was necessarily contingent on circumstances, and subject to the duke's discretion. The latter having expressed his confident expectation of being enabled to afford the desired support, as also of his succeeding in concentrating, very shortly, a sufficient force to assume the offensive, rode back to Quatre Bras.

It was nearly eleven o'clock when General Flahaut, an *aide de camp* of the emperor, after passing through Gosselies, arrived at Frasne, with the following letter from the latter to the marshal:

Au Maréchal Ney.
Mon Cousin—Je vous envoie mon aide de camp, le Général Flahaut,
qui vous porte la présente lettre. Le major général a dû vous donner des

ordres; mais vous recevrez lea miens plus tôt, parceque mes officiers vont plus vite que les siens. Vous recevrez l'Ordre du Mouvement du Jour; mais je veux vous en écrire en détail, parceque c'est de la plus haute importance.

Je porte le Maréchal Grouchy avec les 3e et 4e Corps d'Infanterie sur Sombref. Je porte ma Garde à Fleurus, et j'y serai de ma personne avant midi. J'y attaquerai l'Ennemi si je le rencontre, et j'éclairerai la route jusqu'à Gembloux. Là d'après ce qui ce passera, je prendrai mon parti peutêtre à trois heures après midi, peutêtre ce soir. Mon intention est que, immédiatement après que j'aurai pris mon parti, vous soyez prêt à marcher sur Bruxelles, je vous appuierai avec la Garde qui sera à Fleurus ou à Sombref, et je désirerais arriver a Bruxelles demain matin. Vous vous mettriez en marche ce soir même si je prends mon parti d'assez bonne heure pour que vous puissiez en être informé de jour et faire ce soir trois ou quatre lieues et être demain à sept heures du matin à Bruxelles.

Vous pouvez donc disposer vos troupes de la manière suivante:— Première Division à deux lieues en avant des Quatre Chemins s'il n'y a pas d'inconvénient. Six divisions d'infanterie autour des Quatre Chemins, et une division à Marbais, afin que je puisse l'attirer à moi à Sombref, si j'en avais besoin. Elle ne retarderait d'ailleurs pas votre marche. Le Corps du Comte de Valmy, qui a 3,000 Cuirassiers d'Élite, á l'intersection du chemin des Romains et de celui de Bruxelles, afin que je puisse l'attirer à moi, si j'en avais besoin; aussitot que mon parti sera pris, vous lui enverrez l'ordre de venir vous rejoindre. Je désirerais avoir avec moi la division de la Garde que commande le Général Lefèbvre-Desnouettes, et je vous envoie les deux divisions du corps du Comte de Valmy pour la remplacer. Mais dans mon projet actuel, je préfère placer le Comte de Valmy de manière à le rappeler si j'en avais besoin, et ne point faire de fausses marches au Général Lefèbvre-Desnouettes; puisqu'il est probable que je me déciderai ce soir a marcher sur Bruxelles avec la Garde. Cependant, couvrez la Division Lefèbvre par les deux divisions de cavalrie d'Erlon et de Reille, afin de ménager la Garde; et que, s'il y avait quelque échauffourée avec les Anglais, il est préférable que ce soit sur la Ligne que sur la Garde.

J'ai adopté comme principe général pendant cette campagne, de diviser mon armée en deux ailes et une réserve. Votre aile sera composée des quatre divisions du 2e Corps, de deux divisions de Cavalerie Légère, et de deux divisions du corps de Valmy. Cela ne doit pas être loin de 45 à 50 mille hommes.

Le Maréchal Grouchy aura à peu près la même force, et commandera l'aile droite. La Garde formera la réserve, et je me porterai sur l'une ou l'autre aile, selon les circonstances. Le major général donne les ordres les plus précis pour qu'il n'y ait aucune difficulté sur l'obéissance à vos ordres lorsque vous serez détaché; les commandants de corps devant prendre mes ordres directement quand je me trouve présent. Selon les circonstances, j'affaiblirai l'une ou l'autre Aile en augmentant ma réserve.

Vous sentez assez l'importance attachée à la prise de Bruxelles. Cela pourra d'ailleurs donner lieu à des accidents, car un mouvement aussi prompt et aussi brusque isolera l'Armée Anglaise de Mons, Ostende, etc. Je désire que vos dispositions soient bien faites pour qu'au premier ordre, vos huit divisions puissent marcher rapidement, et sans obstacle sur Bruxelles.

N.

Charleroi, le 16 Juin, 1815.

TRANSLATION

To Marshal Ney

My Cousin—I send you my *aide de camp*, General Flahaut; who brings you the present letter. The major general (Soult) will give you the orders; but you will receive mine sooner, because my officers go quicker than his. You will receive the Order of Movement of the Day: but I wish to write to you respecting it in detail, because it is of the highest importance.

I direct Marshal Grouchy with the Third and Fourth Corps of Infantry on Sombref. I direct my Guard to Fleurus, and I shall be there personally before noon. I shall attack the enemy there if I meet with him, and I shall clear the road as far as Gembloux. There, according to what will happen, I shall make my decision; perhaps at three o'clock in the afternoon, perhaps this evening. My intention is that, immediately after I shall have made my decision, you may be ready to march on Brussels. I will support you with the Guard which will be at Fleurus or at Sombref; and I would desire to arrive at Brussels to morrow morning. You would march this evening even if I make my decision at a sufficiently early hour that you may be informed of it in daylight, and traverse this evening three or four leagues, and be at Brussels tomorrow at seven o'clock in the morning.

You may then dispose your troops in the following manner:—First Division at two leagues in front of Quatre Bras, if in doing so there is no inconvenience. Six divisions of infantry about Quatre Bras; and one division at Marbais, so that I may draw it to myself at Sombref, if I should have need of it. It would not otherwise retard your march.

The corps of the Count de Valmy, which has 3,000 *Cuirassiers d'Élite*, at the intersection of the Roman road with that of Brussels, in order that I may draw it to myself if I should have need of it: as soon as my decision is made, you will send him the order to rejoin you.

I would desire to have with me the division of the Guard commanded by General Lefèbvre-Desnouettes, and I send you the two divisions of the corps of the Count de Valmy to replace it. But in my present design, I prefer to place the Count de Valmy in such a manner as to be able to recall him if I should have need of him; and not to make false marches for General Lefèbvre-Desnouettes: since it is probable that I shall decide this evening to march on Brussels with the Guard. However, cover Lefèbvre's division with the two cavalry divisions of d'Erlon and Reille, in order to spare the Guard; and that, if there shall be any affray there with the English, it may be with the Line rather than with the Guard.

I have adopted as a general principle during this campaign to divide my army into two wings and a reserve. Your wing will be composed of the four divisions of the Second Corps, the two Light Cavalry divisions, and the two divisions of the Corps de Valmy. That ought not to be far from 45,000 to 50,000 men.

Marshal Grouchy will have nearly the same force, and will command the right wing. The Guard will form the reserve, and I shall repair to one or other wing according to circumstances. The major general is giving the most precise orders that there may be no difficulty as regards obedience to your orders when you will be detached; the commanders of corps must take my orders directly from me, when I am present. According to circumstances, I shall weaken the one, or the other, wing in augmenting my Reserve.

You will sufficiently perceive the importance attached to the capture of Brussels. That will otherwise give occasion to incidents: for a movement equally prompt and abrupt will isolate the English Army from Mons, Ostend, &c. I would desire that your dispositions may be well made that, at the first order, your eight divisions may march rapidly and without obstacle upon Brussels.

N.

Charleroi, 16th June 1815

This letter, which was intended to convey to Ney a general notion of Napoleon's intentions, prescribed to him, at the same time, as a principle, that he was to consider his movements subordinate to those of the emperor. The latter intimated his purpose of attacking the enemy at Fleurus, should he find him there, and of pushing on as far as Gembloux, where he would decide upon his plan of further operation, "perhaps at three o'clock in the afternoon, perhaps in the evening;" immediately *after* which Ney was to be ready to march upon Brussels, supported by Napoleon with the Guards, it being the emperor's desire to reach that capital in the morning.

The idea of advancing upon Gembloux, and of capturing Brussels by a coup de main, which could only be effected by a vigorous repulse and signal defeat of the corps of Zieten, and by a successful turning and partial dispersion of those of Pirch and Thielemann, as also by the rapid march of a closely collected force under Ney, proves that Napoleon had either been insufficiently informed as to the general dispositions of his opponents, or had greatly miscalculated the degree of energy and promptitude required in his movements for the execution of such a design.

Very shortly afterwards, Ney received the official Order of Movement to which Napoleon adverted in his letter as having been sent by Soult. It instructed him to put the Second and First *Corps d'Armée*, as also the Third Corps of Cavalry which had been placed at his disposal, in movement upon Quatre Bras; to take up a position at that point; thence to push forward reconnaissances as far as possible on the roads to Brussels and Nivelles, *d'où probablement l'ennemi s'est retiré*"; to establish, should he meet with no impediment, a division with some cavalry at Genappe; and to detach another division towards Marbais, in order to cover the interval between Sombref and Quatre Bras. He was also to desire the general officers commanding the two *corps d'armée* to assemble their troops, collect the stragglers, and order up all the waggons belonging to the artillery and to the hospitals that might still be in the rear.

In pursuance of these instructions, Ney despatched Orders of Movement to Counts Reille and d'Erlon.

Battle of Quatre Bras

The former was desired to put the Second Corps immediately on the march, for the purpose of taking up the following position:—the Fifth Division in rear of Genappe, upon the heights which command that town, the left *appuied* upon the high road; one or two battalions covering all the *débouchés* in advance on the Brussels road; the Ninth Division, following the movement of the Fifth, to take up a position in second line on the heights to the right and left of the village of Bauterlet; the Sixth and Seventh Divisions at Quatre Bras.

It was at the same time intimated to Reille that the three first divisions of d'Erlon's corps were to take post at Frasne; the right division to establish itself at Marbais along with Piré's division of Light Cavalry; that the former was to cover his (Reille's) march towards Brussels, and both his flanks; that two divisions of Kellermann's corps were to take post at Frasne and Liberchies; and that the regiments of the Guard under Generals Lefèbvre-Desnouettes and Colbert were to remain in their actual position at Frasne.

This order had scarcely been sent off to Reille when Ney received from the latter a despatch, dated Gosselies, 16th June, a quarter past ten a.m., announcing his having just received from Girard (whose division was still at Heppignies) a verbal report by one of his officers, to the effect that the enemy continued to occupy Fleurus with Light Cavalry; that hostile masses were observed advancing along the Namur road, the heads of their columns reaching as far as St Amand; that these troops were gradually forming, and gaining ground; that as far as could be judged at that distance, the columns appeared to consist of six Battalions each; and that movements of additional troops were perceived in their rear.

Reille added that General Flahaut, in passing through Gosselies, had made him acquainted with the purport of the orders he was conveying to the marshal, whereupon he had communicated with Count d'Erlon, in order that the latter might follow the movement which he (Reille) had intended to commence as soon as the divisions were under arms, but that in consequence of this report from Girard he would wait for the marshal's further instructions, holding the troops ready to march.

About the same time, orders reached Ney from Napoleon, desiring him to unite the corps under Reille and d'Erlon, and the cavalry corps under Kellermann, which latter, it was stated, was on the point of commencing its march towards him; remarking also, that with these troops he ought to be able to destroy whatever forces the enemy might bring forward; that Grouchy was going to advance upon Sombref; and that the emperor was setting off for Fleurus, to which place the marshal was to address his reports.

In consequence of these instructions, Ney became anxious for the speedy concentration of his troops, and again sent orders to Reille and d'Erlon to move up their divisions. The information which he had obtained concerning the enemy in his front, and Girard's report of the assembling of troops in front of Fleurus, induced him to be cautious in his proceedings, and not to attempt any impetuous onset until he could have all his force more in hand, instead of the greater portion of it being, as it then was, lengthened out in columns of route along the Charleroi high road; and, in this respect, his views were in perfect accordance with the last despatch which he had received from the emperor, enjoining him in the first instance, to unite the two corps of Reille and d'Erlon. Hence, in debouching from his position at Frasne, about one o'clock, his advance was by no means vigorous: it was limited to a gradual pressing forward of the Light troops, and amounted to little more than a reconnaissance.

About two o'clock, Ney, calculating that d'Erlon's corps could not be far in his rear, and hoping that the sound of his cannonade would hasten its march, resolved to attack the enemy's forces which intercepted his advance upon Quatre Bras. Piré's Light Cavalry, constituting a strong line of skirmishers with well disposed supports, covered the advance of the infantry divisions of Bachelu and Foy, whilst that of Jerome followed as a reserve.

The force with which Ney thus entered the field, consisted of three divisions of Reille's corps, of Piré's Light Cavalry, of 4 batteries of Foot, and 1 of Horse, Artillery:
altogether—
    16,189 Infantry
    1,729 Cavalry
    38 Guns

The Prince of Orange's force consisted of de Perponcher's division (with the exception of the 7th Dutch Line Battalion); of 1 battery of Foot, and 1 of Horse, Artillery:
altogether—
    6,832 Infantry
    16 Guns.

It was not long after two o'clock when the Duke of Wellington

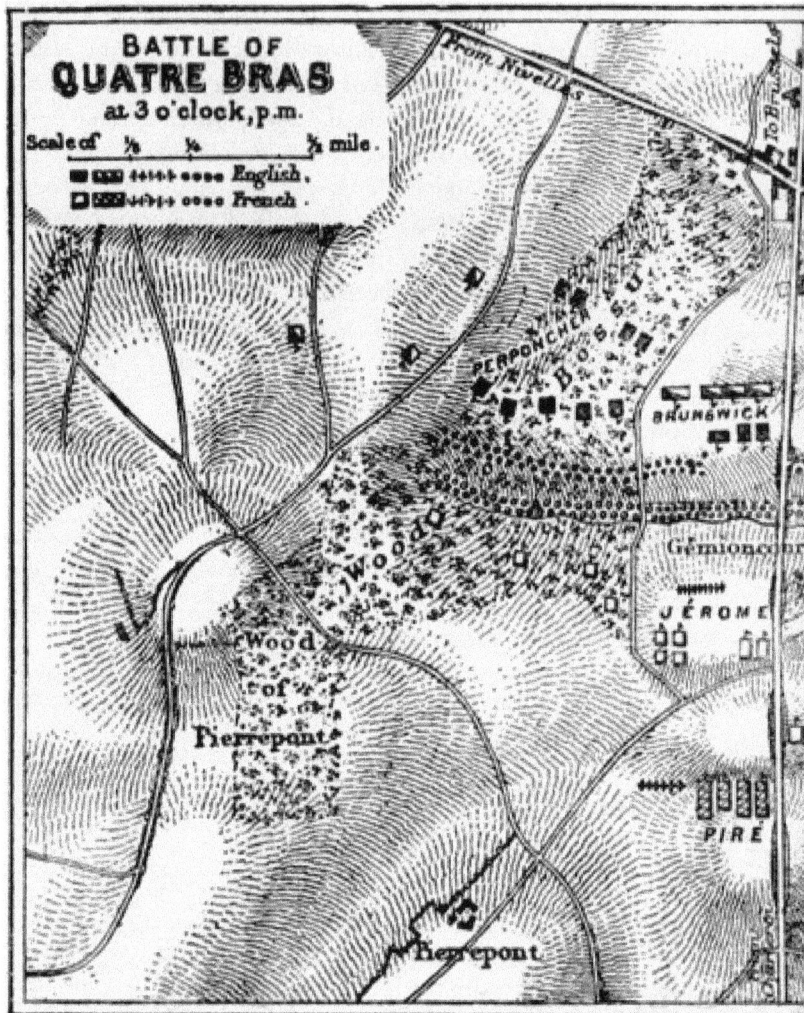

BATTLE OF
QUATRE BRAS
at 3 o'clock, p.m.

Scale of ⅛   ¼   ½ mile.

▬▬ ▮▮ ++++ •••• English.
□ ▭ ++++ •••• French.

From Nivelles

To Brussels

PERPONCHER

BOSSU

BRUNSWICK

Gémioncourt

JÉROME

Wood

Wood
of
Pierrepont

PIRÉ

Pierrepont

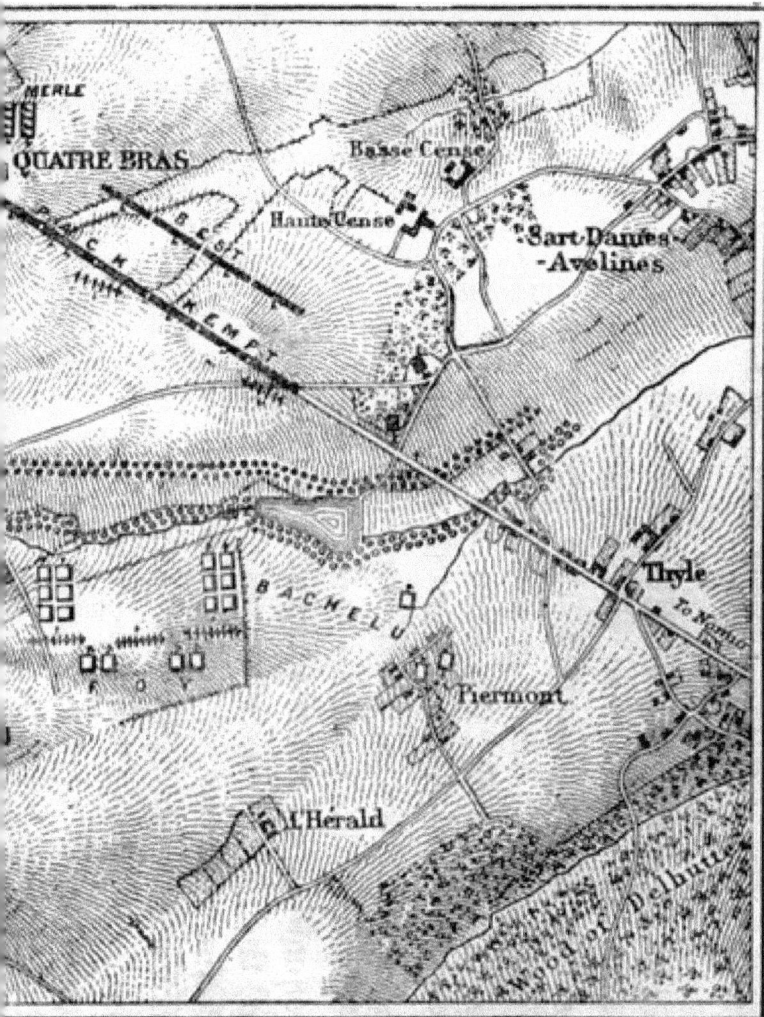

returned to Quatre Bras from the Prussian Army. He observed attentively, with his glass, the movements of the French, and told the Prince of Orange he would be attacked directly.

In a few minutes, the French advanced, and the Dutch-Belgian troops gradually retired; but the prince, aware of the great advantages which the position of Quatre Bras would derive from the possession of the farm of Gemioncourt, adjoining the Charleroi road, as also of the wood of Bossu on the right, and of the enclosures of Piermont on the left, flank, endeavoured, with that view, to make a stand, as soon as his centre reached the first named point. The 5th Battalion of Dutch Militia which occupied this post, successfully withstood several attacks, during which Ney drew up his forces along the ridge which, intersecting the high road in the immediate (French) rear of Gemioncourt, extends on one side towards the wood of Bossu, and on the other in the direction of Piermont.

The vast preponderance of force on the part of the French, was now quite manifest to the Prince of Orange, who found himself compelled to withdraw the main body of his troops into the wood of Bossu, still retaining, however, the post of Gemioncourt. He gave an order to Captain Stievenaar's Foot Battery to fall back and take up a flanking position near the wood. Here this officer, who possessed the highest merit, lost not a moment in reopening his fire, but scarcely had he done so when he was mortally wounded. At the same moment one gun was damaged so as to become useless. The enemy rapidly advanced in such superior force as to compel the battery to resume its retreat. Captain Byleveld's Horse Battery retired by the opposite side of Gemioncourt. One of its limbers blew up, severely wounding an officer, and occasioning the gun attached to it to be relinquished. The French pressed forward with their Light troops; and part of Piré's Light Cavalry, seizing a favourable opportunity, gallantly charged the 27th Dutch Light Infantry, threw it into confusion, and made many prisoners. At this time a portion of Bachelu's infantry division on the right advanced towards the village of Piermont.

It was about half past two, or perhaps a quarter before three o'clock, when the Prince of Orange, whose situation had become extremely critical, as he directed his anxious looks towards that point of the horizon which was bounded by the elevated ground about Quatre Bras, had the inexpressible satisfaction of recognising, by their deep red masses, the arrival of British troops upon the field.

These comprised the Fifth Infantry Division, commanded by

Lieutenant General Sir Thomas Picton, and consisting of the Eighth British Brigade, under Major General Sir James Kempt, the Ninth British Brigade, under Major General Sir Denis Pack, and of the Fourth Hanoverian brigade, under Colonel Best. The head of the column, leaving Quatre Bras on its right, turned down the Namur road, along which the division was speedily drawn up; the British brigades in front, and the Hanoverian Brigade in Second Line. Captain Rettberg's battery of Hanoverian Foot Artillery took post on the right, and Major Rogers's Battery of British Foot Artillery on the left, of the division. The 1st Battalion of the 95th British Regiment, commanded by Colonel Sir Andrew Barnard, was despatched in haste towards the Village of Piermont, of which it was to endeavour to gain possession.

The French, on perceiving the arrival of the British infantry, opened a furious cannonade from their batteries, with a view to disturb its formation, while Ney, anxious to secure the vantage ground of a field which he plainly foresaw, was likely to become the scene of a severe contest, renewed his attack upon Gemioncourt, still bravely defended by the 5th Dutch Militia. Hereupon, Perponcher, having received an order to advance this battalion along the high road, immediately placed himself at its head, as did also the Prince of Orange himself, who rode up to it at the same moment. The manner in which His Royal Highness personally led on his National Militia on this occasion, was distinguished by the most resolute and conspicuous gallantry. The battalion was exposed to a most destructive fire from some guns which the prince seemed determined to capture.

Placing himself frequently at its head, and waving his hat, he presented in his own person so brilliant and heroic an example, that for a considerable time the battalion maintained its ground most bravely against the far superior number of the enemy. It was composed, however, of young and inexperienced soldiers, who had not attained sufficient confidence to fight in anything like deployed order; and, therefore, when, a few minutes afterwards, a swarm of cavalry rushed upon it, it soon lost its compactness, and broke into a confused and hasty retreat; whilst the French infantry succeeded in obtaining possession of the farm, in which they firmly established themselves.

The Duke of Wellington, who now assumed the command, was so much alive to the importance of maintaining Gemioncourt and its enclosures, that he gave directions for its immediate occupation by a British regiment, but the one destined for this service having by some accident been otherwise disposed of, some delay occurred, and the

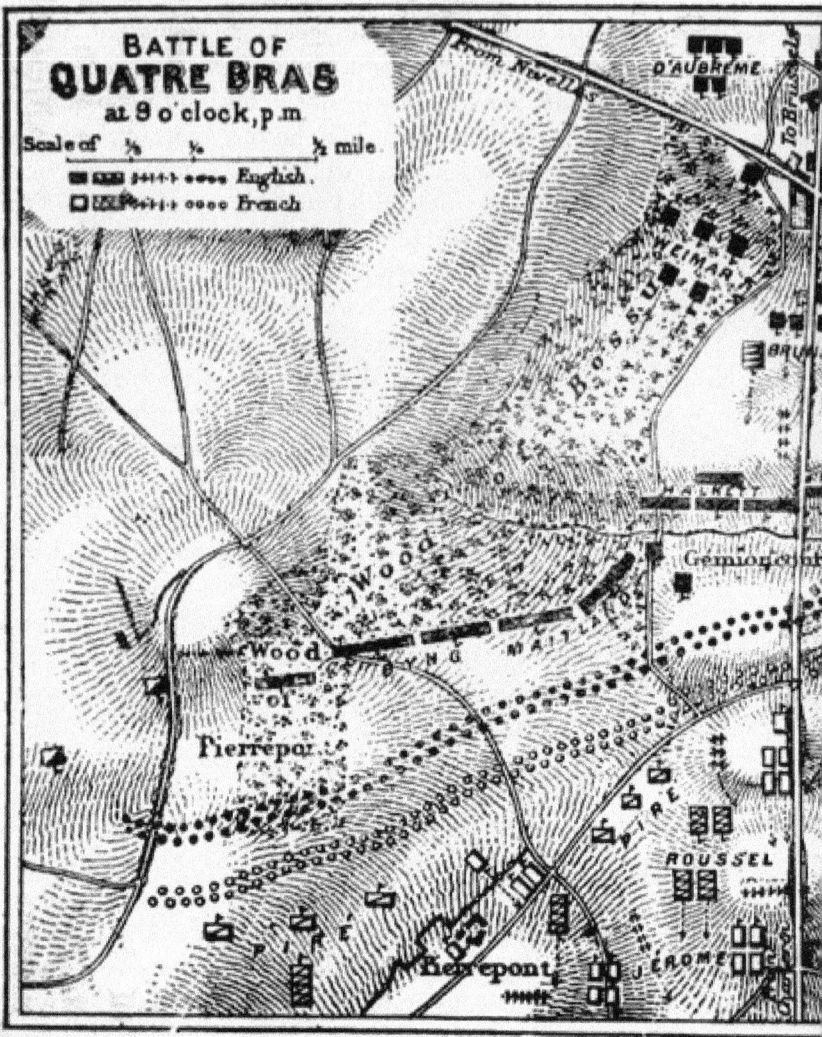

BATTLE OF
QUATRE BRAS
at 9 o'clock, p.m.

Scale of ⅛   ½   ½ mile

☐☐ ☐☐☐ ⊦⊦⊦⊦⊦ ∘∘∘∘ English.
☐ ☐☐☐ ⊦⊦⊦⊦⊦ ∘∘∘∘ French.

From Nivelles

D'AUBREME

WEIMAR
BOSSU
BRUN

HANEY

Gemioncourt

WING MAITLAND

Wood
of
Pierrepon

ROUSSEL

Pierepont

JEROME

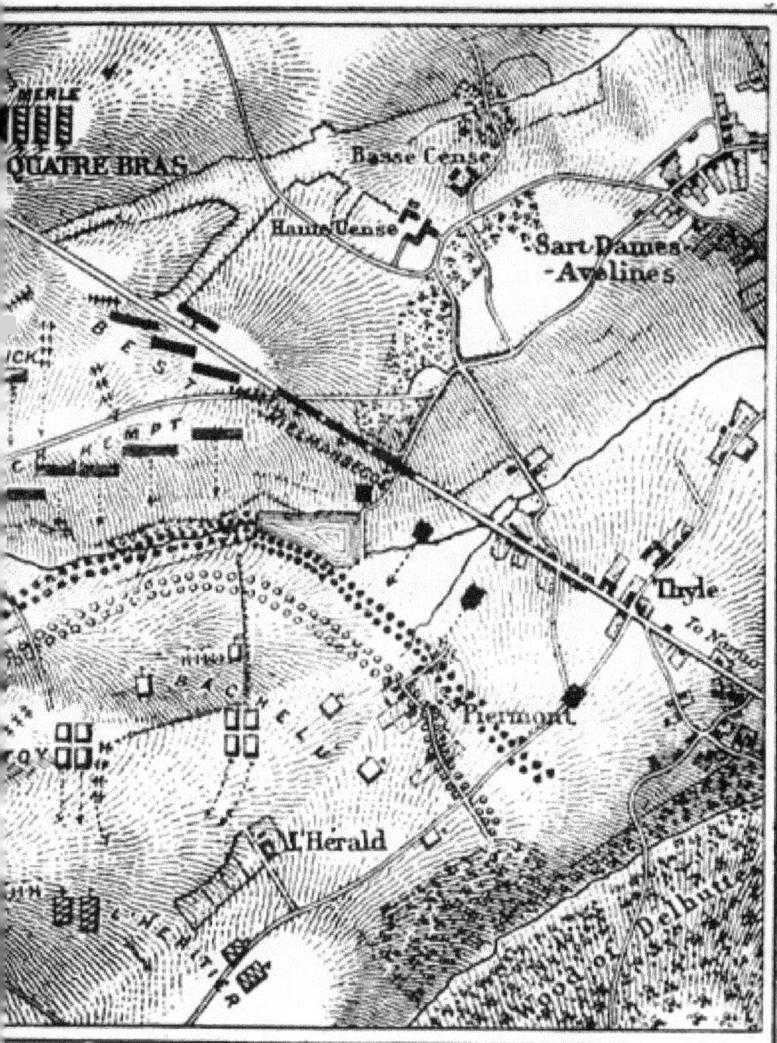

28th British Regiment, commanded by Colonel Sir Charles Philip Belson, was then marched down towards that point, under the guidance of Lieutenant Colonel Gomm, on the staff of the Fifth Division. As the battalion approached the farm, the latter was discovered to be already occupied by the trench, whereupon it was withdrawn to its division.

The Third Dutch-Belgian Light Cavalry Brigade, under General Van Merlen, had shortly before this reached the field, and now advanced to the support of the Dutch infantry retiring from Gemioncourt; but they were met and defeated by Piré's cavalry, and pursued along the high road nearly to Quatre Bras, where they arrived in great disorder; a portion of them coming in contact with the Duke of Wellington himself, and carrying his Grace along with them to the rear of Quatre Bras. The latter, however, succeeded in arresting their further flight, and in bringing them again to the front. The French cavalry did not, on this occasion, follow up the pursuit, evidently hesitating to approach very near to the Allied infantry, the latter appearing well formed, and fully prepared to receive them. The Dutch-Belgian infantry retreated to the wood of Bossu, abandoning four guns to the enemy, who closely pursued them, and now began to penetrate into the wood.

Meanwhile, Bachelu, on the French right, threw a considerable force into Piermont in sufficient time to secure its possession before the 1st Battalion 95th British Regiment had approached the village, and was pushing forward another strong body towards a small wood that lay still more in advance, on the opposite side of the Namur high road, the possession of which along with that of Piermont would have effectually cut off the direct communication between Quatre Bras and Ligny. Here, for the first time in this campaign. the troops of the two nations became engaged. The skirmishers who successfully checked the further advance of the French, and secured the wood, were the 1st Battalion of the British 95th Rifles, whom the old campaigners of the French Army, at least those who had served in the Peninsula, had so frequently found the foremost in the fight, and of whose peculiarly effective discipline and admirable training they had had ample experience.

The possession of Gemioncourt proved of the utmost importance to Ney's position, which now assumed a definite character, and, in a purely tactical point of view, offered great advantages. The southern portion of the wood of Bossu was occupied by his extreme left, while his extreme right was in full possession of Piermont; and these points were connected by a narrow valley extending along his whole front, bounded on either side by a hedgerow, and intersecting the Charleroi road close to Gemioncourt. The outer fence was strongly occupied by his Light troops, ready to cover the formation and advance of his columns of attack, for the support of which by artillery, the Heights constituting his main position in rear of Gemioncourt, offered every facility.

Scarcely had Picton's division taken up its ground, when the Duke of Brunswick's corps arrived upon the field. It was not complete; its artillery (under Major Mahn) and the 1st and 3rd Light Battalions (commanded by Major Holstein and Major Ebeling), having been stationed in distant cantonments, had not yet joined. The 2nd Light Battalion (under Major Brandenstein) was immediately detached to the wood near Piermont on the left of the position, and of which the possession had already been secured by the 1st Battalion of the British 95th Regiment: the two Rifle Companies of the Advanced Guard Battalion (under Major Rauschenplatt) were moved into the wood of Bossu; on the right of which some detachments of cavalry were posted for the purpose of observing the enemy's dispositions in that quarter. The remainder of these troops, by a movement to their left, when close upon Quatre Bras, deployed in rear of, and in a direction parallel to, the Namur road, thus forming a reserve to Picton's division. The absent portion of the corps reached the field in the course of the action, as will hereafter be explained. The Duke of Wellington's force in the field at this moment was as follows:—

		Infantry.	Cavalry.	Guns.
British	{ Eighth Infantry Brigade . .	2,471	...	...
	{ Ninth do. do. . .	2,173	...	...
K. G. Legion .	Battery of Foot Artillery . .	...	...	6
Hanoverians	{ Fourth Infantry Brigade . .	2,582	...	...
	{ Battery of Foot Artillery . .	...	...	6
Brunswickers .	{ Advanced Guard Battalion .	672	...	...
	{ 2 Battalions of the Light Infantry Brigade . . .	1,314	...	...
	{ Line Infantry Brigade . . .	2,016	...	...
	{ Regiment of Hussars . . .	...	690	...
	{ Squadron of Lancers . . .	...	232	...
Dutch-Belgians	{ Second Infantry Brigade (Div.	6,832	...	...
	{ Third Cavalry Brigade . .	...	1,082	...
	{ Half Battery of Horse Artillery	...	...	2
	{ Battery of Foot Artillery . .	...	..	8
	{ Do. Horse do. . .	...	...	8
		18,090	2,004	30

The following is the amount of force which Marshal Ney had actually in the field:—

	Infantry.	Cavalry.	Guns
Fifth Infantry Division . .	5,003	...	...
Sixth do. do. . .	6,591	...	...
Ninth do. do. . .	4,595	...	...
3 Divisional Foot Batteries .	...	...	24
1 Reserve Foot Battery . .	...	...	8
Second Cavalry Division . .	...	1,729	..
1 Battery of Horse Artillery .	...	...	6
	16,189	**1,729**	**38**

The cannonade which had opened against the Fifth British Division as it took up its ground, continued with unabated vigour. The French Light troops were now observed advancing from the enclosures that skirted the foot of their position, and to meet them the Light Companies of the different regiments of Picton's division were immediately thrown forward. On the French extreme right all further progress was checked by the gallant manner in which the 1st Battalion 95th British Regiment, though opposed by a much superior force, retained possession of the Namur road, which they lined with their skirmishers, while the wood in rear was occupied by the battalion reserve and the 2nd Brunswick Light Battalion. On the French left, however, the incessant rattle of musketry in the wood of Bossu plainly indicated by its gradual approach in the direction of Quatre Bras, that the Dutch-Belgian infantry were yielding to the fierce onset of the enemy in that quarter.

The protection which the French would derive from the possession of the eastern portion of this wood for the advance of their masses over the space between it and the Charleroi road, instantly became apparent to the British commander; in fact, the previous pursuit of the Dutch-Belgian cavalry along this road proved the expediency of establishing some restraint to such facility for a hostile advance in that direction; and he therefore requested the Duke of Brunswick to take up a position with a part of his corps between Quatre Bras and Gemioncourt, so as to have his left resting upon the road, and his right communicating with Perponcher's division, part of which was deployed along the skirt of the wood.

The Duke of Brunswick immediately ordered forward the Guard Battalion (under Major Pröstler), the 1st Line Battalion (under Major Metzner), and the two Light companies of the Advanced Guard Battalion, which he posted in close columns upon, and contiguous to, the road, on the ground indicated, and threw out a line of skirmishers connecting these columns with the two *Jäger* companies in the wood. As an immediate support to the infantry, he stationed the Brunswick Hussars (under Major Cramm) and lancers (under Major Pott) in a hollow in their rear: while as a reserve to the whole, the 2nd and 3rd Line Battalions (under Major Strombeck and Major Norrmann) were posted *en crémailère*, contiguously to the houses of Quatre Bras, which important point they were to defend to the last extremity.

Whilst this disposition on the Anglo-Allied right was in progress, two heavy French columns were observed descending into a valley below Gemioncourt, where, under cover of the strong line of skirmishers, which had been for some time engaged with those of Picton's division, they were divided into separate smaller columns of attack. The cannonade from the French heights, which now sensibly quickened, was telling fearfully amidst the Fifth British division; and a fresh impulse having been given to the enemy's Light troops by the near approach of their own attacking columns, the British skirmishers, overpowered by numbers only, were seen darting, alternately and at short distances, to the rear, through the line of smoke that had been raised midway between the contending armies.

At this critical moment, when the rapid progress of the French in the wood of Bossu, and their imposing advance against his left wing, threatened to compromise his disposal of the Brunswick troops on the right of the Charleroi road, Wellington, by one of those electric inspirations of his master mind, resolved not to await the attack, but to meet it. He instantly ordered the advance of Kempt's and Pack's brigades, with the exception of the 92nd Regiment, which (under the command of Lieutenant Colonel Cameron) was to continue at its post on the Namur road, close to Quatre Bras.

During the advance of these two brigades, which was made with admirable steadiness and in the best order, the skirmishers fell back upon their respective battalions, all of which now presented a clear front to the enemy. From the heads of Ney's columns, as well as from the thick lines of skirmishers by which they were connected, a severe and destructive fire was opened and maintained against the British line, along which the gallant Picton, the famed leader of the no less renowned "Fighting Division" of the British Army in the Peninsular Campaigns, was seen galloping from one regiment to another, encouraging his men, and inciting them by his presence and example. The troops significantly responded to his call by those loud and animating shouts with which British soldiers are wont to denote their eagerness to close with their enemies. The interval between the adverse lines was rapidly diminishing: the fire from the French suddenly began to slacken; hesitation, quickly succeeded by disorder, became apparent in their ranks; and then it was, that, animating each other with redoubled cheers, the British Regiments were seen to lower their bristling bayonets, and driving everything before them, to pursue their opponents down to the outer fence of the valley, whence the French line had advanced in the full confidence of triumph.

Kempt's brigade, in consequence of the greater proximity of its original position to that of the enemy, was the first to overthrow the French infantry. The 79th Highlanders, on the left of the line (commanded by Lieutenant Colonel Douglas), made a gallant charge down the hill, dashed through the first fence, and pursued their opponents, who had advanced in two battalion columns, not only across the valley, but through the second fence; and, carried on by their ardour, even ventured to ascend the enemy's position. By this time, however, their ranks were much broken: they were speedily recalled, and as they retraced their steps across the valley, they derived considerable support from the adjoining battalion in the line, the 32nd Regiment (commanded by Lieutenant Colonel Maitland), which was keeping up from the first hedge a vigorous fire against the French, who now lined the second fence. The remaining regiments of both brigades had all in like manner charged down as far as the nearest hedge, whence they inflicted a severe loss upon their enemies as these precipitately retired, with their ranks completely broken and disordered on passing through the enclosure.

On the right of the line, the 42nd Highlanders (commanded by Lieutenant Colonel Sir Robert Macara), and 44th Regiment (commanded by Lieutenant Colonel Hamerton), had advanced to within a very short distance of Gemioncourt, in which, and behind the hedges lining the valley, the French were seeking shelter.

During the progress of this contest on the Anglo-Allied left of the Charleroi road, the Brunswick troops were not permitted to remain in quiet possession of their advanced position on the right, which indeed was well calculated to attract Ney's attention. A battery was immediately drawn up on the opposite height westward of Gemioncourt, from which, as also from the incessant fire maintained by the enemy's skirmishers posted at no great distance from the front of the line, a very destructive fire was maintained against the Brunswick troops. The regiment of Hussars particularly suffered, standing in line, and frequently receiving an entire discharge from the battery. The Brunswickers were, for the most part, young and inexperienced soldiers—in every sense of the word, *raw* troops: and the numerous casualties which befell their ranks in this exposed situation might have produced a fatal influence upon their discipline, but for the example of their prince, whose admirable demeanour was conspicuous on this occasion. Quietly smoking his pipe in front of his line, he gave out his orders as if at a mere field day; and was only restrained from taking offence at the representations made to him by some of his staff of the imminent danger to which he was exposing himself, from a consciousness of the kindly motives by which they were dictated.

At length, the continued havoc created amongst his devoted followers by the fire from the French heights, excited the impatience of the duke himself for at least the means of retaliation; and as his own artillery was still upon the march from its cantonments, he sent to the Duke of Wellington a request to be furnished with some pieces of cannon.

This was immediately acceded to, and four guns were moved forward and posted on the right of the Brunswick infantry; but they had scarcely fired a few rounds when the enemy's cannonade was redoubled; two of the guns were quickly disabled, and several of the horses attached to the limbers were killed. At the same time, two columns of French infantry were seen advancing in succession along the edge of the wood of Bossu, preceded by a battalion in line, and supported by some cavalry, of which description of force there also appeared to be a considerable mass advancing along the Charleroi road. As the French infantry rapidly approached the right of the line of the Brunswick skirmishers, the latter were forced to retire, as were also the Dutch-Belgian infantry that lined the wood at this part of the field.

The Duke of Brunswick, perceiving that the bend of the wood in rear of his regiment of Hussars was likely to impede the freedom of its movements, immediately ordered the latter to proceed to the opposite side of the Charleroi road, and retire towards Quatre Bras, there to remain in readiness to act according to circumstances. Then, placing himself at the head of his lancers, he gallantly charged the advancing infantry, which, however, received them with so much steadiness and good order, and opened upon them so destructive a fire, that the attack completely failed, and the regiment withdrew to Quatre Bras.

Finding the strength of the enemy's forces to be so overpowering, the duke now ordered the infantry posted contiguously to the Charleroi road, also to retire upon the main position. The 1st Line Battalion moved hastily along the road, while the Guard Battalion, with which the duke himself was at this time present, retired across the fields eastward of the isolated House upon the Charleroi road, towards the Allied line, posted upon the road to Namur. Major Pröstler, who commanded the Guard Battalion, rendered himself conspicuous by his exertions to execute this movement in as orderly a manner as possible, but the eager and close pursuit by the French Light troops, now emboldened by success, a shower of round shot upon the column, and the approach of the enemy's cavalry, spread such a panic among these young troops that they fled in confusion, some through Quatre Bras, and others through the Anglo-Allied line on the left of that point; and it was in the moment of attempting to rally his soldiers, not far from the little garden of the house before mentioned, that the Duke of Brunswick was struck from his horse by a shot which killed him.

In the mean time the Brunswick Hussars were ordered forward to cover the retreat of the infantry, and repel the advance of the French cavalry, which was now seen in rapid motion along the Charleroi road, as if incited and emboldened by the loud shouts of triumph sent forth by their Light troops in front. The Hussars, whose order while advancing, was quickly disturbed by a straggling fire from the French infantry, to which their right flank became exposed, failed in producing the slightest check upon the cavalry, and were soon seen wheeling about and in full flight, closely pursued by their opponents.

To the 42nd Highlanders and 44th British Regiment, which were posted on a reverse slope, and in line, close upon the left of the above road, the advance of French cavalry was so sudden and unexpected, the more so as the Brunswickers had just moved on to the front, that as both these bodies whirled past them to the rear, in such close proximity to each other, they were, for the moment, considered to consist of one mass of Allied cavalry. Some of the old soldiers of both regiments were not so easily satisfied on this point, and immediately opened a partial fire obliquely upon the French lancers, which, however, Sir Denis Pack and their own officers endeavoured as much as possible to restrain; but no sooner had the latter succeeded in causing a cessation of the fire, than the lancers, which were the rearmost of the cavalry, wheeled sharply round, and advanced in admirable order directly upon the rear of the two British regiments.

The 42nd Highlanders having, from their position, been the first to recognise them as a part of the enemy's forces, rapidly formed square; but just as the two flank companies were running in to form the rear face, the lancers had reached the regiment, when a considerable portion of their leading division penetrated the square, carrying along with them, by the impetus of their charge, several men of those two companies, and creating a momentary confusion. The long tried discipline and steadiness of the Highlanders, however, did not forsake them at this most critical juncture: these lancers, instead of effecting the destruction of the square, were themselves fairly hemmed into it, and either bayoneted or taken prisoners, while the endangered face, restored successfully repelled all further attempts on the part of the French to complete their triumph. Their commanding officer, Lieutenant Colonel Sir Robert Macara, was killed on this occasion, a lance having pierced through his chin until it reached the brain; and within the brief space of a few minutes, the command of the regiment devolved upon three other officers in succession: Lieutenant Colonel Dick, who was severely wounded, Brevet Major Davidson, who was mortally wounded, and Brevet Major Campbell, who commanded it during the remainder of the campaign.

If this cavalry attack had fallen so unexpectedly upon the 42nd Highlanders, still less had it been anticipated by the 44th Regiment. Lieutenant Colonel Hamerton, perceiving that the lancers were rapidly advancing against his rear, and that any attempt to form square would be attended with imminent danger, instantly decided upon receiving them in line. The low thundering sound of their approach was heard by his men before a conviction they were French flashed across the minds of any but the *old* soldiers who had previously fired at them as they passed their flank. Hamerton's words of command were, "Rear rank, right about face!"—"Make ready!"—(a short pause to admit of the still nearer approach of the cavalry)—"Present!"—"Fire!" The effect produced by this volley was astonishing. The men, aware of their perilous position, doubtless took a most deliberate aim at their opponents, who were thrown into great confusion.

Some few daring fellows made a dash at the centre of the battalion, hoping to capture the colours, in their apparently exposed situation; but the attempt, though gallantly made, was as gallantly defeated. The lancers now commenced a flight towards the French position by the flanks of the 44th. As they rushed past the left flank, the officer commanding the Light Company, who had very judiciously restrained

SIR THOMAS PICTON

DUKE OF BRUNSWICK

THE PRINCE OF ORANGE

NAPOLEON BONAPARTE

his men from joining in the volley given to the rear, opened upon them a scattering fire; and no sooner did the lancers appear in the proper front of the regiment, when the front rank began in its turn to contribute to their overthrow and destruction. Never, perhaps, did British infantry display its characteristic coolness and steadiness more eminently than on this trying occasion.

To have stood in a thin two deep line, awaiting, and prepared to receive, the onset of hostile cavalry, would have been looked upon at least as a most hazardous experiment; but, with its rear so suddenly menaced, and its flanks unsupported, to have instantly faced only one rank about, to have stood as if rooted to the ground, to have repulsed its assailants with so steady and well directed a fire that numbers of them were destroyed—this was a feat of arms which the oldest or best disciplined corps in the world might have in vain hoped to accomplish; yet most successfully and completely was this achieved by the gallant 2nd Battalion of the 44th British Regiment, under its commander, Lieutenant Colonel Hamerton.

In this attack occurred one of these incidents which, in daring, equal any of the feats of ancient chivalry.

A French lancer gallantly charged at the colours, and severely wounded Ensign Christie, who carried one of them, by a thrust of his lance, which, entering the left eye, penetrated to the lower jaw. The Frenchman then endeavoured to seize the standard, but the brave Christie, notwithstanding the agony of his wound, with a presence of mind almost unequalled, flung himself upon it—not to save himself, but to preserve the honour of his regiment. As the colour fluttered in its fall, the Frenchman tore off a portion of the silk with the point of his lance; but he was not permitted to bear the fragment beyond the ranks. Both shot and bayoneted by the nearest of the soldiers of the 44th, he was borne to the earth, paying with the sacrifice of his life for his display of unavailing bravery.

In the meantime, the leading portion of Piré's Light Cavalry, from which the lancers that attacked the 42nd and 44th British Regiments had been detached, as already described, continued its advance along the high road towards Quatre Bras, driving in the Brunswick Hussars, who were now galloping confusedly upon the 92nd Highlanders then lining the ditch of the Namur high road contiguous to Quatre Bras. Pursued by the *Chasseurs à Cheval*, and finding no opening for their passage, they made for the right flank of the regiment: and, as they were flying past, the grenadier company was wheeled back upon the

117

road so as to oppose a front at that point to the flank of the pursuing cavalry, upon which the Highlanders now poured a most destructive volley. The shock thus occasioned to the French cavalry was immediately perceptible; but though thrown into confusion, the main body soon reformed, and retired with much steadiness and regularity.

The front of the column, however, impelled by the furious ardour with which it had advanced, or, perhaps, imagining itself still followed and supported by the main body, dashed in amongst the houses of Quatre Bras, and even advanced to some distance beyond them, cutting down several stragglers whom they found there, principally belonging to the routed Brunswick Infantry, as also groups of wounded. Many of them rushed through the large opening into the farmyard of Quatre Bras, which was situated immediately in rear of the right of the 92nd. A few daring fellows finding they had proceeded too far to lie able to retire by the same direction in which they had advanced, wheeled round suddenly at the point where the high roads intersect each other, and galloped right through the grenadier company of the Highlanders, shouting, and brandishing their swords, and receiving a fire from some of the rear rank of the regiment as they dashed along the road.

None of them escaped: one, an officer of the *Chasseurs à Cheval*, had already reached the spot where the Duke of Wellington was at that moment stationed in rear of the Highlanders. Some of the men immediately turned round and fired: his horse was killed, and at the same moment a musket ball passed through each foot of the gallant young officer. Those of the French *chasseurs* who had entered the farmyard, finding no other outlet, now began to gallop back, in small parties of two or three at a time, but few escaped the deadly fire of the Highlanders.

About this time, Kellermann reached the field, with the Eleventh Heavy Cavalry Division under Lieutenant General l'Heritier. This augmented Ney's forces to the following amount:

	Infantry.	Cavalry.	Guns.
Force already in the Field	16,189	1,865	38
Eleventh Cavalry Division	...	1,743	...
1 Battery of Horse Artillery	...	...	6
	16,189	3,608	44

The French infantry upon the extreme Left had by this time possessed themselves of the greater portion of the wood of Bossu, from the Allied rear of which numerous groups of wounded and runaways were now seen to emerge; indeed, it soon became evident that no dependence could be placed on the continued occupation of the wood by the Dutch-Belgian forces, and that the whole brunt of the battle would have to be borne by the British, Hanoverian, and Brunswick forces. Upon the extreme French right, all attempts to turn the opposite flank of the Allies were successfully checked by the steadiness and gallantry of the 95th British Regiment, supported by the 2nd Brunswick Light Battalion.

Ney, although he had failed in his first general attack upon the Anglo-Allied line, had fully ascertained that the raw troops of which the Dutch-Belgian and Brunswick cavalry in the field were composed, were totally incapable of competing with his own veteran warriors of that arm, and he therefore determined to take advantage of Kellermann's arrival for the execution of a vigorous cavalry attack. Retaining General Piquet's brigade in reserve, he combined, for this purpose, General Guyton's brigade, consisting of the 8th and 11th Cuirassiers, with Piré's Light Cavalry division; and also taking advantage of his greatly superior artillery force, he caused the attack to be preceded and covered by a tremendous cannonade, occasioning great havoc in the ranks of the Anglo-Allied infantry, the range for which the French gunners had by this time ascertained with fearful precision.

It was not long before the British battalions most in advance were warned of the approach of hostile cavalry by the running in of their skirmishers; and scarcely had they formed their squares when the batteries respectively opposed to them having ceased their fire, a rushing sound was heard through the tall corn, which, gradually bending, disclosed to their view the heads of the attacking columns; and now began a conflict wherein the cool intrepidity with which British infantry are accustomed to defy the assaults of cavalry was exemplified. A rolling fire from the muskets of the 42nd Highlanders and 44th British Regiment, given at a moment when the enemy's horsemen were almost close upon their bayonets, though most destructive in its effects upon their own immediate opponents did not check the general attack. These two diminutive squares, now completely surrounded by the French cavalry, seemed destined to become a sacrifice to the fury with which a rapid succession of attacks was made upon them; no sooner was one squadron hurled back in confusion, than another rushed impetuously forward upon the same face of a square, to experience a similar fate; and sometimes different faces were charged simultaneously.

A strong body of *cuirassiers* now passed the right flank of the two regiments, along the high road, with an evident intention of making another attempt upon Quatre Bras.

Picton, who had been watching with intense anxiety the contest maintained by the 42nd and 44th British Regiments in their exposed situation, and who had become convinced of the utter hopelessness of obtaining any efficient support from the Allied cavalry then in the field, could no longer restrain his impatience to fly to the rescue of the squares; and, as a substitute for cavalry, he decided upon immediately assailing that of the enemy with his own infantry. With this view, he united the Royals (under Lieutenant Colonel Colin Campbell) and the 28th Regiment, both of which corps were at that moment standing in column at quarter distance.

Led on by both Picton and Kempt, the united column, with loud shouts, advanced into the midst of the enemy's cavalry; the whole extent of ground along its front appeared to swarm with lancers, *chasseurs à cheval*, and *cuirassiers*, a considerable portion of whom were now seen rapidly forming for an attack upon the column; but Picton constantly on the alert, and at the same time desirous of arriving at such a distance as would enable him to present an efficient flank fire in support of the 44th Regiment, continued advancing until the last moment, when he suddenly formed it into a square.

The repeated and furious charges which ensued, were invariably repulsed by the Royals and the 28th, with the utmost steadiness and consummate bravery; and although the lancers individually dashed forward and frequently wounded the men in the ranks, yet all endeavours to effect an opening, of which the succeeding squadron of attack might take advantage, completely failed. The ground on which the square stood was such that the surrounding remarkably tall rye concealed it in a great measure, in the first attacks, from the view of the French cavalry until the latter came quite close upon it; but to remedy this inconvenience, and to preserve the impetus of their charge, the lancers had frequently recourse to sending forward a daring individual to plant a lance in the earth at a very short distance from the bayonets, and they then charged upon the lance flag as a mark of direction.

The advance of the Royals and the 28th had been almost immediately followed, under the same form, by that of the 32nd Regiment, which, having reached a convenient distance, halted, and formed square so as to support, at the same time, by a flank fire, the Royals and 28th, and the square of the 79th Highlanders, which latter regiment constituted a connecting link with the 95th British Regiment upon the extreme left.

Upon the advance of the regiments belonging to Kempt's and Pack's British Brigades, Best's Hanoverian Brigade occupied the Namur road in their rear, along which the *Landwehr* Battalions Lüneburg, Osterode, and Münden (respectively commanded by Lieutenant Colonel Ramdohr, Major Reden, and Major Schmid) were deployed, while the *Landwehr* Battalion Verden (under Major Decken), also in line, was posted somewhat in advance.

In this position, Picton's division sustained repeated assaults of the French cavalry, which attacked the squares simultaneously, and in every direction: as a portion rushed upon one square, other squadrons passed on to assail the next; some parties, taking advantage of sinuosities of the ground, awaited, like birds of prey, the favourable moment for pouncing upon their victims; no sooner was one attacking squadron driven back and dispersed by a stream of musketry from the face of a square, than a fresh party would rush from its cover upon the same ranks, in the vain hope that the means of breaking its onset had been expended; but a reserved fire never failed to bring down upon it a similar fate. Viewed from a little distance, the British squares could at times be scarcely discerned amidst the surrounding cavalry; and as the latter was frequently observed flying back from sudden discharges of musketry, a spectator might easily have imagined the squares to be so many immense bombs, with every explosion scattering death and confusion among the masses that rushed so daringly into their fatal vicinity.

The French Cavalry, by its repeated failures to make any impression on the British Infantry by the manner in which it had passed through and through the intervals between the Squares, and in which the charging squadrons when dispersed had got intermingled, was now in great disorder—lancers, *chasseurs*, and *cuirassiers*, were mixed together and crossing one another in every direction, seeking out their respective corps. To retire and reform had therefore become with them an absolutely necessary measure; but this afforded no respite to the devoted squares, against which the batteries upon the French heights now played with terrific effect.

During the French attack of the British squares on the eastern side of the Charleroi road, a considerable body of *cuirassiers* advanced along the latter, with the evident design of making another attack upon the Anglo-Allied centre at Quatre Bras. The Belgian cavalry, which was again ordered forward, endeavoured to check this movement, but with no better effect than that which attended its former attempt; in fact, it retired sooner, charged and pursued by the *cuirassiers*, against whom a rapid fire was now opened from the 92nd Highlanders, who still lined the ditch of the Namur road, close to Quatre Bras, a fire so destructive in its effects that the steel clad warriors were completely staggered, and the order of their advance so thoroughly shaken that they were compelled to retire in confusion.

In addition to the furious cannonade to which they were subjected, the foremost of Picton's British battalions, more especially the 42nd and 44th Regiments, were exposed to a rapid and destructive fire, which, as soon as the enemy's cavalry had been withdrawn, was opened upon them by the French troops advancing from the enclosures of Gemioncourt. To check this, skirmishers were thrown forward, but from the want of sufficient ammunition, they could reply but very feebly to the fire of their opponents, who, not suffering the same disadvantage, were picking them off as fast as they could load. Their line soon became fearfully thinned, and finally their ammunition was totally exhausted, to which circumstance the officer on whom the command of them had devolved (Lieutenant Riddock, 44th Regiment) called the attention of Sir Denis Pack, who ordered him to close his men to their centre and to join his own Regiment.

He had just executed the first part of the order, when the French cavalry having rallied and reformed, renewed their attacks upon the British squares. Squadrons of *cuirassiers* and lancers, in their onward course, swept past Lieutenant Riddock and his party, while others intercepted his direct line of retreat. He instantly formed four deep, and with his front rank at the charge, he made good his way through the enemy's cavalry, as far as the south face of the square formed by the 44th Regiment; which, however, was so hotly pressed at that moment as to be unable to receive him, whereupon he ordered his men to lie down close to their bayonets, until a favourable opportunity should offer for their admission within the square.

A repetition of the former scene on this part of the field now took place, and the attacks, which were conducted with similar impetuosity, were met by a resistance equally undaunted. As if to overawe the square formed by the Royals and 28th British Regiments, the

French cavalry now made a simultaneous attack upon three of its faces, and these consisted mainly of the latter Corps. Picton, who was again in the square, upon perceiving the approach of this apparently overwhelming force, suddenly and emphatically exclaimed, "28th! remember Egypt!" They answered him with a loud cheer, and reserving their fire until the cavalry had approached within a few yards of the square, their muskets were coolly and deliberately levelled at their assailants, who in the next moment were hurled back in wild disorder, horses and riders tumbling over one another, and creating indescribable confusion. Similar in their results were all the attacks made upon the other British squares, which maintained their ground with the same unshaken steadiness and gallantry.

These repeated charges by the French cavalry, though conducted by veteran soldiers, with admirable order and compactness, and though affording innumerable instances of individual gallantry and daring, were certainly not carried on in a manner calculated to ensure success over infantry distinguished by such high training and such undaunted bravery as the British proved themselves to possess on this memorable occasion. There was no indication of a systematic attack upon any particular point by a rapid succession of charging squadrons—no *forlorn hope like* rush upon the opposing bayonets by the survivors of a discharge of musketry levelled at a leading squadron, and that rush followed up with lightning-like rapidity by the next squadron, which, in spite of the intervening space encumbered with the bodies of men and horses overthrown in the first charge, would thus obtain the greatest chance of effecting by its own weight and compact order, a breach in the square at the point originally selected for the assault.

No such system of attack was attempted; but, on the contrary, it almost invariably happened that the leading squadron no sooner received the fire from the point attacked, than it either opened out from the centre to the right and left, and retired, or, it diverged altogether to one flank, leaving the succeeding divisions, in both cases, to observe the same movement; and, in this manner, the whole of the attacking force exposed itself to a far more extended range of fire and consequent loss, than if it had pursued the more daring, and at the same time, more decisive, mode of attack just described.

Whilst a considerable portion of the French cavalry was thus fruitlessly assailing the British squares, a body of lancers, which had advanced considerably in the rear of those squares, made a sudden and unexpected charge upon the Hanoverian Landwehr Battalion Verden, which was then, as previously explained, deployed a short distance in front of the Namur road: it was completely successful, and the greater part of the battalion was cut down by the lancers, who, emboldened by this triumph, were preparing to cross the Namur road, where a well directed fire opened upon them by the Landwehr Battalions Lüneburg and Osterode, lying concealed in the ditch by which it was lined, threw them into disorder, and forced them to a precipitate retreat.

The whole of the French cavalry was now withdrawn for the purpose of reforming its broken and disordered ranks, leaving the Anglo-Allied infantry to be again assailed by a vigorous cannonade from the Heights above Gemioncourt. The only movement on the part of the Anglo-Allied forces was the advance of the Brunswick Guard Battalion and 2nd Line Battalion in front of Quatre Bras, by the right of the Charleroi road, as a precautionary measure against any flank attack that might be attempted from the wood of Bossu upon the advanced battalions of Picton's right.

It was long past five o'clock. The French infantry in the wood of Bossu was continually making progress towards the Namur road, across which increased numbers of the Dutch-Belgian troops, to whom the defence of the wood had been entrusted, were seen hastily retiring. In Piermont, the French Light troops had been reinforced, and they were now evidently preparing for a more vigorous attack upon the extreme left of Wellington's forces; whilst certain movements in the vicinity of Gemioncourt gave intimation of an intended renewal of the attack upon Quatre Bras. All prospect of the Anglo-Allied cavalry encountering Ney's veteran dragoons with any chance of success had entirely vanished; whilst, on the other hand, the latter were on the point of being reinforced by the arrival of another cavalry division. Pack's brigade had expended nearly the whole of its ammunition; its exposed position, and the continued cavalry charges in its rear having precluded the transmission of the necessary supply. The Brunswickers had been greatly discouraged by the death of their prince; and the losses sustained by all the troops engaged had already been truly frightful.

It was at this very moment, when Wellington's situation had become so extremely critical, that two infantry brigades of the Third Division, under Lieutenant General Sir Charles Alten, most opportunely reached the field of action by the Nivelles road. They were the Fifth British Brigade, commanded by Major General Sir Colin Halkett, and the First Hanoverian Brigade, under Major General Count Kielmansegge; and were accompanied by Major Lloyd's battery of British Foot Artillery, and by Captain Cleeves's battery of Hanoverian Foot Artillery.

By the arrival of these troops Wellington's force was augmented as follows:—

		Infantry.	Cavalry.	Guns.
	Force already in the Field	18,090	2,004	30
British {	Fifth Infantry Brigade .	2,254	...	...
	Battery of Foot Artillery	...	...	6
King's German Legion	Do. do. do. .	...	...	6
Hanoverians . .	First Infantry Brigade .	3,189	...	...
Dutch-Belgians .	7th Dutch Line Battalion	731	...	...
		24,264	2,004	42

About the same time, Ney's troops were reinforced by the remaining division of Kellermann's corps of Heavy Cavalry, so that his whole force was constituted as follows:—

	Infantry.	Cavalry.	Guns.
Force already in the field . .	16,189	3,472	44
Twelfth Cavalry Division . .	...	1,502	...
1 Battery of Horse Artillery .	...	...	6
	16,189	4,974	50

Ney, on perceiving the arrival of this reinforcement to the Anglo-Allied troops, despatched a peremptory order to d'Erlon to hasten to his support and join him without a moment's delay; and having well calculated the advantages he still retained, he resolved upon a hold and vigorous effort to secure the victory.

The greater portion of the wood of Bossu was now in his possession; and this circumstance appeared to him to present the means of establishing himself at Quatre Bras, and of thus enabling him effectually to turn Wellington's right flank, and cut off his line of retreat upon Brussels. With this view he had already greatly reinforced his infantry in the wood through which he had even ordered the advance of two batteries, in a direction parallel to, and within a very short distance of, its eastern boundary, so that they might be prepared to act upon the plain, as soon as circumstances rendered such a proceeding advisable or expedient. He now also threw forward additional Light troops to strengthen his extreme right in the vicinity of Piermont; whilst his cavalry, so vastly superior, both in numbers and in efficiency, to that which the British commander had brought into the field, constituted his main central force, and compensated in a great measure for the deficiency created in this point of his line by the drawing off of the infantry to the flanks.

The two French batteries above alluded to as having advanced along the interior of the wood of Bossu, suddenly opened a destructive fire from the edge of the latter upon the Brunswick troops posted on the right of the Charleroi road, just as Lloyd's Battery arrived at Quatre Bras. The duke instantly ordered the advance of this battery into the open space between the Charleroi road and the wood, for the purpose of silencing the French guns; but before the British artillerymen could unlimber, several horses of the battery were killed, wheels were disabled, and, from the proximity of the enemy's guns, some of the gunners were literally cut in two by the round shot with which they were so closely assailed. Nevertheless, the battery succeeded, not only in silencing its opponents, but also in forcing back into the wood a French column of infantry, which, advancing directly towards the Brussels road, had endeavoured to turn its right flank: after which brilliant services, Lloyd, perceiving no adequate support, judged it prudent, in the then crippled state of his battery, to retire to his former post, abandoning two guns for which he had not a sufficient number of horses remaining, and which consequently could not be recovered until the termination of the action.

Halkett's Brigade, shortly after passing Quatre Bras, was ordered to bring up its left shoulders; and, entering the rye fields in front of the Namur road, it proceeded some little distance in advance, and halted.

Kielmansegge's Brigade continued its march along the Namur road, and received orders to strengthen the extreme left, as also to support, and, where necessary, to relieve the exhausted British battalions, which had withstood the fiercest onsets of a daring and well organised cavalry, and had endured the incessant cannonade maintained against them by the well served batteries on the French heights.

It was during the advance of the Third British Division to take up its ground—Halkett proceeding directly to the front, and Kielmansegge moving along the Namur road to the left—and under cover of the heavy cannonade which was maintained against the Allied line at this time, that again a column of French infantry advanced from out of the wood, towards the Brussels road, and entering the latter by the isolated house southward of Quatre Bras, established itself in and about that building and its enclosures.

Shortly afterwards, another column advanced in support of the former one, which then emerged from its cover, and began to ascend that part of the Anglo-Allied position occupied by the 92nd Highlanders. On perceiving this, Major General Barnes, Adjutant General to the British forces, who had just ridden up to the right of the regiment, placed himself very conspicuously at the head of the Highlanders, waving his hat, and exclaiming, "92nd, follow me!" In an instant the latter sprang out of the ditch in which they had hitherto been posted, and with great gallantry and steadiness charged down the slope. The French infantry hastily fell back, until having gained the partial shelter afforded them by the isolated house and its enclosures, they opened a most destructive fire upon the Highlanders, who nevertheless slackened not their pace, but drove the French out of their cover.

Their commanding officer, Colonel Cameron, here received his death wound, and having lost the power of managing his horse, the latter carried him at its utmost speed along the road until he reached Quatre Bras, where his servant was standing with his led horse, when the animal, suddenly stopping, pitched the unfortunate officer on his head. The supporting column, however, securing the garden opposite to the house and on the right of the road, seemed resolved to make a stand against the further advance of the Highlanders; but the latter, by a judicious disposition of their force in three divisions—one towards each flank of the garden, and the other directly to the gate in front—and again uniting as soon as these points were secured, once more rushed upon their foes with the bayonet, displaying, under a terrific fire, the most undaunted bravery.

As soon as the French turned their backs, the 92nd poured upon them a volley which proved most destructive, and continued their advance, pursuing the enemy along the edge of the wood, into which they finally retired upon perceiving a disposition on the part of the French cavalry to charge, and finding themselves exposed to a heavy cannonade which was rapidly thinning their ranks to a fearful extent. Subsequently, in consequence of their very severe loss, they were withdrawn through the wood to Quatre Bras.

Again the French skirmishers were creeping up the slope from the Gemioncourt enclosures, and Pack, who had united the remains of the 42nd and 44th Regiments into one battalion, made the best show of resistance in his power to their teasing *tiraillade*; but being aware how very small a quantity of ammunition remained in his men's pouches, his anxiety on this point became extreme, the more so as he had good reasons for apprehending fresh attacks of cavalry. His advanced position in the immediate proximity of the formation of the enemy's columns of attack, naturally kept him on the look out for effective British support; and on observing the head of Halkett's Brigade, as the latter was advancing from Quatre Bras, he instantly despatched an *aide de camp* to that general, with a message, that his own brigade had expended nearly the whole of its ammunition, and that if he did not offer him a support, he would be under the necessity of almost immediately abandoning his position. Halkett at once acceded to the proposal by sending forward the 69th British Regiment, and desiring its commanding officer, Colonel Morice, to obey any orders he might receive from General Pack.

In pursuance of orders received from the duke, Halkett moved the remainder of his brigade into the space between the wood of Bossu and the Charleroi road, fronting the French left wing. Here he found the Brunswick infantry retiring with precipitation: he immediately put himself in communication with their commanding officer, Colonel Olfermann, and by aid of the support which his brigade presented to their view, he succeeded in bringing them up under cover, in the ditch which, traversing the space between the wood and the high road, ran nearly parallel with the enemy's line.

Leaving his brigade in the position he had taken up, in support of the Brunswickers and of Pack's Brigade, and pending the arrival of further instructions from the duke, Halkett galloped to the front, near-ly beyond the farm of Gemioncourt, for the purpose of ascertaining, if possible, the disposition and intentions of the enemy. He was not kept long in suspense, Ney's arrangements for another general attack hav-ing been concluded; and, observing the cavalry destined to advance against the Allies on both sides of the Charleroi road in motion, he turned round his horse and hastened to dispose his brigade in such a manner as to render it fully prepared to brave the coming storm. On his way, he sent an intimation to Pack of his discovery, and Orders to the 69th Regiment to prepare forthwith to receive cavalry.

A sudden and heavy cannonade had already opened from the French heights—a sure prelude to the attack which was about to take place—and the 69th Regiment was in the act of forming square, when the Prince of Orange rode up to it and asked what it was doing. Colonel Morice explained that he was forming square in pursuance of the instructions he had received; upon which His Royal Highness, remarking that he did not think there was any chance of the cavalry coming on, ordered him to reform column, and to deploy into line.

During this last movement a strong body of French *cuirassiers*, taking advantage of the surrounding high corn, and of the circumstance of the regiment lying in a hollow, approached unperceived quite close to the spot, and rushing suddenly and impetuously upon a flank, succeeded in completely rolling up the regiment, riding along and over the unfortunate men, of whom great numbers were cut down, and in the midst of the confusion thus created, captured and carried off one of the colours; in defence of which Major Lindsay, Lieutenant Pigot, and Volunteer Clarke, highly distinguished themselves, and were desperately wounded. Some officers and men took shelter in the square formed by the 42nd and 44th Regiments; the mounted officers gained the other side of the road, pursued by about twenty of the enemy, and escaped by riding through one of the Hanoverian battalions lining the Namur road.

The 30th Regiment, which had also been deployed into line by the orders of the Prince of Orange, most fortunately discovered, in sufficient time, the approach of cavalry (notwithstanding the extraordinary height of the rye, which greatly impeded all observation), formed square with remarkable rapidity, and, reserving their fire until the very last moment, they completely dispersed and drove off a body of Piré's lancers, and a portion of Kellermann's *cuirassiers*, which troops had made a charge upon them, enveloping two faces of their square. Picton, who, from the opposite side of the high road, was an eye witness of this scene, was so much pleased with the perfect steadiness of the regiment, that, seizing a favourable opportunity of galloping up to it, he called for the commanding officer, and told Lieutenant Colonel Hamilton that he should report to the duke the gallant conduct of his corps. Indeed the steadiness and gallantry of the 30th in this battle were so conspicuous as also to draw upon them the well merited commendations of the Prince of Orange, and Generals Alten, Halkett, and Kielmansegge.

The 73rd Regiment (under Colonel Harris), and the Brunswickers, were equally on the alert; but the French cavalry, on finding them prepared, diverged towards the high road.

The 33rd Regiment (under Lieutenant Colonel Elphinstone), had formed square upon its leading company (the grenadiers) at the moment the latter had reached some rising ground; in which position it became a conspicuous mark for the fire, at point blank distance, of a

French battery which opened upon it with great spirit. It was deemed advisable to deploy it into line, in which formation the regiment advanced towards the two Brunswick battalions then fiercely engaged with the enemy's Light troops near the skirt of the wood; but upon approaching the latter, a report was spread along the line that French cavalry was in its rear, whereupon the regiment rushed precipitately into the wood, within which it was speedily reformed.

Whilst that portion of Kellermann's dragoons which had dispersed the 69th Regiment, were sweeping gallantly onwards in their bold career along the high road towards Quatre Bras, the greater body of this corps advanced into the open space on the right of that road. Here Picton's gallant little bands found themselves again involved in one general onset of cavalry, made with a violence and fury which seemed to betoken a desperate resolve to harass the devoted squares to the last extremity, and to carry everything by main force. At the same time a dense cloud of skirmishers, bursting forth from the enclosures of Piermont, threatened to turn the extreme left of the Anglo-Allied Army; whilst the French infantry in the wood of Bossu, close upon the northern boundary of the latter, equally endangered its extreme right.

At this moment, Ney's prospects were bright enough to justify his hopes of success, and he hailed the captured colour, presented to him by the Cuirassier Lami of the 8th Regiment, as the harbinger of victory. In fact, on whatever point of his line Ney now directed his view, his operations were full of promise as to the result.

It was certainly an anxious moment to the British chief: but frightfully crippled as were his resources by the failure and hasty retreat of the great bulk of the Dutch-Belgian infantry, by the evident inferiority and utter helplessness of his cavalry, and by the dreadfully severe losses already inflicted upon his British regiments, he surveyed the field of slaughter, and calculated upon the extent to which the British and German infantry would enable him to bear up against the attack along his whole line, until he might detect some favourable opening, or seize some critical moment, to deal an effective counter stroke.

The arrival of Lloyd's British, and Cleeves's German, Batteries, attached to Alten's division, had already made a most important addition to the duke's artillery force; the former took post in front of Quatre Bras on the right, the latter on the left, of the Charleroi road.

Almost immediately afterwards, Major Kuhlmann's Battery of Horse Artillery of the King's German Legion, belonging to the First

Division, which it had preceded on the Nivelles road, reached the Field, and moved rapidly to the point of intersection of the Brussels and Nivelles road, where it came into action, at the very moment the *cuirassiers* who had fallen upon Halkett's Brigade were advancing in mass along the former road towards Quatre Bras.

Two guns under Lieutenant Speckmann were posted so as to bear directly upon the French column, and completely to enfilade the road; and as the *cuirassiers* approached with the undaunted bearing that betokened the steadiness of veterans, and with the imposing display that usually distinguishes armoured cavalry, a remarkably well directed fire was opened upon them: in an instant the whole mass appeared in irretrievable confusion; the road was literally strewed with corses of these steel clad warriors and their gallant steeds; Kellermann himself was dismounted, and compelled like many of his followers to retire on foot.

It was at this moment that Colonel Laurent, who had been despatched from the Imperial headquarters, reached Ney, with a pencilled note requiring the marshal to detach the First Corps towards St Amand. Having fallen in with the head of the column of that corps, he had taken upon himself to alter the direction of its march; and, on coming up with Count d'Erlon, who had preceded his corps, and was then in front of Frasne, he showed him the note, and explained to him where he would find the head of his column. Shortly afterwards, General d'Elcambre, Chief of the Staff to the First Corps, arrived to report the movement which was in course of execution.

Ney now saw clearly that at the very moment he required the aid of d'Erlon's Corps, not only to counterbalance the arrival of reinforcements which had joined Wellington, but to give an efficient support to the renewed general attack he had projected, that corps had been placed beyond his reach, and that he must, in all probability, continue to fight the battle without any addition to the force he had already in the field. Nevertheless, he did not allow the circumstance to suspend the execution of his operations; and, with the hope of yet securing the assistance of the First Corps, he sent back General d'Elcambre, with a peremptory order for its return towards Quatre Bras.

It was soon after this that Ney received another despatch from Napoleon, dated at two o'clock. From its general tenor it was evidently written previously to the departure of Colonel Laurent with the order for the flank movement of d'Erlon's corps, and therefore the bearer of it must have taken longer time than was necessary in conveying it to the marshal. It announced that the Prussians were posted between Sombref and Bry, and that at half past two Grouchy was to attack them with the Third and Fourth *Corps d'Armée*, and expressed the emperor's wish that Ney should also attack whatever enemy might be in his front, and, after having repulsed the latter, fall back in the direction of Ligny, to assist in enveloping the Prussians.

At the same time it stated, that should Napoleon succeed in defeating the latter beforehand, he would then manoeuvre in Ney's direction, to support in like manner the marshal's operations. It concluded by requesting information both as to Ney's own dispositions and those of the enemy in his front. This despatch reached Ney at a moment when he was most seriously engaged, when the issue of the battle was extremely doubtful, and the probability of his being enabled to afford the support required by Napoleon most questionable.

Upon the extreme left of the Anglo-Allied forces, the advance of the French Light troops from Piermont and its vicinity was met in a most determined and gallant manner by the head of Kielmansegge's Hanoverian Brigade (which after having moved along the Nivelles road, exposed to the continued fire from the batteries on the French heights, had just reached that part of the field), in conjunction with the 1st Battalion 95th British Rifles, and the 2nd Brunswick Light Battalion. The most determined efforts were made by the enemy to turn the Anglo-Allied Flank. The French infantry had already gained the high road, and were boldly pressing forward, when the British Rifles, the Brunswick Light infantry, and the Hanoverian Field Battalion Lüneburg (under Lieutenant Colonel Klencke) dashed in amongst them. The contest was obstinate and severe; but the Allied Light troops having been reinforced by the Hanoverian Field Battalion Grubenhagen (under Lieutenant Colonel Wurmb), gradually obtained the ascendancy, and, dislodging their opponents from one enclosure after another, continued steadily advancing, and gaining ground.

Along the whole front of the central portion of the Anglo-Allied Army, the French cavalry was expending its force in repeated but unavailing charges against the indomitable squares. The gallant manner in which the remnants of Kempt's and Pack's Brigades held their ground, of which they surrendered not an inch throughout the struggle of that day, must ever stand preeminent in the records of British infantry.

To relieve them as much as possible from the severe pressure they experienced, now that their ammunition was almost entirely exhausted, some of the Hanoverian battalions were judiciously thrown forward so as to afford them a close, immediate, and efficient, support, while others continued to line the Namur road; a disposition for which the arrival of Kielmansegge's Brigade had presented the ready means, and which imposed an impregnable barrier to any further advance of the French cavalry, whose ranks were now thoroughly disordered, and their numbers greatly diminished, by their perseverance in a contest the hopelessness of which began to appear but too evident.

During that part of the battle just described, Ney received a further despatch from the emperor by Colonel Forbin Janson. It was dated a quarter past three, and announced to the marshal that Napoleon was at that moment seriously engaged. It desired Ney to manoeuvre immediately so as to turn the right of the Prussians and fall upon their rear, and contained the remark that the latter would thus be taken *en flagrant délit* at the moment they might be endeavouring to join the English. The impossibility of Ney's complying with these directions was already sufficiently apparent.

At this time, Wellington received an addition to his forces by the arrival of the 1st and 3rd Brunswick Light Battalions, and the Brunswick Brigade of artillery under Major Mahn, consisting of a battery of Horse, and another of Foot, Artillery. The guns were immediately posted close upon the Namur road, at a short distance to the left of Quatre Bras; and their fire, combined with that of the British and German batteries, soon produced a very perceptible effect upon the French artillery. The infantry reinforced the 1st and 3rd Brunswick Line Battalions occupying the houses of Quatre Bras.

The most important reinforcement, however, was the arrival, at nearly the same moment—about half past six o'clock—of the First British Division, under Major General Cooke, consisting of the First Brigade of Guards, commanded by Major General Maitland, and the Second Brigade of Guards, commanded by Major General Sir John Byng.

Their line of march having been by the Nivelles road, they came very opportunely upon the most critical point of the Anglo-Allied position, namely, its extreme right, just at the moment when the French Light troops, having driven out the Dutch Belgian infantry, showed themselves in force along the northern boundary of the wood of Bossu, and some of their skirmishers had almost gained the high road.

Wellington's force was still further augmented by the recently arrived troops as follows:—

		Infantry.	Cavalry.	Guns
British . . .	Force already in the Field .	24,264	2,004	42
	First Infantry Division . .	4,061	...	...
	Battery of Foot Artillery . .	...	...	6
K. G. Legion .	Do. Horse do. . .	...	...	6
	1st and 3rd Light Battalions	1,344	...	...
Brunswick . .	Battery of Foot Artillery .	...	...	8
	Do. Horse do. . .	...	...	8
		29,669	2,004	70

Ney's force actually present continued as before:—

Infantry.	Cavalry.	Guns.
16,189	4,974	50

The Prince of Orange, who had galloped along this road to meet the Guards, immediately ordered the Light Companies under Lieutenant Colonel Lord Saltoun, to enter the wood. They rushed forward with a loud cheer, and commenced a brisk fire on their opponents, who were soon made sensible of the superior description of force now brought against them. The remainder of the brigade speedily followed, and the loud, sharp, animated rattle of musketry, which was progressing rapidly into the very heart of the wood, plainly indicated that even in this quarter, where the French had hitherto been the most successful, and whence they might not only have molested the Anglo-Allied troops on the eastern boundary of the wood, but have most seriously endangered the right of the British position, they were now encountering a most vigorous and determined resistance.

Halkett's Brigade, with the Brunswickers, resolutely maintained the ground on which they had been charged by the French cavalry. As the latter retired, the Light Companies of the brigade, with a portion of the Brunswickers on the right, and some Hanoverian Riflemen on the left, advanced in pursuit. The French threw forward a line of *tirailleurs* to check them, and a brisk fire was maintained on both sides. The cannonade on this side of the field was also kept up with great spirit. At length the French cavalry advanced, forcing back Halkett's skirmishers upon their respective columns, on which they then charged. Their attack, however, was not made with much energy, and, upon their being uniformly repulsed, the Light troops resumed their former ground. Halkett pushed forward his battalions to the line of his skirmishers, and then moving towards his right, in the direction of the ravine, which descends from the wood, drove across the rivulet a body of French infantry, from which a portion of his brigade had suffered a severe fire. In this part of the affair one of Picton's battalions—the Royals—co-operated. The two Brunswick battalions continued boldly to advance even beyond this line, resting their right close upon the wood.

In the meantime, Byng's Brigade had closely followed up Maitland's in support, having previously sent forward its Light Companies under Lieutenant Colonel MacDonell round by Quatre Bras, skirting the eastern border of the wood. The spirited and determined nature of the advance of the British Guards not admitting of that restraint which, considering the many intricate parts of the Wood, was essential for the preservation of order, led to great confusion in their ranks by the time they reached the southern extremity, after having fairly driven out the French; and in this state they ventured to pursue the enemy on the open ground, but were quickly repulsed by his reserves; and the French artillery poured so destructive a fire into this portion of the wood, that Maitland deemed it advisable to withdraw the 2nd Battalion (under Colonel Askew) to the rivulet, where it was immediately joined from the rear by the other battalion of his brigade (the 3rd, under Colonel the Hon. William Stuart).

The time which would have been occupied in restoring the order and regularity that had been so completely lost during the progress of these battalions through the wood, was considered too precious for that purpose at such a moment, and the brigade was ordered to form line to its left, outside the wood, the men falling in promiscuously as fast as they emerged from their cover, and extending the line into the plain between the wood and the Brussels road. Thus formed, the line advanced, though but for a short distance, when it opened and continued a brisk fire, under which the French infantry, in its immediate front, deployed with the utmost steadiness and gallantry. This advance had been followed by the Brunswick Guard Battalion, which was now manoeuvring to form on the left of Maitland's Brigade.

The French cavalry, which had been watching for an opportunity to charge the brigade, now made a dash at its left flank. When the irregular formation of the latter, which has been already explained, is considered, it is evident that any attempt to form Square at that moment would have involved the British Guards in inextricable confusion, and have rendered them an easy prey to the French horsemen. Rapid as was the advance of the latter, its object was frustrated in a manner which testifies the extraordinary discipline of the men of that brigade. Mere discipline it was not; it was an instinctive momentary impulse, which seemed to animate the whole corps with the sole conviction, that the only step to be taken, the only chance left for safety, consisted in a general and instantaneous movement to the ditch which bounded the wood on their right.

This was accomplished with complete success, and the French cavalry, which had advanced in full confidence of an easy triumph, were hurled back in confusion by a volley from the ditch, which the brigade had lined with a rapidity, a dexterity, and a precision, quite wonderful; while at the same moment, the Brunswick battalion threw itself into square, and received the cavalry with a steadiness, and gallantry, which won for it the admiration of the British who witnessed the manoeuvre. The flanking fire which was thus brought to bear so suddenly on the French cavalry by the Brunswickers, and the destructive front fire so deliberately poured in amongst them by the British Guards from the ditch, fairly drove them out of this part of the field.

More to the left, the French were retiring before Halkett in perfect order, covered by their skirmishers. As that general's brigade neared the farmhouse of Gemioncourt, Major Chambers of the 36th Regiment, an experienced officer, incited by the desire of capturing a post which had been throughout the day a *point d'appui* to the French centre, led on two companies of his corps towards it. They made a gallant rush into the courtyard, but were met by a smart fire which forced them back. Major Chambers, however, rallied his men in the orchard; and having instructed them how to proceed in their attack, the place was instantly carried.

The further advance upon the Anglo-Allied left had, in the meantime, kept equal pace with that on the right. Ney had been compelled to yield the strongholds by aid of which he had hoped to force the duke's position: his Infantry had been driven out of Piermont and the enclosures in front of his right, as also out of the wood of Bossu on his left: Gemioncourt, also, in front of his centre, had been captured; while the plain between the two positions, over which his cavalry had executed innumerable charges—charges that were occasionally suspended merely that the scattered bands might rally afresh to renew the onslaught with redoubled vigour, and that his artillery might pour upon the devoted squares its destructive missiles, by which each was shattered to its very centre,—was now completely cleared from the presence of a single horseman.

It was long after sunset, and darkness was approaching, when Wellington, now that his flanks and centre were relieved from the severity of a pressure of such long duration, led forward his troops to the foot of the French position. The loud shouts which proclaimed the triumphant advance of his forces on either flank were enthusiastically caught up and responded to by those who constituted the main central line, and who had so resolutely withstood the impetuous of the battle shock by which they had been so repeatedly assailed.

Ney, convinced of the futility, if not imminent hazard, of protracting the contest, withdrew the whole of his forces, and concentrated them on the Heights of Frasne, throwing out a strong line of picquets, to which Wellington opposed a corresponding line, having the southern extremity of the wood of Bossu on the right, the enclosures south of Piermont on the left, and Gemioncourt in the centre, for its main supports.

The French picquets manifested an extraordinary degree of vigilance; the slightest movement on the side of the Anglo-Allied picquets instantly attracted attention, and was noticed by a concentrated fire from the watchful sentries of the enemy. No movement, however, of any consequence was made on either side during the night. The wearied combatants sought that rest of which they stood so much in need, and the silence in which the Anglo-Allied bivouac soon became hushed, was only disturbed by the arrival of additional reinforcements, consisting principally of British cavalry.

Ney was joined by the First Corps, after the termination of the action. At nine o'clock, d'Erlon presented himself to the marshal for the purpose of reporting to him his proceedings, and of receiving his orders, after which the corps was bivouacked in the rear of Frasne; with the exception, however, of Durutte's division (the Fourth), and Jaquinot's Light Cavalry Brigade, which d'Erlon had left on the field of Ligny; in front of the extreme right of the Prussian Army; a measure which he had deemed advisable in order to prevent the enemy from debouching into the plain between Bry and the wood of Delhutte.

It is singular that Napoleon, who at Fleurus held so powerful a reserve as that consisting of the Imperial Guard and the Sixth Corps, and who was in perfect ignorance of the true state of affairs at Quatre Bras, should have ventured to withdraw from Ney a force amounting to more than one half of that which he had originally placed at his disposal. It was decidedly a false step, from which no advantage resulted on his own Field of Battle, whilst there can be very little doubt that it lost him that of Quatre Bras.

The losses sustained in this battle by the Anglo-Allied Army in killed, wounded, and missing, were as follows:—

British	2,275
Hanoverians	369
Brunswickers	819
	———
	3,463 men.

To these must be added the loss of the Dutch-Belgian troops, amounting probably to about 1,000 killed and wounded, which makes the entire loss of the Anglo-Allied Army equal to about 4,463 men.

The French loss amounted to about 4,000 killed, wounded, and missing.

Such was the Battle of Quatre Bras: a battle in which the British, the Hanoverian, and the Brunswick, infantry, covered itself with imperishable glory; to estimate the full extent of which we must constantly bear in mind, that the whole brunt of the action fell upon that infantry; that throughout the greater part of the day it was totally unaided by any cavalry, that arm of the Allies in the field having, at the outset, proved itself incompetent to engage with the French; and, lastly, that it was completely abandoned in the latter part of the action by the Second Dutch-Belgian Infantry Division, amounting to no less than 7,533 men.

When the imagination dwells upon that which constitutes one of the most prominent features of the battle—the manner in which Picton, on finding there was no cavalry at hand wherewith to charge effectively that of the enemy, led on the British infantry, and dashed into the midst of the French masses, maintaining his ground in defiance of their repeated assaults, invariably scattering back their charging squadrons in confusion, and this, too, in the face of a splendid cavalry headed by a Kellermann, whose fame and merit were so universally acknowledged.

The defeat sustained by the French was certainly not attributable, in the slightest degree, to any deficiency on their part, of either bravery or discipline. Their deportment was that of gallant soldiers, and their attacks were all conducted with an admirably sustained vigour, which could leave no doubt on the minds of their opponents as to the sincerity of their devotion to the cause of the emperor.

In a strategical point of view, both parties gained certain important advantages, and lost others which had been comprised within their respective plans of operation.

Ney had succeeded in preventing the junction of the Anglo-Allied Army with the Prussians, and might have obtained still more important results, had he not been deprived of the services of d'Erlon's Corps, the arrival of which he had been so fully led to expect.

Wellington, though he had been compelled to relinquish all hope of being enabled to afford that aid to Blücher which, in the morning, he had proffered to him, yet, by maintaining his ground at Quatre Bras sufficiently long to admit of the arrival of reinforcements, he completely succeeded in frustrating the grand object of Ney's movements, which had been to defeat the Anglo-Allied troops thus advancing, in detail, and also to operate upon Blücher's right flank.

And now that he had gained the battle, and secured the important point of Quatre Bras, upon which the remainder of his troops were advancing, and where the greater portion of them would arrive in the evening and during the night, he was perfectly ready and willing, should the Prussians prove victorious at Ligny, to renew the contest on the following morning, by attacking Ney with his collected force; and then, if successful by a junction with Blücher's right, to operate upon Napoleon's left, so as to bring the great mass of the combined armies to bear directly upon the main body of the French; or, in case of a defeat of the Prussians, to make good his retreat along his principal line of operation, in such a manner, as to secure a position between Quatre Bras and Brussels, favourable for a co-operation of Blücher's forces with his own, and for presenting a bold and determined stand against the further advance of the French emperor.

Orders were now forwarded for the movement of Clinton's division on the following morning, at daybreak, from Nivelles to Quatre Bras: and of Colville's division, at the same hour, from Enghien to Nivelles. The reserve artillery was directed to move at daybreak, on the following morning, to Quatre Bras, there to receive further orders; and the Tenth Infantry Brigade, under Major General Sir John Lambert, was directed to march, at the same hour, from Assche to Genappe, there to remain until further orders.

The tremendous roar of artillery in the direction of Ligny gave a sufficient intimation to the duke that a great battle had taken place in that quarter, but as it seemed to continue stationary, and only erased as night set in, he was doubtful of the result, and remained in this state of suspense and uncertainty until the following morning; the officer who had been despatched in the night to Quatre Bras from the Prussian headquarters with the expected communication, having been surprised in the dark, and made a prisoner by the French.

Battle of Ligny

CHAPTER 6

Battle of Ligny

Prince Blücher having ascertained, on the morning of the 16th, that his communication with the left division of the Duke of Wellington's forces by Quatre Bras continued uninterrupted, resolved upon accepting battle in the position in rear of Fleurus, which had been previously fixed upon as the one most eligible, in the event of the enemy's adoption of that line of operations respecting which all doubt and uncertainty had now ceased. Its importance in a strategical point of view, apart from tactical considerations, was manifest. Wellington having, on his part, selected Quatre Bras as the point whereon to concentrate his forces, the position in question, connected as it was with the latter by a paved road over an extent of not more than six or seven miles, offered great facility for co-operation and mutual support upon whichever point the great mass of the French Army might be directed.

Should it prove tenable, then, considered in conjunction with the advance of the Russians from the Rhine, the whole line of the Meuse below Namur, and the communications with Aix la Chapelle and the Prussian States, were effectually secured. If, on the other hand, either position should be forced by the enemy, then Mont St Jean and Wavre, upon parallel lines of retreat towards Brussels and Louvain, would likewise offer the means of co-operation on the south side of the forest of Soignies; and supposing Blücher willing to risk for a time his communication with the right bank of the Meuse, concentric lines of retreat upon Brussels would bring the two armies in combined position in the immediate front of that capital.

Supposing also that Napoleon's plan had been to advance by Mons, the concentration of the Prussian forces could not have been effected upon a more favourable point than that of Sombref, whence they could have advanced in support of their Allies, leaving a sufficient portion of Zieten's corps to watch the approaches by Charleroi: and, finally, had the French emperor directed his main attack by Namur, the retreat of Thielemann's corps would have secured time for effecting the concentration of the First, Second, and Third Prussian *Corps d'Armée*, if not also of the Fourth, while the Duke of Wellington's forces might have assembled at Quatre Bras, for the purpose of meeting any secondary attack from the Charleroi side, and of forming a junction with the Prussian Army.

The position itself comprises the heights of Bry, Sombref, and Tongrines, contiguous to the high road connecting Namur with Nivelles, by Quatre Bras, and to the point of junction of that road with the one from Charleroi, by Fleurus. These heights are bounded upon the south-west and western sides, or right of the position, by a ravine, through which winds a small rivulet along the villages of Wagnelé, St Amand la Haye, and St Amand, near the lower end of which last, it unites with the greater rivulet of the Ligny; and, along the whole of the south side, or front of the position, by a valley, through which flows the Ligny, and in which lie, partly bordering the stream itself, and partly covering the declivities, the villages of Ligny, Mont Potriaux, Tongrenelles, Boignée, Balatre, and Vilrets. At the last named point, another small rivulet falls into the Ligny on quitting a deep ravine, which commences northward of the village of Botey, and thus tends to the security of the extreme left of the position.

The extreme right, however, resting upon the Namur road, in the direction of Quatre Bras, was completely *en l'air*. The heights in rear of St Amand, Ligny, and Sombref, are somewhat lower than those on the opposite or Fleurus side of the valley; and, from the nature of the ground, troops, particularly artillery, are more exposed on the former than on the latter, where the undulations afford better cover. The descent from either side into the villages of Wagnelé, St Amand la Haye, and St Amand, is gentle: between the latter point and Mont Potriaux the sides of the valley descend more rapidly: and below that Village they become steep, particularly about Tongrines, Boignée, and Balatre: while the ground above commands alternately from side to side. Above Mont Potriaux, the bed of the valley is soft, and occasionally swampy: below that point it partakes still more of this character.

The buildings in the villages are generally of stone, with thatched roofs, and comprise several farmhouses with courtyards, presenting great capabilities for defence. St Amand and Boignée are the most salient points of the position, the central portion of which retires considerably, particularly near Mont Potriaux.

In the morning of the 16th, the First Corps (Zieten's) occupied that portion of the position which is circumscribed by the villages of Bry, St Amand la Haye, St Amand, and Ligny. The four brigades of this corps had been very much mixed up together when occupying these villages during the night, which will account in some measure for the promiscuous manner in which their several battalions appear to have been distributed during the battle. The main body of the corps was drawn up on the height between Bry and Ligny, and upon which stands the farm and windmill of Bussy, the highest point of the whole position. Seven battalions of the Second Brigade (General Pirch II.) were formed immediately in rear of this farm; the 28th Regiment and 2nd Westphalian Landwehr in the First, and the 2nd and 3rd Battalions of the 6th Regiment in the Second, Line; while the 3rd Battalion of the latter regiment occupied the farm itself, which was put into a state of defence.

Two battalions of the Fourth Brigade (General Count Henkel), namely, the 2nd Battalions of the 19th Regiment and of the 4th Westphalian Landwehr, stood on the slope between the Second Brigade and Ligny; while the remaining four battalions of the brigade—the 1st and 3rd of the 19th Regiment, and the 1st and 3rd of the 4th Westphalian Landwehr—were charged with the defence of Ligny. The village of Bry was occupied by the 3rd Battalions of the 12th and 24th Regiments, belonging to the First Brigade (General Steinmetz); and the 2nd Battalion of the 1st Westphalian Landwehr was posted in rear of the village in support. The 1st and 3rd Companies of the Silesian Rifles, attached to this brigade, were distributed about the intersected ground between Bry and St Amand la Haye.

The remainder of the First Brigade was posted on the height in the rear of St Amand, its right resting on St Amand la Haye; the 1st and 2nd Battalions of the 12th Regiment on the right, and the 1st and 2nd Battalions of the 24th Regiment on the left, forming a First, and the 1st and 3rd Battalions of the 1st Westphalian Landwehr forming a Second, Line. The defence of St Amand was confided to three battalions of the Third Brigade (General Jagow)—the 1st and 2nd of the 29th Regiment, and the 2nd Battalion of the 3rd Westphalian Landwehr. The remaining six battalions of this brigade were posted in reserve northward of Ligny, and near the Bois du Loup. The 2nd and 4th Companies of the Silesian Rifles were thrown into Ligny.

The reserve cavalry of Zieten's Corps continued in advance, upon the Fleurus high road, watching the movements of the enemy.

It was eight o'clock when these dispositions were completed; and about eleven o'clock, Pirch's corps, which more than an hour before had quitted its bivouac near Mazy, was formed up in reserve to Zieten. The Fifth Brigade (General Tippelskirchen) stood across the high road, near its intersection with the old Roman road, in the customary Prussian brigade order of three lines of columns of battalions at deploying intervals, and had in its front the two batteries, Nos. 10 and 37. The Sixth Brigade (General Krafft) was posted in similar order in the rear of the farm of Bussy, and in left rear of Bry. The Seventh Brigade (General Brause) stood more to the left: it had only the 14th Regiment then present, for the 22nd Regiment and the Elbe Landwehr did not rejoin it until one o'clock in the afternoon. The Eighth Brigade (Colonel Langen) was ordered to remain upon the high road leading from Sombref to Fleurus, until the arrival of the Third Corps (Thielemann's). One of its battalions—the 3rd of the 21st Regiment—as also two squadrons of the Neumark Dragoons attached to this corps, had been left in the line of outposts beyond the Meuse, towards Philippeville; and did not rejoin it until the 20th of June.

The reserve cavalry of Pirch's corps, under General Jürgass, was stationed in rear of the high road, and on the west side of Sombref.

The twelve pounder batteries, Nos. 4 and 8, and the Horse Batteries, Nos. 5 and 18, remained in reserve, near Sombref.

Thielemann's corps, which had quitted Namur about seven o'clock in the morning, had reached Sombref before twelve. It was immediately assigned its position in that part of the field which lies between Sombref and Balatre, and was posted in columns upon both high roads, here to remain available for either a movement to the right, or for the occupation of the position in left front of Sombref, along the heights in rear of the Ligny rivulet.

Such were the dispositions made by Blücher previously to Napoleon's advancing from Fleurus. The occupation of Ligny and St Amand—the most salient part of the position—by Zieten's corps, and the posting of the reserve cavalry of the latter in the intervening space between those villages and Fleurus, were justly calculated to secure for the Prussian commander ample time for further developing his line of battle in such a manner as the direction and mode of his opponent's attack might render most expedient.

In the morning of the 16th, the French troops which lay along the

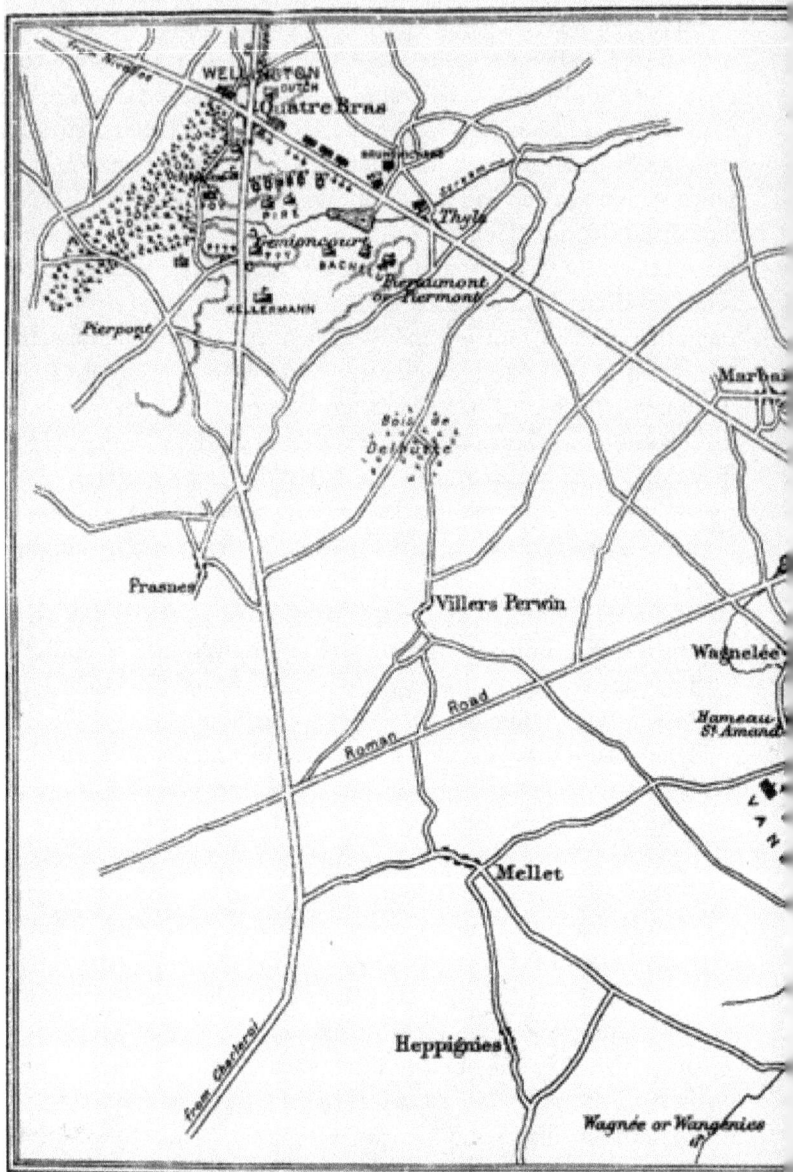

BATTLES OF
LIGNY AND QUATRE BRAS
JUNE 16TH, 1815.

Scale, 1:68,420 (1 mile = 92 inch)

NOTE: from the high ground at Quatre Bras, troops on the field of Ligny could be seen with a glass.

Allies........ ▆▆▆ ▆▆▆ French

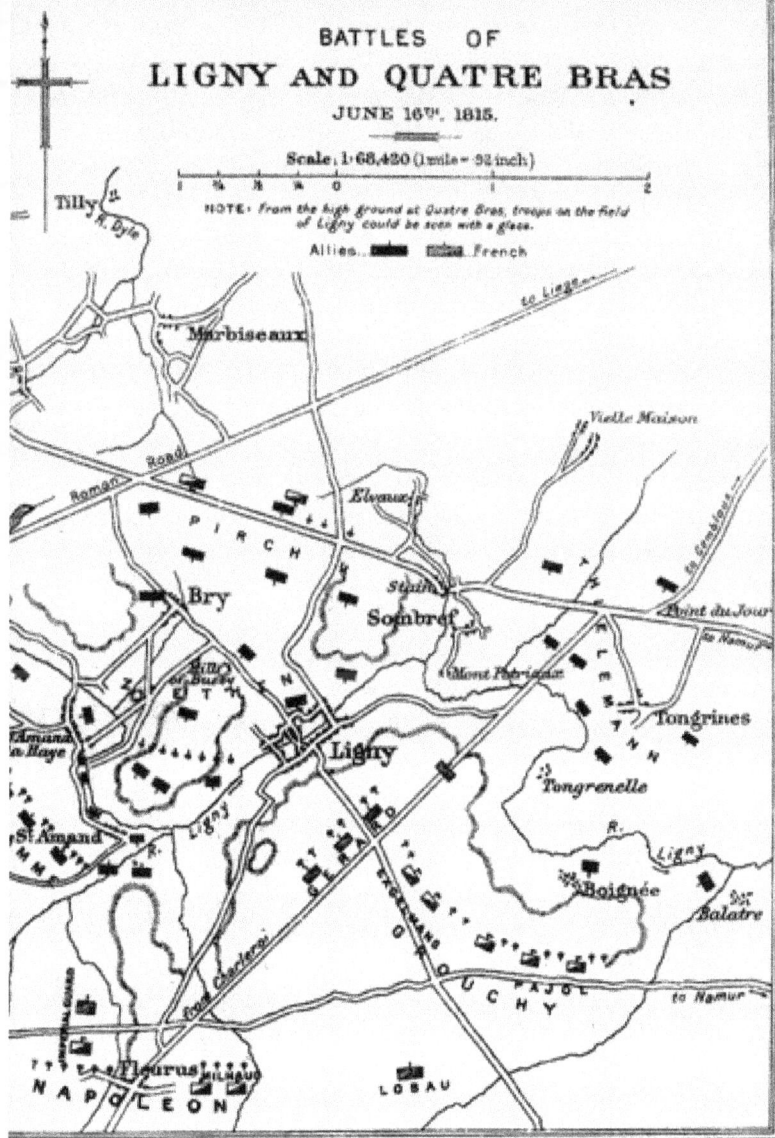

Tilly

R. Dyle

Marbiseaux

to Liege

Vielle Maison

Roman Road

PIRCH

Elvaux

Bry

Stain

Sombref

Point du Jour

to Namur

Mont Potriaux

St. Amand

la Haye

Ligny

St. Amand

R. Ligny

Tongrines

Tongrenelle

R. Ligny

Boignée

Balatre

to Namur

OUCHY

PAJOL

NAPOLEON

Fleurus

LOBAU

Sambre, and which belonged to that main portion of the Army which was more immediately under the orders and guidance of Napoleon, quitted their bivouacs, and marched to join their leading columns, the position of which in front of Fleurus was described in the fourth chapter.

It was past ten o'clock when these troops debouched in two columns from the Fleurus Wood—the one along the high road, the other more to the right—and drew up in two lines within a short distance of Fleurus. In the first line Pajol's Light, and Excelmans' Heavy, Cavalry, formed the right, and Vandamme's corps, the left wing; while Gérard's corps which had not received the order to march until half past nine o'clock, arrived much later, and occupied the centre. Girard's division was detached some little distance on the extreme left. The Imperial Guard and Milhaud's corps of *cuirassiers* constituted the Second line. More than an hour was passed in this position before the arrival of the emperor, who then rode along the line of vedettes, and reconnoitred the enemy's dispositions.

It appeared to Napoleon that Blücher had taken up a position perpendicular to the Namur road, and had, in this way, completely exposed his right flank; whence he inferred that the prince placed great reliance upon the arrival of auxiliary forces from the Duke of Wellington's Army.

A single glance at the Prussian position, as it has been described, will suffice to prove that the French emperor was in error as regarded Blücher's assumed line of battle, and that so far from its having been perpendicular to, it was, in the general military acceptation of the term, parallel with, the Namur road. At the same time it is proper to remark, that he may have been misled by the massing of the Prussian troops between the salient point of the position, St Amand, and the road in question, as well as by the direction of the line of the occupied villages of St Amand, Ligny, and Sombref . It must also be acknowledged that although the inference was incorrectly drawn, it accorded in substance with the real fact, that Blücher did rely upon the arrival of a portion of Wellington's forces by the Namur road from Quatre Bras.

Napoleon having returned from his reconnaissance, immediately gave his orders for the advance of the army, and for the disposition of each individual corps in his intended line of battle.

Impressed with the important advantage which, according to his assumed view of Blücher's position, might accrue from a vigorous and well timed attack upon the right and rear of the Prussians, while vigorously assailing them himself in their front, he directed Soult to address to Ney the despatch, dated two o'clock, to which reference was made in the preceding chapter, acquainting the marshal that in half an hour thence he proposed attacking Blücher, posted between Sombref and Bry, and desiring that he would, on his part, also attack whatever might be in his front, and that after having vigorously repulsed the enemy, he should move towards the emperor's field of battle, and fall upon the right and rear of the Prussians; adding, at the same time, that should the emperor be first successful, he would then move to the support of the army at Quatre Bras.

The French Light troops moved forward against Fleurus, of which place they gained possession between eleven and twelve o'clock, and then opened from their Light Artillery a cannonade upon the Prussian cavalry posts taken up by the 6th Uhlans. The latter immediately retired, and formed upon the left of the Brandenburg Dragoons, which regiment had been placed in front of the Tombe de Ligny, along with the Horse Battery No. 2, in support. The Brandenburg Uhlans were also in support, but more to the rear, and on the left of the high road.

At this time, Napoleon was on the height of Fleurus, again reconnoitring the Prussian position; and it was also about the same period that Wellington joined Blücher in person near the mill of Bussy.

As soon as Röder perceived the imposing array of the French columns in full advance, he ordered the immediate retreat of his cavalry, which he covered with the 6th Uhlans and the Brandenburg Dragoons, together with two pieces of Horse Artillery. He sent the main body, which he had stationed in a hollow, in rear of the Tombe de Ligny, as also the remainder of the artillery, across the Ligny, with directions to take post between the village of that name and Sombref. He himself continued with the above two regiments, and the two guns, near the Tombe de Ligny, until he received orders also to retire.

In the mean time, the main body of the French Army advanced in great regularity in columns of corps. The left column, consisting of the Third *Corps d'Armée* under Vandamme, to which was attached the infantry division under Lieutenant General Girard belonging to Reille's corps (then with Ney), being destined to advance against St Amand, the most salient point of the Prussian position, and therefore having the shortest distance to pass over, was the first to take up its ground, preparatory to attack. Whilst thus engaged in making its preliminary dispositions for this purpose, it was cannonaded by the Prussian bat-

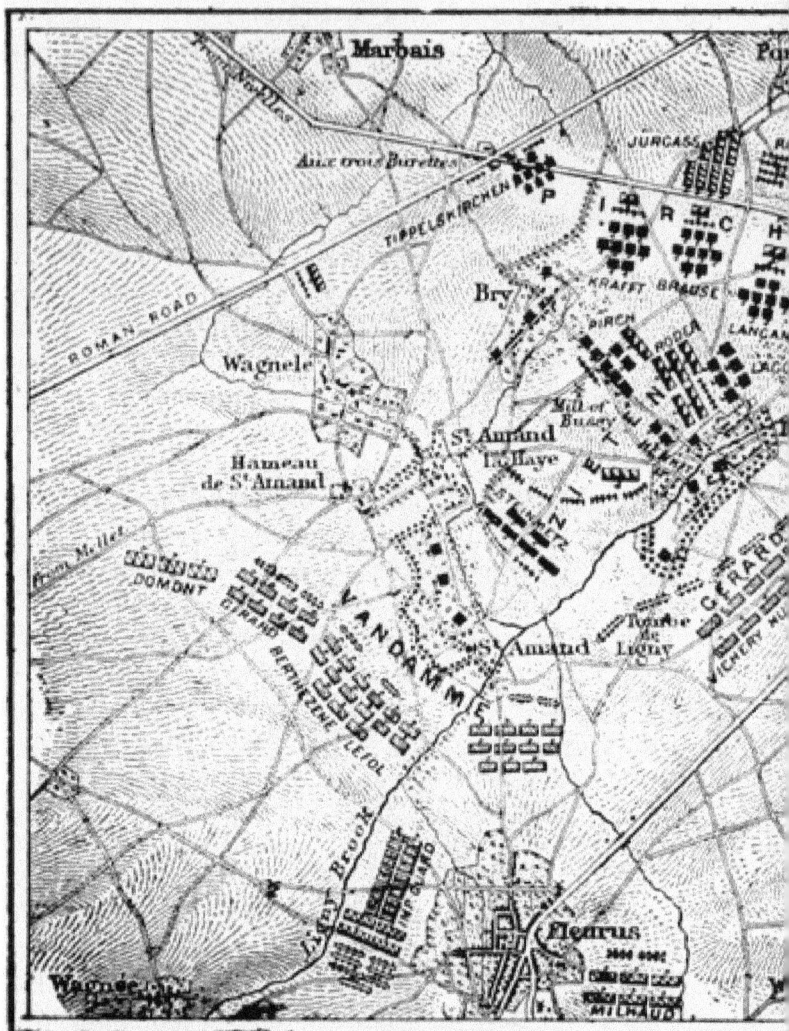

Marbais

JURCASS...

Aile croix Burettes

TIPPELSKIRCHEN

ROMAN ROAD

Bry

KRAFFT BRAUSE

PIRCH

LANGA...

Wagnele

Miller et Bussy

St Amand
La Haye

Hameau
de St Amand

from Millet

DOMONT

VANDAMME

St Amand

GÉRARD

Tombe
de Ligny

VICHERY

BERTEZENE TEROI

Ligny Brook

LIGNY GUARD

Wagnée

Fleurus

MILHAUD

BATTLE OF LIGNY
at ½ past 2 o'clock, p.m.
SCALE
0 ¼ ½ ¾ 1 Mile
Prussians
French
Vieille Maison
To Gembloux
Humrée
BORCKE
STULPNAGEL
Sombref
Botey
Le Point du Jour
THIELEMANN
To Namur
Tongrines
Mont Potriaux
KAMPFEN
HOBE
Ligny Br.
Tongrenelles
Ligny Br.
Balatre
Boignee
EXCELMANS
GROUCHY
Old road to Namur
PAJOL
Velaine sur les Termes

teries posted on the heights in rear of the village. Girard's division took post on the left of Vandamme's corps, and Domon's Light Cavalry division on the left of Girard.

The centre column, consisting of the Fourth *Corps d'Armée*, under Gérard, advanced along the Fleurus high road, and took up, somewhat later, a position upon the heights fronting Ligny, and parallel to the general direction of that village; its left being near the Tombe de Ligny, and its right resting on an eminence southward of Mont Potriaux.

The right column, under Grouchy, comprising the cavalry corps of Pajol and Excelmans, moved by its right, and took post, as did also the Light Cavalry division under Lieutenant General Maurin, belonging to the Fourth *Corps d'Armée*, on the right of Gérard, and showing front towards the villages of Tongrines, Tongrenelle, Boignée, and Balatre. Grouchy disposed this cavalry so as to protect Gérard from any attempt which the Prussians might make to debouch in his rear from Mont Potriaux or Tongrenelle; as also to watch any hostile movements on their left, and to divert their attention from the centre. Pajol's corps, which was formed on the right, detached along the cross road which leads to Namur. The villages of Boignée and Balatre being situated on the French side of the valley, and occupied by Prussian infantry, Grouchy was supplied with two battalions from Gérard's corps. The 1st and 2nd Squadrons of the 3rd Kurmark Landwehr Cavalry belonging to Thielemann's corps, which had been posted in advance, upon the Fleurus road, retired skirmishing until they reached the barrier at the bridge, whither they were pursued by the French cavalry. Here, however, the latter were checked and driven off by the 3rd Battalion of the 4th Kurmark Landwehr, belonging to Colonel Luck's Brigade.

The Imperial Guard and Milhaud's *Cuirassiers* were halted in reserve, the former on the left, and the latter on the right, of Fleurus.

The numerical strength of the French emperor's forces prepared to engage with the Prussian Army amounted to:—

Infantry,	43,412
Cavalry,	12,614
Artillery,	6,856
	———
Total,	62,882 men, with 204 guns.

If to this we add Lobau's corps, which was on the inarch from Charleroi, the total amount of available force was:—

BATTLE OF LIGNY

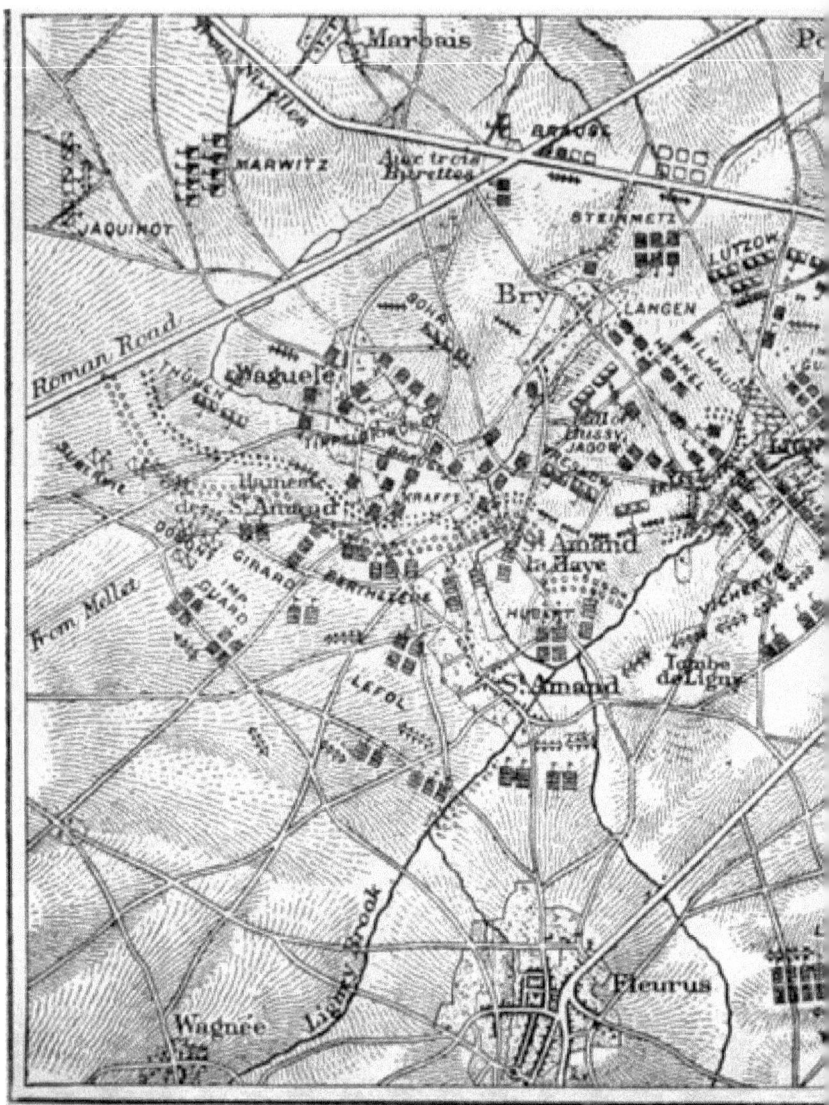

Marbais

MARWITZ

Avc trois
Burettes

JAQUINOT

STEINMETZ

LUTZOW

Roman Road

Bry

LANGEN

HENKL

Waguele

Hamens
do S.Amand

KRAFFT

Brissy
JAGO

St Amand
la Haye

GIRARD

BERTHEZENE

HUBERT

VICHERYE

From Mella

LAFOL

Tombe
de Ligny

S.Amand

Ligny Brook

Fleurus

Waguee

BATTLE OF LIGNY

at ½ past 8 o'clock p.m.

SCALE

0   ¼   ½   ¾   1 Mile

Prussians

French

Infantry,	51,564
Cavalry,	12,614
Artillery,	7,788

Total, 71,966 men, with 242 guns.

The Prussian Army in the Field amounted to:—

Infantry,	73,040
Cavalry,	8,150
Artillery,	3,437

84,617

Deduct loss of First Corps on 15th June, 1,200

Total, 83,417, with 224 guns.

As soon as the direction of the enemy's movements for attack became sufficiently manifest, Blücher made such further disposition of his force as appeared to him requisite to meet that attack.

He ordered the batteries of the First *Corps d'Armée* (Zieten's) to be suitably posted for impeding the enemy's advance. The three heavy batteries of the corps were immediately drawn up on the height between Ligny and St Amand. They were supported by the battery of the First Brigade, posted in rear of St Amand. Somewhat later, when the direction of attack by Gérard's corps became more developed, the battery of the Third Brigade was placed on the right of Ligny, near a quarry, and the battery of the Fourth Brigade on the left of the village, upon the declivity descending to the rivulet.

The battery of the Second Brigade, the Foot Battery No. 1, and the Horse Battery No. 10, remained in reserve. Of the remaining horse batteries of the corps, one continued with the cavalry under General Röder (which was posted in a hollow, as before stated, between Ligny and Sombref), and the other was with the 1st Silesian Hussars, which regiment had been detached in observation on the right flank of the army, and posted between the northern extremity of the village of Wagnelé and a large pond contiguous to the old Roman road.

By the time the action commenced in front of St Amand and Ligny—half past two o'clock—Blücher was satisfied that no necessity existed for any movement of his Third *Corps d'Armée* to the right; and he therefore ordered it to proceed from the position it had hitherto held in columns upon the two high roads near Sombref, and form the left wing of his line of battle; resting its right upon Sombref, and occupying the heights, at the foot and on the declivities of which are situated the villages of Mont Potriaux, Tongrines, Tongrenelle, Boignée, Balatre, Vilrets, and Botey.

The Ninth Brigade (General Borke) was formed in brigade order in rear of Sombref and northward of the Namur high road, having detached one of its battalions (the 3rd of the 8th Regiment) with the Foot Battery No. 18, to Mont Potriaux, where the former posted itself on the north, and the latter took up a favourable position on the south, side of the church. The Eleventh Brigade (Colonel Luck) with the twelve pounder Battery No. 7, stood across the Fleurus high road, in front of the junction of the latter with the Namur road upon the height of Le Point du Jour, having detached the 3rd Battalion of the 4th Kurmark Landwehr into the valley, where it occupied the houses in its immediate vicinity.

Four battalions of the Tenth Brigade (Colonel Kämpfen) were drawn up on the height of Tongrines, resting their right on this village, and having in their front the Foot Battery No. 35, and at a short distance from their left, the Horse Battery No. 18. The remaining two battalions of the brigade were detached, the 3rd Battalion of the 27th Regiment, to occupy Tongrines and the castle of Tongrenelle, and the 3rd Battalion of the 2nd Kurmark Landwehr, to hold the villages of Boignée and Balatre. The 2nd Battalion of the 3rd Kurmark Landwehr, belonging to the brigade, as also two squadrons of the 6th Kurmark Landwehr Cavalry, and two squadrons of the 9th Hussars, attached to this corps, still continued in the line of outposts in the vicinity of Dinant, to observe Givet; and rejoined on the morning of the 17th of June.

The Twelfth Brigade (Colonel Stülpnagel) with the Horse Battery No. 20, was formed in Brigade order, in reserve, near the windmill, on the height of Le Point du Jour. The reserve cavalry of this corps, with the Horse Battery No. 19, was posted on the extreme left of the position between Botey and Vilrets, whence it detached the 3rd Squadron of the 7th Uhlans to Onoz, in observation.

This position and the order of battle which was thus developed, were well calculated to answer the object which Blücher had in view, namely, to hold his ground long enough to gain sufficient time for the arrival of at least a portion of Wellington's forces, expected to join the Prussian extreme right by the Namur road; as also, perhaps, for the arrival and co-operation of Bülow's corps, in rear of Thielemann, by the Gembloux road. In either of these cases, if not previously favoured by the circumstances of the general battle about to take place, such a marked accession to his strength would enable him to assume the offensive; whilst, in the first mentioned, Wellington would effectually prevent a junction between Napoleon's and Ney's forces.

The position had been long before selected, and the whole of the ground had even been surveyed, with a view to meet the contingency which had now actually occurred; but then it must be remembered, that in this design the co-operation of the Fourth Corps d'Armée was fully contemplated, whereas the latter had now become a doubtful question: and hence it was that Blücher, was led to place more reliance upon a direct support from Wellington, than would otherwise have been the case.

To accept a battle, notwithstanding the absence of Bülow's corps, was undoubtedly the wisest course. The enemy's force in the field did not appear to exceed that of the Prussians; and therefore, considering the nature of the position, the contest would, in all probability, become protracted, perhaps until the arrival of Bülow; perhaps, also, until the close of day, without any distinct advantage being gained by either party. In the former case, the required preponderance might instantly give a decidedly favourable turn to the scale; in the latter, the junction of the Fourth Corps during the night would enable Blücher on the following morning to attack his opponent with every prospect of success, and either to relieve Wellington, if necessary, from any pressure in his front, or so to combine his further operations with those of the British commander, should the latter have held his ground and concentrated his army, as to lead to the complete overthrow of both Napoleon's and Ney's forces.

To have declined the contest, and retired so as to effect a junction with his Fourth Corps, he must still, if he wished to act in close concert with Wellington, have abandoned his direct communication with the Meuse and the Rhine, whence he drew all his supplies; a result which might as well be trusted to the chances of a battle.

These considerations were also, in all probability, strongly seconded by a desire on the part of the Prussian commander, and one perfectly in keeping with his ardent character, to take every possible measure to oppose Napoleon's advance.

In a tactical point of view, the position was undoubtedly defective. Nearly the entire of the ground situated between the line of villages of Ligny, St Amand, and Wagnelé, and the great Namur road, was exposed to the view of the enemy; and as there was every probability of a protracted village fight along the front of the position, the supports and reserves required to maintain a contest of that nature, would necessarily be subjected to the full play of the batteries on the opposite heights. Upon the space above mentioned every movement could be detected from the French side; where, on the contrary, the undulations were such as to admit of the concealment of the disposition of considerable masses of troops.

The defect in this respect was subsequently made strikingly manifest by the fact that the gradual weakening of the Prussian centre for the purpose of reinforcing the right, was closely observed by Napoleon, who took advantage of the insight thus obtained into his opponent's designs, by collecting in rear of the heights of Ligny that force with which, when he saw that the Prussians had no reserve remaining, he so suddenly assailed and broke the centre of their line.

Napoleon's dispositions having been completed, the battle commenced, about half past two o'clock, with an attack upon the village of St Amand, by Lieutenant General Lefol's division of Vandamme's corps. The attack, which was made in three columns, proved successful; the three battalions of the 29th Prussian Regiment which defended it, were compelled, after a stout resistance, to yield to greatly superior numbers, and were driven out of the village. General Steinmetz, whose brigade was posted in rear of St Amand, pushed forward all the sharpshooters of the 12th and 24th Regiments to their support.

These, however, being unable to make head against the enemy, who already made a disposition to debouch from the village, the 12th and 24th Regiments were led forward to renew the contest. In the meantime, just as the French appeared at the outlet of the village, a shower of grape and canister was poured right down amongst them from the Foot Battery No. 7. Immediately upon this, both battalions of the 12th Regiment descended into the ravine, rushed upon the enclosures, and, driving the enemy's shattered infantry before them, regained possession of the village. The 24th Regiment advancing by wings of battalions—the one in line and the other in column of reserve respectively—supported this attack upon the left, and established itself in the lower part of St Amand.

In the course of this short prelude, the batteries ranged along the little eminences which rose on either side of the valley of the Ligny, opened a furious cannonade along the whole extent of the front lines of the contending armies. Ligny, as also St Amand (when repossessed by the Prussians), both of which lay so directly under the French guns, seemed devoted to destruction. Their defenders, sheltered in a great degree by stone walls, hollow ways, and banked up hedges, appeared perfectly motionless while the deluge of shot and shell poured fast and thick around them; but no sooner did those in Ligny discover a dusky mass emerging from the clouds of smoke which enveloped the heights above them, and wending its course downwards upon the lower portion of the village, than they rushed out of their concealment, and lining with their advanced skirmishers the outermost enclosures, prepared to meet the onset which would probably bring them into closer contact with their enemies, and lead to a struggle in which physical strength and innate courage, combined with individual skill and dexterity, might effect a result unattainable by a recourse to projectiles alone. It was the 2nd Battalion of the 19th Prussian Regiment, which, issuing from its cover, where it had stood in column, rapidly deployed, and, by a well directed volley, shook the advancing mass, which it then threw into disorder by following up this advantage with a well sustained fire.

Twice was this attack repeated on the part of Gérard's troops, but with a similar result. A second column now advanced against the centre of the village, and shortly afterwards a third was launched against the upper part of it, near the old castle; but their attempts to penetrate within its precincts proved equally futile, and the four Prussian battalions of Henkel's Brigade gallantly maintained the post of Ligny. As the French column withdrew, their Batteries played with redoubled energy upon the village, and fresh columns prepared for another assault.

The troops of Vandamme's corps renewed the attack upon St Amand with the utmost vigour; and forcing back the 12th and 24th Prussian Regiments, which suffered most severely, penetrated into the village, where the fight became obstinate, and the fire most destructive. Steinmetz had only two more battalions of his brigade remaining at his disposal—the 1st and 3rd Battalions of the 1st Westphalian Landwehr—and these he pushed forward into the village, to restore confidence to the defenders, whose numbers were so fearfully reduced, and, if possible, to stem the progress of the assailants. They had scarcely got fairly into action, however, when their commanding officers were wounded, and both battalions gave way before the furious onset of the French, the 3rd Battalion leaving numbers of its men killed, along the outlets of the village.

The whole brigade, which, within a short period, had suffered a loss of 46 officers and 2,300 men, having rallied in rear of St Amand, retired into position between Bry and Sombref, and the three battalions which had first occupied the village, marched to rejoin the Third Brigade; whilst the loud shouts of "*Vive l'Empereur!*" which immediately followed the cessation of the sharp rattle of the musketry, heard even amidst the incessant thunder of the artillery, proclaimed the triumph of the French infantry.

In the meantime, another assault was made upon Ligny, whose defenders had been reinforced by the two remaining battalions of Henkel's Brigade. The French now changed their mode of attack. They advanced simultaneously against the centre with the view of gaining the churchyard, and against the lower end of the village in order to turn the left flank of the defenders; and taking advantage of the unusually great height of the corn, their line of skirmishers, strengthened by whole battalions so as to give it a decided superiority over that of the Prussians, approached so cautiously and silently as to continue unperceived until they suddenly possessed themselves of the outermost hedges and gardens. A hand to hand contest ensued, and the Prussians, pressed in front by superior numbers, and taken in flank at the same time, were forced to yield. Presently, however, stimulated by the combined exertions of the commanding officers, Majors Count Gröben, Kuylenstierna, and Rex, they recovered themselves, rallied, and again faced their enemies.

The battle, on this part of the field, now presented an awful, grand and animating spectacle, and the hopes of both parties were raised to the highest state of excitement. Intermingled with the quick but irregular discharge of small arms throughout the whole extent of the village, came forth alternately the cheering "*En avant!*" and exulting "*Vive l'Empereur!*" as also the emphatic "*Vorwärts!*" and the wild "*Hourrah!*" whilst the batteries along the heights, continuing their terrific roar, plunged destruction into the masses seen descending on either side to join in the desperate struggle in the valley, out of which there now arose, from the old castle of Ligny, volumes of dark thick smoke, succeeded by brilliant flames, imparting additional sublimity to the scene.

The Prussians gradually gained ground, and then pressing forward upon all points of the village, succeeded in clearing it of the French; who, in retreating, abandoned two guns which had been moved close down to the principal outlet on that side. General Jagow's Brigade

BATTLE OF LIGNY

(the Third) had made a change of front to its left, and approached the village; the 3rd Battalions of both the 7th and 29th Regiments had been detached to the right, to protect the Foot Batteries Nos. 3 and 8, and to remain in reserve; the four remaining battalions descended into the village as a reinforcement.

Beyond an occasional cannonading, the action on the eastern side of the field, between the corps of Grouchy and of Thielemann, was comparatively languid: being limited to a contest, varied in its results, for the possession of the village of Bognée, and subsequently, of those houses of Tongrines which were situated along the bottom of the valley; as also to some skilful manoeuvring on the part of Grouchy with his cavalry, with a view of menacing the Prussian left.

In the meantime, the French maintained possession of St Amand, but Zieten's twelve pounder batteries, which were now moved forward, presented a formidable obstruction to their debouching from that village.

Napoleon directed General Girard, on the extreme left, to take possession, with his division, of St Amand la Haye; and this operation having been successfully accomplished, gave the French the advantage of outflanking from thence any attack upon St Amand itself.

Blücher ordered General Pirch II. to retake this village; whereupon the latter advanced with his brigade from the height of Bry, and withdrew the 1st Battalion of the 6th Regiment from the windmill of Bussy, which was then occupied by the 2nd Battalion of the 23rd Regiment (Eighth Brigade), and near to which the 1st Westphalian Landwehr Cavalry remained during the whole of the action.

At the same time, the Prussian chief, fully sensible of the very critical position in which he would be placed, were the French, following up the advantages they had already gained upon his right, to debouch from St Amand and St Amand la Haye in sufficient force to overpower Zieten's corps, and thus cut off his communication with Wellington; he decided upon occupying the village of Wagnelé, whence repeated attacks might be directed against the enemy's left flank; and, with this view, he desired General Pirch I., who commanded the Second Corps, to detach the Fifth Brigade (General Tippelskirchen's) to the latter village, and to place it under the orders of General Jürgass, who was also sent to that part of the field, with Lieutenant Colonel Sohr's Brigade of cavalry (consisting of the 3rd Brandenburg, and 5th Pomeranian, Hussars), together with two squadrons of the 6th Neumark Dragoons, and the Horse Battery No. 6.

Colonel Marwitz, of Thielemann's corps, was also ordered to join these troops with two regiments of his brigade, the 7th and 8th Uhlans. The brigade of General Brause (the Seventh), which had been rejoined by detached battalions, was pushed forward as far as the Roman road, to occupy the position vacated by the advance of General Tippelskirchen's Brigade, to which it was to act as a support in case of necessity.

It was four o'clock when General Pirch II. who had formed his brigade for the attack of St Amand la Haye, having his left flank protected by the 12th Regiment, which had reassembled in rear of St Amand, moved his front line against the former village. As it advanced, however, its ranks were dreadfully shattered by the fire from the French artillery, nor were they less thinned by that of the musketry as they entered the village; and such was the determined resistance on the part of the French, that they were unable to penetrate beyond the centre of the village; and though reinforced by the 1st Battalion of the 6th Regiment, from the second line, they found it quite impracticable to drive the enemy out of a large building which was surrounded by a stone wall, and which formed the point of connection between the two villages.

The Prussians having got into great disorder, and being closely pressed by the French, were compelled to abandon the village, in order to collect their scattered remnants, and to reform. General Girard, whose division had, under his own immediate guidance, so gallantly maintained the village, fell mortally wounded on this occasion.

Blücher now decided on a renewed attack upon St Amand la Haye, in order to occupy the front of Girard's division, while he should carry into effect his previously projected movement against the enemy's left flank; and, anxious to ensure the due execution of his instructions and to direct the attacks himself, he repaired in person to this part of the Field. General Tippelskirchen's Brigade, having advanced along the Roman road, was already formed in brigade order, in rear of Wagnelé, while Jürgass had posted his cavalry more to the left, and opposite to the interval between that Village and St Amand la Haye, whence he could with considerable advantage fall upon the enemy, should the latter venture to debouch in that direction.

These movements did not escape the watchful eye of Napoleon, who detached a division of the Young Guard and a battery of the same corps in support of his left wing, as also General Colbert's Brigade of lancers from Count Pajol's corps, to reinforce the cavalry on the left, and to preserve the communication with Ney.

When all was ready for the attack, Blücher, who felt how much depended on its result, galloped up to the leading battalions, and thus earnestly and impassionately ordered the advance :—

"Now, lads, behave well! don't suffer the *Grande Nation* again to rule over you! Forward! In God's name—forward!"

Instantly his devoted followers rent the air with their re-echoing shouts of "*Vorwarts!*"

Nothing could surpass the undaunted resolution and intrepid mien which Pirch's battalions displayed as they advanced against, and entered, St Amand la Haye, at a charging pace; they completely swept the enemy before them; while Major Quadt, who commanded the 28th Regiment, supported by some detachments of the 2nd Regiment (from Tippelskirchen's Brigade) gained possession of the great building. The 1st Battalion of the 6th Regiment, after having forced its way right across the village, sallied forth from the opposite side, in pursuit of the enemy, with a degree of impetuosity which its officers had the utmost difficulty in restraining, while numbers of the men were on the point of plunging into the very midst of the French reserves.

The cavalry on the right of the village seemed to have caught up the intrepid spirit and enthusiastic devotion of the infantry; and, as if impatient to join in the struggle, a squadron of the Brandenburg Uhlans supported the attack of the village by a charge upon the enemy's cavalry: after which, the remainder of this regiment, with the 1st Kurmark Landwehr Cavalry, advanced under General Treskow, into the plain on the left of the village, of which the whole contour now bristled with the bayonets of the 46th Regiment, while the 28th Regiment held the post of the great building, which it had so gallantly carried, and the 2nd Westphalian Landwehr stood in second line, as a reserve.

So completely absorbed was the attention of the twelve pounder Battery No. 6, which stood in a somewhat isolated position, by the contest in St Amand la Haye, which it covered by its fire, that it had not noticed the stealthy advance of a troop of the enemy's horsemen, wearing the uniform of the Light Artillery of the Guard, and most unexpectedly found itself attacked in flank by these bold adventurers. This give rise to a curious scene, for the Prussian gunners, in the first moment of surprise, could only defend themselves with their rammers and handspikes; but with these they plied the intruders with so much adroitness and resolution as to hurl their leaders to the ground, and force the remainder to betake themselves to a hasty flight.

Prince Blücher had, in the meantime, on perceiving Colbert's French lancers hovering upon, and stretching out beyond, his extreme right, ordered General Pirch to detach two more cavalry regiments— the Queen's Dragoons and the 4th Kurmark Landwehr Cavalry—as a reinforcement to the cavalry of Zieten's Corps.

The nearly simultaneous attack upon Wagnelé by Tippelskirchen's Brigade, previously mentioned as having taken post in rear of that village, was not attended with an equal degree of success. The 1st and 2nd Battalions of the 25th Regiment advanced in column through the centre of Wagnelé; but on debouching, the 2nd Battalion, which led the advance, was suddenly assailed by a fire from the French skirmishers who lay concealed in the high corn. Although its order was thus considerably disturbed; it succeeded, nevertheless, in effecting its deployment. The 1st Battalion also deployed, but, in doing so, its left wing covered the right of the 2nd Battalion; and while executing a second movement, intended to clear the front of the latter, the French battalions pressing forward, drove in the Prussian skirmishers upon the regiment, which consisted mostly of young soldiers; when, notwithstanding the conspicuously meritorious exertions of all their officers, they were overthrown and dispersed in such a manner that it became impracticable to lead them back into action in any other way than by separate detachments.

The 3rd Battalion of this regiment shared nearly the same fate; for, having plunged into the high corn, it received a volley which disordered its ranks, and killed its three senior officers; and although it maintained for some time a fire in return, it was eventually compelled to retire, as were also the 1st and 2nd Battalions of the 5th Westphalian Landwehr, under precisely similar circumstances. The brigade was reformed, under the protection of the 2nd Prussian Regiment, which now advanced from the reserve, boldly encountered the enemy, and aided by the efficacious fire of the Foot Battery No. 10, stemmed the further progress of the French, and thus gained time for the remaining Battalions to reform in rear of Wagnelé. Upon the advance, however, of a French column towards its left flank, it fell back as far as the entrance into the village.

The French now renewed their attacks upon St Amand la Haye, and made their appearance simultaneously in front and in both flanks of that village. The fight again became desperate. Pirch's Brigade had, however, exhausted both its ammunition and its strength, when Blücher pushed forward the 3rd Battalion of the 23rd Regiment (from the Eighth Brigade—Colonel Langen's), and soon afterwards the 3rd Battalion of the 9th Regiment, together with the whole of the 26th Regiment (from the Sixth Brigade—General Krafft's); whereupon General Pirch withdrew his battalions, which had suffered so severely, to the rear of Bry. The Foot Battery No. 3, belonging to Pirch's Brigade, had at an earlier period moved to its left, and had taken up a position near the quarries on the right of Ligny, by the side of the Foot Battery No. 8, of Jagow's Brigade.

While the struggle in the villages in front of the Right of the Prussian position continue to wear an indecisive and unsettled aspect; let us return for a moment to Ligny, which we left in possession of Count Henkel's Fourth Prussian Brigade, supported by the Third Brigade under General Jagow.

The 1st and 2nd Battalions of the 7th Regiment (of Jagow's Brigade) were ordered to traverse the village, and to advance in column against the enemy. Just as they debouched, they found in their immediate front, several French battalions, in close column, moving directly against the village. Both parties at once came to a halt; the Prussians without being able to deploy in the defile, and the French without attempting to do so, probably unwilling to lose the time which such a movement would require. A fire of musketry commenced which lasted half an hour, and caused much loss. Other battalions now hastened across the village, but all at once, a rumour flew rapidly among them, that the French were in possession of the churchyard, and in a moment several muskets were aimed in that direction, and either thoughtlessly or nervously discharged.

Those battalions that were in front, at the outlet of the village, became alarmed by this unexpected tiring in their rear. At the same time, a discharge of grape, from some guns suddenly brought forward by the French, in their immediate front, augmented their confusion, and forced them to a retreat. They were closely pursued by the enemy, whose skirmishers made a dash at the colour of the 2nd Battalion of the 7th Regiment, which they would have captured but for the noble and determined gallantry with which it was defended.

General Krafft, from whose brigade (the Sixth) five battalions had already been detached, namely, four for the defence of St Amand la Haye, and one in aid of that of Ligny, now received Blücher's order with his remaining four battalions (the 1st and 2nd of the 9th, and the

1st and 3rd of the 1st Elbe Landwehr), to drive the enemy out of the latter village. The Foot Battery No. 15, was posted between the left of Ligny and the Bois du Loup, and the Foot Battery No. 37, was directed towards St Amand. The other batteries posted between Ligny and St Amand received orders to retire accordingly as they expended their ammunition, for the purpose of refitting; and they were successively relieved by the Foot Battery No. 1, the Horse Battery No. 10, and the twelve pounder Batteries Nos. 4 and 8. The Horse Battery No. 14 was advanced across the stream between Ligny and Sombref, and took post on the other side of the valley, where it was much exposed to the enemy's fire, and lost 19 Gunners and 53 horses.

General Krafft moved forward, in the first instance, only two battalions, and kept the others in reserve; but all of them soon became engaged; for the French, though driven back at first, received considerable reinforcements.

The fight throughout the whole village of Ligny was now at the hottest: the place was literally crammed with the combatants, and its streets and enclosures were choked up with the wounded, the dying, and the dead: every house that had escaped being set on fire, was the scene of a desperate struggle: the troops fought no longer in combined order, but in numerous and irregular groups, separated by houses either in flames, or held as little forts, sometimes by the one, and sometimes by the other party; and in various instances, when their ammunition failed, or when they found themselves suddenly assailed from different sides, the bayonet, and even the butt, supplied them with the ready means for prosecuting the dreadful carnage with unmitigated fury. The entire village was concealed in smoke; but the incessant rattle of the musketry, the crashing of burning timbers, the smashing of doors and gateways, the yells and imprecations of the combatants, which were heard through that misty veil, gave ample indication to the troops posted in reserve upon the heights, of the fierce and savage nature of the struggle beneath.

In the meantime, the relieving batteries on the Prussian side, which had arrived quite fresh from the rear, came into full play, as did also a reinforcement, on the French side, from the artillery of the Imperial Guard. The earth now trembled under the tremendous cannonade; and as the flames, issuing from the numerous burning houses, intermingled with dense volumes of smoke, shot directly upwards through the light grey mass which rendered the village indistinguishable, and seemed continually to thicken, the scene resembled for a time some violent convulsion of nature, rather than a human conflict—as if the valley had been rent asunder, and Ligny had become the focus of a burning crater.

Long did this fierce and deadly strife continue without any material advance being made on either side. At length the French gained possession of a large house, as also of the churchyard, into which they brought forward two pieces of cannon. General Jagow vainly endeavoured with the 7th Regiment to retake this house. The 1st Battalion of the 3rd Westphalian Landwehr displayed the most inflexible perseverance in its endeavours to drive the French out again from the churchyard: it made three unsuccessful attempts to cross an intervening ditch, and subsequently tried to gain a hollow way, which lay in the flank of that post, but falling upon the French reinforcements that were advancing towards it, they were compelled to abandon the enterprise.

Fresh victims were still required to satiate the "King of Terrors," who might be said to hold a gala day in this "Valley of Death." Blücher had ordered Colonel Langen's Brigade (the Eighth) to follow in succession that of General Krafft. The position vacated by the former, in front of Sombref, was taken up by Colonel Stülpnagel's Brigade (the Twelfth) of Thielemann's corps, and the chain of skirmishers of the latter brigade extended along the rivulet as far as Ligny. As soon as Colonel Langen had reached the immediate vicinity of Ligny, he posted the 1st and 2nd Battalions of the 21st Regiment upon an eminence near the village, and the Foot Battery No. 12, covered by two squadrons of the 5th Kurmark Landwehr Cavalry, upon the left of the road leading Ligny. The 21st Regiment made no less than six different attacks, partly in conjunction with the other troops that fought in Ligny, and partly isolated, without succeeding in disturbing the position of the enemy in that portion of the village which lies on the right bank of the Ligny.

Colonel Langen, observing the increased fury and obstinacy of the fight in Ligny, detached thither also the 1st Battalion of the 23rd Regiment, and the 2nd of the 3rd Elbe Landwehr: he then took up a position, with the remainder of his brigade, near the mill of Bussy, into which he threw the 2nd Battalion of the 23rd Regiment. The 1st Battalion of this corps, having formed two columns, rushed into the village, and, after crossing the stream, received a sharp fire from the windows of the houses on the opposite side. The left column of the battalion stormed a farmhouse, of which, after it had burst in the gates with hatchets, it gained possession, and thus protected the advance of the right column.

At this moment, Napoleon's final and decisive attack commenced on this point; but previously to entering upon an account of it, it will be necessary to resume the narrative of the contest along the remainder of the line of battle.

On the right, Tippelskirchen's Brigade (the Fifth) was ordered to renew the attack upon St Amand la Haye; and, as an auxiliary movement, a bold push was to be made upon the group of houses in rear of that village, and of Wagnelé, called the Hameau de St Amand. Both of the 3rd Battalions of the 2nd and 25th Regiments, under Major Witzleben, advanced against the latter point, while the 1st and 2nd Battalions of the 2nd Regiment, the 3rd Battalion of the 5th Westphalian Landwehr, and a Battalion of the 25th Regiment made a direct attack upon St Amand la Haye. Both movements were supported by the Foot Batteries Nos. 10 and 37, and Colonel Thümen was detached, with the Silesian Uhlans, and the 11th Hussars, to cover the right of the brigade: the 1st and 2nd Squadrons of the 5th Kurmark Landwehr Cavalry were posted in reserve.

The 3rd Battalion of the 2nd Regiment opened the attack upon the Hameau de St Amand, and being well protected on their right by the 11th Hussars, carried it by storm. The French appeared determined to regain this point, which from its position, was, in fact, the key to the defence of the three villages of St Amand, St Amand la Haye, and Wagnelé; and the struggle for its possession was most obstinate and sanguinary. All the battalions of Tippelskirchen's Brigade became successively engaged. Four times was St Amand la Haye lost and retaken by the 2nd Regiment, which suffered severely. General Jürgass ordered forward the Horse Battery No. 6, on the right of which the Foot Battery No. 10 then took post. The Silesian Uhlans and the 11th Hussars suffered considerably from their exposure to the enemy's artillery.

Colonel Thümen was killed at their head, by a cannon shot, and was succeeded by Lieutenant Colonel Schmiedeberg, who ordered both these regiments to make a change of front to the right; when the Prussian lancers dashed forward to meet the advance of a French regiment, which they completely defeated, and having followed up the attack with a vigorous pursuit, fell all at once among the enemy's reserves; but they immediately recovered themselves, and rallied with great celerity, order, and precision.

About this time, the Light Cavalry Brigade of Colonel Marwitz, already mentioned as having been ordered from the left, reached the right flank, and was formed up in two lines: also the four battalions that had been detached from General Krafft's Brigade, arrived upon the right of St Amand la Haye, and came into action. The battle on both sides on this part of the field continued to rage with unabated violence, and with such indefatigable ardour did the Prussians continue the struggle, that when the fire of their infantry skirmishers was observed to slacken, from the men having expended their ammunition, the soldiers of the 11th Hussars rushed into the midst of them, and supplied them with such cartridges as they had of their own; an act of devotion to which many of them fell a sacrifice. General Jürgass ordered forward the brigade (Seventh) of General Brause in support of that of General Tippelskirchen, which had suffered a very severe loss.

When General Brause had, at an earlier period, taken post at the Trois Burettes, upon Tippelskirchen advancing from that point to Wagnelé (as previously explained), he stationed both the 3rd Battalions of the 14th and 22nd Regiments upon an eminence on the left of the high road, for the purpose of keeping up the communication with Tippelskirchen; and he pushed on the other two battalions of the 14th Regiment towards Bry, that they might be nearer at hand, if required, for the contest in the villages of Wagnelé and St Amand la Haye, while the two squadrons of the Elbe Landwehr Cavalry, attached to his brigade, kept a look out upon both sides of the road. These two battalions, thus posted, caught the eye of Blücher as he looked round for the nearest available force, and he immediately ordered them to advance, and join in the contest; and General Brause, on being made acquainted with this disposition, led forward the 3rd Battalions of the 14th and 22nd Regiments, and the 1st Battalion of the 2nd Elbe Landwehr, while the four remaining battalions of his brigade, making a change of front to their left, formed up, in reserve, in rear of the Namur road.

On approaching the more immediate scene of the action, General Brause came upon the 3rd Battalion of the 9th Regiment, which had expended all its ammunition: he procured for it a fresh supply, and ordered it to return into the village, along with the 2nd Battalion of the 14th Regiment; while the 1st Battalion of this regiment threw itself into St Amand la Haye, and relieved the 2nd Regiment, which now retired, as did also the remainder of Tippelskirchen's Brigade to the rear of Wagnelé, where it reformed.

Here, in these villages on the right, as well as at Ligny, the fight never slackened for a moment: fresh masses, from both sides, poured in among the burning houses as often as the fearfully diminished numbers and dreadfully exhausted state of the combatants rendered relief imperatively necessary; partial successes on different points were constantly met by corresponding reverses on others; and so equally were the courage, the energies, and the devotion of both parties balanced, that the struggle between them appeared, from its unabated vigour, likely to continue until the utter exhaustion of the one should yield the triumph to the greater command of reserves possessed by the other.

The anxiety at that time on the part of Blücher for the arrival of either a portion of Wellington's forces, or Bülow's corps, was extreme; and frequently, as he cheered forward his men in their advance to take part in the contest, did he address them with the exhortation, "Forward, lads! we must do something before the English join us!" In fact, his only reserve remaining was the Ninth Brigade (General Borcke's), the withdrawal of which would greatly expose his centre; and Napoleon, who had already entertained a suspicion that such was the case, resolved upon terminating the sanguinary combat in the valley, by boldly advancing a portion of his own intact reserves, consisting of the Guard and Lobau's corps (which had just arrived and was posted on the right of Fleurus) against the Prussian centre.

For the execution of his project the French emperor destined the Imperial Guard, with Milhaud's corps of *cuirassiers* in support. He wished to conceal this movement as much as possible from the enemy, and caused it to be made to the right, along the rear of the corps of Gérard, a portion of whose batteries were ordered to be withdrawn, for the purpose of affording greater protection to the Guard, by diverting the enemy's fire to other points, and of deceiving him as to the real object of the movement, if observed previously to the actual execution of the emperor's design.

This far-famed band of veteran warriors, and Milhaud's splendid corps of mailed *cuirassiers*, were in full march towards the lower extremity of Ligny, where they were to cross the stream, when, all at once, they were halted by an order direct from the emperor, who had decided upon suspending the movement, until he should ascertain the result of an incident that had occurred upon his extreme left, and which had placed him for the time in considerable doubt and anxiety respecting its real nature.

He had received a message from Vandamme, informing him that a strong column, composed of infantry, cavalry, and artillery, was advancing towards Fleurus; that it had at first been looked upon as the corps detached from Ney's forces, until it was discovered that it moved by a different road from that along which those troops had been expected, and in a direction towards the French left rear, instead of the Prussian extreme right; that Girard's division had been consequently induced to fall back, and take up a position to cover Fleurus; and that the effect produced upon his own corps by the sudden appearance of this column was such, that if His Majesty did not immediately move his reserve to arrest its progress, his troops would be compelled to evacuate St Amand and commence a retreat.

This intelligence could not fail to create alarm in the mind of the French emperor, who concluded that the corps in question had been detached against his rear, as a diversion in favour of Blücher, from the army of Wellington, who had probably obtained some signal triumph over Ney. Another officer arrived from Vandamme, reiterating the account previously given. Napoleon instantly gave the order for the halt of the Imperial Guard; and despatched one of his *aides de camp* to reconnoitre the strength and disposition of the column, and to discover the object of its movement.

The commencement of the march of the Imperial Guard and Milhaud's *Cuirassier* corps towards Ligny, had been conducted with so much skill, and the manoeuvring of these troops at one point in their line of march to shelter themselves from the fire of the Prussian batteries, to which they had become suddenly exposed, bore so much the appearance of a retrograde movement, accompanied as it was by the withdrawal of a portion of the guns of Gérard's corps, that the Prussians were completely deceived by it. Intelligence was hastily conveyed to Blücher that the enemy was retreating; whereupon he ordered the march of all the remaining disposable battalions of Colonel Langen's Brigade (the Eighth) upon St Amand, to enable him to take advantage of the circumstance by pressing upon the enemy's left.

In the meantime, Colonel Marwitz had been menaced by the advance of a considerable line of cavalry and a battery, which latter annoyed him but little. This cavalry did not, however, seem much disposed to risk a close encounter: once it put forward a detachment, which was overthrown by two squadrons of the 7th and 8th Uhlans, and then a regiment of French *Chasseurs à Cheval* fell upon the skirmishers of the 2nd Regiment of Infantry, but was driven back by two squadrons of the 5th Kurmark Landwehr Cavalry. Colonel Marwitz had been ordered by General Jürgass to send out patrols in different directions from the right flank, for the purpose of seeking out the communication with the Duke of Wellington's forces. These brought in prisoners, from whom it was ascertained that a whole French corps, the First, under Count d'Erlon, was in that vicinity.

Subsequently, French cavalry were perceived between Mellet and Villers Perruin; whereupon Colonel Marwitz, who had been reinforced by two squadrons of the Pomeranian Hussars, ordered a change of front of his brigade in this direction, then deployed his eight squadrons in two lines, with considerable intervals, and withdrew them, alternately, towards the high road; followed, though not vigorously, by three French regiments of cavalry and a battery, comprising Jaquinot's Light Cavalry Brigade, attached to d'Erlon's corps. As he approached the *chaussée*, the 2nd and 3rd Battalions of the 2nd Elbe Landwehr, as also the 3rd Battalion of the 22nd Regiment, advanced to his support.

Until about six o'clock the action along that part of the line which extended from Sombref to Balatre, had not been carried on with any degree of energy, and the occupation of the opposing forces was generally limited to mutual observation. Now, however, the French infantry (of which only a small portion was attached to Grouchy's cavalry), penetrated as far as the precincts of the village of Tongrines; but Colonel Kämpfen's Brigade (the Tenth), having been successively reinforced by all the battalions of Colonel Luck's Brigade (the Eleventh) excepting one which was left in reserve, the French were easily repulsed, and the Prussians maintained full possession of all this portion of their original position.

It was about seven o'clock when the *aide de camp* returned from his reconnaissance, and reported to Napoleon that the column in the distance which had caused so much uneasiness proved to be d'Erlon's corps; that Girard's division, upon being undeceived, had resumed its position in the line of battle; and that Vandamme's corps had maintained its ground.

This movement of d'Erlon's corps admits of being satisfactorily explained. Napoleon, having received information that d'Erlon had been left in reserve in front of Gosselies, and inferring, perhaps, from this circumstance that Ney was sufficiently strong to be able to hold his ground at Quatre Bras, without further aid than what he had at hand, resolved upon employing this corps upon the Prussian right flank; but in the meantime, d'Erlon had, in pursuance of instructions from Ney, continued his march towards Quatre Bras; and having himself proceeded in advance, had reached Frasne, at which place Colonel Laurent found him, and communicated to him the emperor's order for the march of his corps upon St Amand; adding that on coming up with the head of his column, he had taken upon himself to change its direction of march into that of St Amand. D'Erlon hastened to comply with Napoleon's wishes, and despatched General d'Elcambre, his chief of the staff, to make known the movement to Marshal Ney.

His route from Frasne towards St Amand, the point prescribed by the order, lay through Villers Perruin, and the movement was altogether one of a retrograde nature. Hence the direction of the column, as seen in the distance, was well calculated to alarm the troops of the French extreme left; as also to excite surprise in the mind of Napoleon, who having formed no expectation of the arrival of any French troops in the field by any other direction than that from Gosselies upon St Amand, or perhaps from Quatre Bras upon Bry, also participated in the opinion that the column in question, under its attendant circumstances and general disposition, could be no other than that of an enemy.

As d'Erlon debouched from Villers Perruin, and advanced upon the prescribed point, St Amand, he threw out his cavalry (Jaquinot's) to his left, for the protection of this flank; and it was before this cavalry that the Prussian Brigade, under Colonel Marwitz, retired in the manner already explained, a movement which fully restored confidence to Girard's division.

All at once this column was observed to halt, to indicate an indecision in its intentions, and finally to withdraw from the field. D'Erlon had in fact just received from Ney a peremptory order to join him without delay, with which he resolved to comply, probably concluding that he was bound to do so from the circumstance of his having been in the first instance placed under the marshal's immediate command; having ascertained also from the emperor's *aide de camp* that he was not the bearer of any instructions whatever from Napoleon as to his future movements, and that the appearance of his corps upon that part of the field of battle had been quite unexpected. This pressing order had been despatched by Ney immediately previous to the arrival of Colonel Laurent on the heights of Gemioncourt.

If the first appearance of this column had caused alarm and perplexity among the troops of the French left wing, the apprehensions it excited on the Prussian right, when its cavalry was observed to advance and to drive back Colonel Marwitz' Brigade, which had been sent towards it *en reconnaissance* (as already explained), were still greater; and its equally unexpected disappearance (with the exception of its cavalry, and a portion of its infantry), at a moment when it was felt that its vigorous co-operation must have rendered the issue of the battle no longer doubtful, was looked upon as a particularly fortunate turn of affairs; and Blücher's hopes revived as he prepared to carry into effect his meditated attack upon the French left flank.

There did not appear on the part of Napoleon any eagerness to resume the movement of the Imperial Guard towards the lower extremity of Ligny, but rather an anxiety to await calmly the most favourable moment for his projected attack. Doubtless he had discovered the march of the remaining battalions of Colonel Langen's Brigade, from Sombref towards St Amand, as a further reinforcement to the Prussian right, and calculated upon paralysing the attack which Blücher was evidently preparing against his left flank, by executing a sudden and vigorous assault on the Prussian centre, with a preponderating mass of fresh troops.

At length, towards eight o'clock, the emperor gave the order for the Guard and Milhaud's corps of *cuirassiers* to resume their march. The same, precautions were observed as before for masking the movement as much as possible, and so successfully, that Thielemann, on observing a French battery opposite Tongrines entirely withdrawn, and Grouchy's lines of cavalry presenting a diminished extent of front, and conceiving, at the same time, that the contest in Ligny was assuming a change favourable to the Prussians, concluded that the moment had then arrived in which an attack might be made with every probability of success, upon the right flank of the enemy. He had only one brigade remaining of the cavalry of his corps, namely that of Colonel Count Lottum; the other brigade, under Colonel Marwitz, having been, as already explained, for some time detached to the extreme right of the Prussian Army. General Hobe, who commanded this Cavalry Division, had previously moved forward Count Lottum's Brigade and posted it in rear of Colonel Kämpfen's Infantry Brigade. Thielemann now desired him to advance with Lottum's Brigade and the Horse Battery No. 19, along the Fleurus high road.

In carrying this order into effect, General Hobe posted the battery, in the first instance, close to the twelve pounder Battery No. 7, which stood across the Fleurus high road, about midway between the junction of the latter with the Namur road and the bridge over the Ligny. A cannonade was opened from this point upon the French guns on the opposite height, to which the latter replied with great spirit, and one of the guns of the battery was dismounted. The remaining guns were now advanced rapidly along the high road, preceded by two squadrons of the 7th Dragoons: on getting into position, two of the guns continued upon the road itself, on which the French had also posted two pieces, but scarcely had the squadrons formed up, and the battery fired a few rounds, when they were furiously attacked by the 5th and 13th French Dragoons of Excelmans' cavalry corps: in an instant they were thrown into confusion; the two guns upon the road escaped, while the remainder fell into the hands of the French dragoons, who closely pursued the Prussians.

General Borcke (commanding the Ninth Brigade) observing this *mêlée* upon the Fleurus road, immediately pushed forward the 1st and 3rd Battalions of the 1st Kurmark Landwehr, and posted them in rear of the hedges and walls running parallel with the high road, so as to flank the enemy's cavalry; the 2nd Battalion of the same regiment followed this movement, and was finally stationed upon the road. In order to support these battalions, and to preserve the communication with Colonel Stülpnagel's Brigade (the Twelfth) on his right, he occupied Mont Potriaux and its outlets with the remainder of his brigade, excepting the 1st and 2nd Battalions of the 8th Regiment, which he held in reserve.

The 5th and 13th French Dragoons finding themselves likely to be thus seriously impeded both in front and on their left, and finally experiencing on their right a cannonade from the two batteries attached to Colonel Kämpfen's Brigade, which had moved forward from the height above Tongrines to the rise of ground south of Tongrenelle. retired from this part of the field.

It will be recollected that Colonel Stülpnagel's Brigade, on relieving that of Colonel Langen in front of Sombref, had extended a chain of skirmishers along the stream as far as Ligny: these were now reinforced by both the 3rd Battalions of the 31st Regiment and the 6th Kurmark Landwehr, with the 3rd Battalion of the 5th Kurmark Landwehr in reserve. The 1st and 2nd Battalions of the Kurmark Landwehr were posted on the height between Sombref and Bois du Loup, having on their right and somewhat in advance, two squadrons from each of the 5th and 6th Regiments of Kurmark Landwehr Cavalry, together with two guns from the Foot Battery No. 12. The remaining four battalions of the brigade were in reserve immediately in front of the enclosures of Sombref.

It was nearly eight o'clock, when General Krafft despatched an *aide de camp* to the rear with a message stating, that it was only by dint of extraordinary efforts that the troops in Ligny could hold out against the enemy, who was continually advancing with fresh reinforcements. General Count Gneisenau (the Chief of Staff of the Prussian Army), in the absence of the prince, sent word that the village must be maintained, at whatever sacrifice, half an hour longer.

About the same time, General Pirch II. sent word to Blücher that his brigade, in defending St Amand la Haye, had expended the whole of its ammunition, and that even the pouches of the killed had been completely emptied. To this the prince replied, that the Second Brigade must, nevertheless, not only maintain its post, but also attack the enemy with the bayonet.

In fact, the exhaustion of the Prussian troops was becoming more manifest every moment. Several officers and men, overcome by long continued exertion, were seen to fall solely from excessive fatigue. No kind of warfare can be conceived more harassing to the combatants than was the protracted contest in the villages which skirted the front of the Prussian position. It partook also of a savage and relentless character. The animosity and exasperation of both parties were uncontrollable. Innumerable individual combats took place. Every house, every court, every wall, was the scene of a desperate conflict. Streets were alternately won and lost. An ungovernable fury seized upon the combatants on both sides, as they rushed wildly forward to relieve their comrades exhausted by their exertions in the deadly strife—a strife in which every individual appeared eager to seek out an opponent, from whose death he might derive some alleviation to the thirst of hatred and revenge by which he was so powerfully excited. Hence no quarter was asked or granted by either party.

When it is considered that a very great portion of the Prussian Army consisted of young soldiers, who were under fire for the first time, their bravery and exertions in maintaining so lengthened a contest of this nature, with the veteran warriors of the French Army, cannot fail to be regarded with the highest admiration.

Such were the distribution and the state of the Prussian troops throughout their line, when Napoleon arrived near the lower extremity of Ligny, with a formidable reserve. This consisted of eight battalions of the Guard, of Milhaud's Corps of Heavy Cavalry, comprising eight regiments of *cuirassiers*, and of the *Grenadiers à Cheval* of the Guard. It was not, however, his sole reserve; for most opportunely Lobau's corps had just arrived and taken post on the right of Fleurus. The troops which the French emperor held thus in hand ready to launch as a thunderbolt against the weakened centre of the Prussian line of battle, were perfectly fresh, not having hitherto taken any part whatever in the contest, and they might justly be styled the flower of his army.

It was this consciousness of the vantage ground he then possessed which, upon his perceiving the comparatively unoccupied space in rear of Ligny, called forth from him the remark to Count Gérard, "They are lost: they have no reserve remaining!" He saw that not another moment was to be delayed in securing the victory which was now within his grasp, and gave his last orders for the attack at the very time when Blücher, whose right had just been strengthened by the arrival of the remaining three battalions of Colonel Langen's (the Eighth) Infantry Brigade, was making his dispositions for vigorously assailing the French Army in its left flank.

The projected movement that was to decide the battle was preceded, at about half past eight o'clock, by the rapid advance of several batteries of the Guard, which opened a must destructive tire upon the Prussians posted within, and formed in the immediate rear of, Ligny. Under cover of this cannonade, Gérard, with Pecheux's infantry division, reinforced the troops that still maintained that half of the village which lay on the right bank of the rivulet, and pushed forward with a determination to dislodge the enemy from the remaining portion on the left flank. While the Prussian infantry in rear of Ligny were in movement for the purpose of relieving their comrades who were already giving way before this renewed attack, they suddenly perceived, on the French right of the village, a column issuing from under the heavy smoke that rolled away from the well served batteries which had so unexpectedly opened upon them, and, which continued so fearfully to thin their ranks; and, as the mass rapidly advanced down the slope with the evident design of forcing a passage across the valley, they could not fail to distinguish both by its well sustained order and compactness, and by its dark waving surface of bearskins, that they had now to contend against the redoubted Imperial Guard. Ligny being thus turned, the Prussian infantry, instead of continuing its advance into the village, was necessitated, by its inferiority of numbers, to confine its operations to the securing, as far as possible, an orderly retreat for the defenders of the place.

Notwithstanding their dreadfully exhausted and enfeebled state, and their knowledge that a body of fresh troops was advancing against them, a body, too, which they knew was almost invariably employed whenever some great and decisive blow was to be struck, they evinced not the slightest symptom of irresolution, but, on the contrary, were animated by the most inflexible courage. The sun had gone down, shrouded in heavy clouds, and rain having set in, the battlefield would speedily be enveloped in darkness; hence the Prussians felt that it required but a little more perseverance in their exertions to enable them to counterbalance their deficiency of numbers upon any point of their Line by a stern and resolute resistance, sufficient to secure for the entire of their army the means of effecting a retreat, unattended by those disastrous consequences which a signal defeat in the light of day might have entailed upon them.

The 21st Regiment of Infantry boldly advanced against the French column, with a determination to check its further progress; but soon found itself charged in flank by cavalry that had darted forward from the head of a column which, by the glimmering of its armour, even amidst the twilight, proclaimed itself a formidable body of *cuirassiers*. It was, in fact, Milhaud's whole corps of *cuirassiers*, which had effected its passage on the other side of the village. The 9th Regiment of Infantry fought its way through a mass of cavalry, whilst Major Wulffen, with two weak squadrons of the 1st Westphalian Landwehr Cavalry, made a gallant charge against the French infantry, which received it with a volley at a distance of twenty paces. The Prussian infantry compelled to evacuate Ligny, effected its retreat in squares, in perfect order, though surrounded by the enemy, bravely repelling all further attacks, made in the repeated but vain attempts to scatter it in confusion.

Blücher, who had arrived upon the spot from his right, having, in consequence of this sudden turn of affairs, been under the necessity of relinquishing his meditated attack upon the French left, now made a last effort to stem the further advance of the enemy, and, if possible, to force him back upon Ligny. The rain having ceased, it became lighter, and the enemy's columns being more clearly discernible, the prince immediately ordered the advance of three regiments of the cavalry attached to the First *Corps d'Armée*, namely, the 6th Uhlans, the 1st West Prussian Dragoons, and the 2nd Kurmark Landwehr Cavalry. These regiments, which constituted the only cavalry force immediately at hand, had for some time been posted in reserve, and had suffered severely from their exposure to the fire from the French artillery. Lieutenant General Röder directed the 6th Uhlans to make the first charge. The regiment was led on by Lieutenant Colonel Lützow, to whose brigade it belonged. In the charge which was directed upon the enemy's infantry, Lützow and several of his officers fell under a volley of musketry.

The regiment, which was about 400 strong, lost on this occasion 13 officers and 70 men. A second attack, made by the 1st West Prussian Dragoons, and supported by the 2nd Kurmark Landwehr Cavalry, seemed to offer a fair prospect of penetrating the French Infantry, when the former regiment was unexpectedly charged in flank by the enemy's *cuirassiers*, and completely dispersed. The Westphalian, and 1st Kurmark Landwehr Cavalry, with several other squadrons of the *landwehr*, were collected together, and formed a mass of twenty four squadrons, with which a further attack was made upon the enemy, but without success.

The cause of this failure is to be attributed not to the want of sufficient cavalry, for indeed there was an ample number for the purpose, but to the confusion and disorder consequent upon the surprise which the enemy's attack had occasioned, and which was augmented by the darkness that had set in upon the field. Nor was the failure caused by the absence of that most essential requisite in a charge of cavalry, good example on the part of the officers who lead the well set squadrons into the midst of an enemy's ranks.

Blücher himself, seeing that the fate of the day depended solely on the chance of the cavalry at hand succeeding, while there was yet light, in hurling back the French columns into the valley which they had so suddenly and so resolutely crossed, rallied his routed horsemen; and placing himself at their head, charged, in his old Hussar style, with the full determination of restoring, if possible, that equal footing with the enemy which had hitherto been so gallantly maintained. The French firmly stood their ground, and the charge proved ineffectual. As Blücher and his followers retired to rally, they were rapidly pursued by the French *cuirassiers*.

At this moment, the prince's fine grey charger—a present from the Prince Regent of England—was mortally wounded by a shot, in its left side, near the saddle girth. On experiencing a check to his speed, Blücher spurred, when the animal, still obedient to the impulse of its gallant master, made a few convulsive plunges forward; but on feeling that his steed was rapidly losing strength, and perceiving at the same time the near approach of the *cuirassiers*, he cried out to his *aide de camp*:—"Nostitz, now I am lost!" At that moment the horse fell from exhaustion, rolling upon its right side, and half burying its rider under its weight. Count Nostitz immediately sprang from his saddle, and holding with his left hand the bridle of his own horse, which had been slightly wounded, he drew his sword, firmly resolved to shed, if necessary, the last drop of his blood in defending the precious life of his revered general. Scarcely had he done so, when he saw the *cuirassiers* rushing forward at the charge.

To attract as little as possible their attention, he remained motionless. Most fortunately, the rapidity with which the *cuirassiers* advanced amidst the twilight, already sensibly obscured by the falling rain. precluded them from recognising, or even particularly remarking, the group, although they swept so closely by that one of them rather roughly brushed against the *aide de camp's* horse. Shortly afterwards, the Prussian cavalry having rallied, and reformed, in their turn began to drive back the French. Again the thunder of their hoofs approached, and again the flying host whirled past the marshal and his anxious friend; whereupon the latter. eagerly watching his opportunity as the pursuers came on, darted forward, and seizing tire bridle of a non-commissioned officer of the 6th Uhlans, named Schneider, ordered him and some files immediately following, to dismount and assist in saving the prince.

Five or six powerful men now raised the heavy dead charger, while others extricated the fallen hero, senseless and almost immoveable. In this state they placed him on the non-commissioned officer's horse. Just as they moved off, the enemy was again pressing forward with renewed speed, and Nostitz had barely time to lead the marshal, whose senses were gradually returning, to the nearest infantry, which received the party, and, retiring in perfect order, bade defiance to the attacks of its pursuers.

The Horse Battery No. 2, which had supported these cavalry attacks by directing its fire against the left flank of the enemy, became, all at once, surrounded by French dragoons. These vainly endeavoured to cut the traces, and the Prussian artillerymen defended themselves so well that they succeeded in effecting the escape of the battery through an opening in the enclosures of Bry. The Foot Battery No. 3, however, was overtaken in its retreat by the enemy's cavalry, between the windmill and Bry, and lost one of its guns.

During these cavalry attacks, the Prussian infantry, already exhausted, and broken up into separate divisions by the desperate contest in the valley, had collected together at the outlets of the villages. Some of the Regiments presented a remarkable degree of steadiness and good order. At length the cavalry brigade of General Treskow, then comprising the Queen's and the Brandenburg Dragoons, and the Brandenburg Uhlans, were brought forward, and made several attacks upon the French infantry and *cuirassiers*. Colonel Langen advanced, at the same time, from near the windmill, with the only battalion of his brigade remaining at his disposal, the 2nd of the 23rd Regiment, under the guidance of General Pirch I., and covered by the cavalry of General Treskow; but all his efforts proved unavailing.

He himself was wounded, and then driven over by a gun. The battalion, however, by continuing in admirable order, enabled General Pirch I., on whom, at this time, the defence of Ligny had devolved, to effect the retreat of the troops from the village. General Jagow retired, with a part of his brigade to Bry, and immediately occupied this point. Some battalions of General Krafft's Brigade (the Sixth) fell back from Ligny, towards the high road, leaving Bry on their left; others still more to the left towards Bry.

General Pirch II., whose brigade (the Second) had been posted by the prince in rear of St Amand la Haye, preparatory to a renewed attack, was upon the point of proceeding to support the Seventh and Eighth Brigades, then seriously engaged, when lie observed the retreat towards Bry. He immediately withdrew his brigade to this point, where he supported and facilitated the retreat of the troops from the village, with the assistance of the twelve pounder Battery No. 6, and the Foot Battery No. 34, as also of the Westphalian Landwehr Cavalry, under Major Wulffen, to which latter corps several dragoons that had become separated from their own regiments, attached themselves.

General Grolman, the quartermaster general of the Prussian Army, foreseeing the consequences of the line having been thus broken by the enemy, hastened to Bry, and desired General Pirch II. to cover the retreat by means of the troops here collected together. He then proceeded in the direction of Sombref, and finding near this place two battalions of the 9th Regiment (Sixth Brigade) he posted them in rear of a hollow road, leading from Bry towards Sombref. These battalions had, in their retreat from Ligny, defeated several attempts on the part of the enemy's cavalry to break them. Grolman, on perceiving a twelve pounder had stuck fast in this hollow road, ordered the battalions to advance again in front of the latter, to assist in extricating the battery, and to protect its retreat; which was immediately accomplished within view of the French cavalry.

It was at this critical period of the battle, that the 2nd Battalion of the 1st Westphalian Landwehr, which still continued in reserve, in rear of Bry, under the command of Captain Gillnhaussen, appeared upon the height in front, where it particularly distinguished itself. In the first place it succeeded in effectually checking, by its vigorous fire, the French *cuirassiers*, who were in pursuit of the Prussian infantry. Then it drove back French cavalry which was on the point of making a fresh attack upon the Prussian dragoons. Afterwards it successfully withstood three charges by the French cavalry of the Guard. General Grolman now ordered this battalion to join the 9th Regiment near Sombref; and, with the latter, to take up a position at the junction of the cross road from Ligny with that from Bry to Sombref. This position, which was in rear of the before mentioned hollow road, was maintained until past midnight.

Such were the circumstances resulting from the French having forced the Prussian line at Ligny, and pursued in the direction of Bry: it is now necessary to explain what occurred at that time, at, and in the vicinity of Sombref.

The First Brigade, which had been placed in reserve, was ordered to take post, in squares, upon the high road to Sombref, to check the pressure of the enemy's cavalry. Subsequently, when the direction of the retreat was decided upon, it fell back upon Tilly. The Fourth Brigade, with the exception of one or two battalions, advanced again through Sombref towards Ligny, just as the French cavalry pushed towards the high road. The battalions of the brigade formed squares, and fell back upon the high road, whence they continued their further retreat.

At the time the French troops were debouching from Ligny, Colonel Stülpnagel's (the Twelfth) Brigade was posted in front of Sombref; and Colonel Rohr had just pushed forward towards Ligny with the 2nd Battalion of the 6th Kurmark Landwehr, when he perceived three French cavalry regiments advancing against the right wing of the brigade; whereupon he gradually retired, and the whole brigade threw itself into Sombref, just as the French cavalry made an attack at the entrance of the village, and captured the two guns of the Battery No. 12, which had been posted there. Major Dorville faced about the rear division of the 6th Kurmark Landwehr Cavalry, and gallantly attacked the French cavalry, in the hope of checking their progress; but the lances of his brave followers were shivered against the cuirasses of their opponents, and for a moment the former could only defend themselves with their broken poles. The Prussian infantry, however, hastened forward in support; the French were driven out of the village; and one of the lost guns was retaken.

Every exertion was now made to secure the possession of Sombref. General Borcke (Ninth Brigade) sent thither two battalions of the 1st Kurmark Landwehr; which, during this movement, fired upon the flank of the enemy's cavalry as the latter fell back. The defence of the entrance into the village from the side of Ligny was confided to the 2nd Battalion of the 6th Kurmark Landwehr, under Colonel Rohr.

About this time, General Jürgass received orders to cover with his cavalry (of the Second Corps) the retreat of the Prussian infantry from St Amand la Have and Wagnelé. General Brause, perceiving that the enemy had attacked Colonel Marwitz' cavalry brigade, on his right, and endangered his communication with the rear, hastened with the Fusilier battalions of the 22nd Regiment (which had continued in reserve in rear of St Amand la Have) towards the high road, upon which the greater part of the Seventh Brigade had by this time been collected. The Prussians, on retiring from St Amand la Have, were closely followed by the French. The 1st Battalion of the 14th Regiment was still in the Hamlet of St Amand when it received the order to retire.

During its retreat it was attacked whilst in a hollow way. It immediately showed a front on each flank, and succeeded in driving back the enemy. General Jürgass now sent forward the 4th Squadron of the Brandenburg Hussars to attack the enemy's *tirailleurs*, who were beginning to advance from out of St Amand la Haye. The latter were immediately forced back upon the village. Somewhat later, however, the French *tirailleurs* poured forth in greater numbers from out of Wagnelé, and threw themselves upon the right flank of the retreating troops. A *mêlée* ensued, in which General Jürgass was shot in the shoulder.

When the centre of the Prussian Army had been broken by the French cavalry, and the Prussian commander had been placed so completely *hors de combat*, Lieutenant General Count von Gneisenau, the chief of the staff, having undertaken the direction of affairs, ordered the retreat of the First and Second Corps upon Tilly; and despatched Colonel Thile with directions to Thielemann, that if he could not effect a direct retreat upon Tilly, he was to retire upon Gembloux, there to unite with Bülow, and then effect a junction with the rest of the army.

The occupation of Bry by General Pirch II. offered a safe point of retreat to the disordered Prussian battalions; and, now that it had become quite dark, Pirch led all the troops from this post towards Marbais, where they reformed, and whence, soon afterwards, under the command of Lieutenant General Röder, they continued the retreat upon Tilly. Marwitz' Cavalry Brigade, which was not pursued with much vigour by the enemy, fell back to the rear of the battalions formed up to cover its movement, and now joined the rest of the cavalry of the right wing, in the general retreat.

The Fifth Infantry Brigade was in full retreat upon Marbais when the 1st and 2nd Battalions of the 22nd Regiment still continued posted on the high road, not far from the Trois Burettes. The good order and perfect steadiness of these Battalions, which were commanded by Major Sack, completely checked the further advance of the French Cavalry, and greatly facilitated the retreat of the Prussian troops.

After General Jürgass was wounded, the command of the rear guard devolved upon Lieutenant Colonel Sohr, of whose brigade (the Brandenburg and Pomeranian Hussars) it consisted. He executed this duty with great success, falling gradually back upon the cavalry posted in advance of Tilly by Lieutenant General Zieten; who then took command of the whole of the cavalry employed in protecting the retreat.

During the retreat of the centre of the Prussian Army, which had been effectually broken, and of its right from St Amand and Wagnelé, which, in consequence of Blücher's previous dispositions for his contemplated attack upon the French left, was better prepared to sustain a reverse of this kind; the left wing, under Thielemann, maintained its position, and contributed not a little, by its firm countenance, in diffusing a considerable degree of caution into the French movements in advance.

This was strikingly exemplified by the conduct of the 1st and 2nd Battalions of the 30th Prussian Regiment. They were posted at Mont Potriaux, and although their knowledge of what was passing on other points of the line was very imperfect, still it sufficed to prompt their commander to cross the rivulet, and undertake, if not a vigorous attack, at least a demonstration, which, now that darkness had almost covered the field, would tend to impede, perhaps to paralyse the French movements against the Prussian centre, Having effected their passage, they met at first but a feeble opposition from a line of skirmishers: a French regiment of dragoons then advanced very close upon the 2nd Battalion, but was driven off; whereupon both these battalions pushed forward, and gained a height which was occupied in force by the enemy. Here they sustained two more cavalry attacks, which proved equally unsuccessful. A mass of infantry belonging to Lobau's corps, having its flanks covered by parties of cavalry, now advanced against the 1st Battalion; but having, in the dark, exposed a flank to the battalion, it was also repulsed.

Major Dittfurth, however, finding himself in too isolated a position, did not deem it prudent to advance further upon ground which he knew to be in full possession of the enemy, and therefore retraced his steps.

A renewed attempt was made, at the same time, by the French Light Cavalry Brigade under General Vallin, to push forward along the high road towards Sombref, and gain possession of the barrier; but the attack was as abortive as had been the former one upon this point.

With the darkness of night, now rapidly deepening, the din of battle, which had been terrific and incessant until the last faint glimmering of twilight, became gradually hushed: its expiring sounds still issuing from the heights in front of Bry, whence the flashes from the fire of artillery, and from that of skirmishers along the outskirts of this village (held by General Jagow with the 1st and 2nd Battalions of the 9th Regiment, and the 2nd Battalion of the 1st Westphalian Landwehr), indicated to the French Army the extreme verge of its advance; while the still more vivid flashes emitted from the rattling musketry fire of the two battalions of the 30th Regiment, which had so gallantly sallied forth out of Mont Potriaux, under Major Dittfurth, as previously described, as also from the Prussian guns which defended the approach to Sombref, and frustrated the renewed attack along the high road inwards that point, plainly intimated that the Prussian left wing (Thielemann's corps) still firmly maintained itself in a position whence it might seriously endanger the flank of any further movement in advance against the centre.

Vandamme's corps (the Third) bivouacked in advance of St Amand, Gérard's Corps (the Fourth) in front of Ligny, the Imperial Guard upon the heights of Bry, Grouchy's cavalry in rear of Sombref, and Lobau's corps (the Sixth in rear of Ligny. This possession of the field of battle, and the capture of 21 pieces of cannon, were the only advantages of which the French could boast as the immediate result of so severe a struggle. With these, however, it would seem that their emperor was fully satisfied: if he had entertained any idea of pursuit, it was now abandoned; he took no measures for watching the movements and prying into the designs of his adversary: but left his troops resting in their bivouacs, offering no molestation whatever to the Prussians, whilst he in person returned to Fleurus, where he passed the night.

The contrast between the circumstances of the two armies during the night was very striking; for whilst the victors were indulging in perfect repose, the vanquished were completely on the alert, seizing every possible advantage which the extraordinary quietude of their enemies afforded during the precious hours of darkness; and never, perhaps, did a defeated army extricate itself from its difficulties with so much adroitness and order, or retire from a hard fought field with so little diminution of its moral force.

The Prussian commander was carried to Mélioreux. about six miles in rear of Ligny, and the headquarters were established there for the night.

Thielemann still retained possession of his original position in the line of battle; and General Jagow, with several detached battalions belonging to Zieten's corps, occupied Bry and its immediate vicinity. From this position the latter general quietly effected his retreat about an hour after midnight, taking the direction of Sombref, and thence proceeding to Gembloux, presuming, in all probability, that the general retreat would be towards the Meuse. It was not until three o'clock in the morning, when the field of battle had been completely evacuated by the remainder of the Prussian Army, that Thielemann commenced his retreat, which he conducted slowly, and in perfect order, to Gembloux; near which Bülow's *Corps d'Armée* (the Fourth) had arrived during the night.

The loss of the Prussian Army on the 15th and 16th of June, amounted in killed and wounded to about 12,000 men: that of the French to between 7,000 and 8,000. But few prisoners were taken on either side.

In consequence of this defeat, Blücher was compelled, in order to maintain and secure his close communication with Wellington, to abandon the line of the Meuse between Namur and Liege; but his orderly and unmolested retreat afforded him sufficient time to remove all his stores and material from these points to Maestricht and Louvain, which now constituted his new base of operations.

It was not, however, a defeat which involved the loss of every advantage previously gained. Blücher was *not* driven from the field: but, on the contrary, he maintained it during the night, with the exception of the villages of Ligny and St Amand in his front; thus facilitating the orderly retreat of his own army, and, at the same time, affording a considerable degree of security to the direct line of retreat of the Duke of Wellington.

The defeat certainly compelled the latter to retire on the following morning, whatever might have been his success at Quatre Bras; but so long as Blücher had it in his power to fall back in such a manner as to effect his junction the next day with Wellington, the advantage which accrued to the common object of the two commanders was of the highest importance. They would then unite after the concentration of each army had been accomplished; hitherto, they had been compelled to meet their opponents before they had succeeded in collecting their respective forces. If, however, Wellington had been unable to maintain his ground against Ney, and Napoleon had in this manner succeeded in beating both armies in detail; or, if the Prussian defeat had been followed up by a vigorous pursuit, the loss of the Battle of Ligny might have placed both armies in a critical position.

The struggle at Ligny was undoubtedly of a most desperate and sanguinary character. It was, almost throughout, one continued village fight; a species of contest which, though extremely harassing and destructive to both parties engaged, was that most likely to prove of a long duration, and consequently to afford a better prospect of relief by the promised support from Wellington, or by the hoped-for junction of Bülow.

It remains a question whether Blücher, had he confined himself during the latter part of the action to the same defensive system he had so successfully carried on up to that time, instead of detaching his reserves to the right, and preparing for an attack upon the enemy's left, might not have fully maintained his original position until dark, and thus have saved his army from defeat. By the arrival of Bülow's corps during the night, he would then have been prepared to meet his opponent on the following morning with a greatly preponderating force; whilst, on the other hand, Wellington, having concentrated a considerable portion of his army, would have been placed in an equally advantageous position as regards the already vanquished enemy in his own front.

When it is considered that along the whole extent of Blucher's line, the French had not gained any material advantage upon one single point, and that the Prussians continued to hold their ground with most exemplary firmness; the circumstance of his not having delayed the collecting of his reserves, for a grand attack upon the enemy's left, until actually joined by either the British or Bülow's troops, can scarcely be explained except by a reference to the peculiar character of the Prussian chief, whose natural fiery temperament led him, in all probability to seize with avidity the first prospect which opened itself of a favourable opportunity of aiming a deadly thrust at his hated foe, rather than to adhere to that comparatively passive kind of warfare which so ill-suited his own individual inclination and disposition.

Napoleon had undoubtedly gained the victory from the moment he succeeded in penetrating the Prussian centre; but it was not distinguished by that brilliant success, or by those immediate and decisive advantages, which might have been anticipated from the admirable manner in which the attack had been prepared, and the care with which it was concealed from the Prussians, at a moment when they had no reserve remaining, and when the co-operation of the British on their right, or the arrival of Bülow's corps from Hannut, had become quite impracticable. This appears the more surprising when we reflect that he had a considerable corps of cavalry under Grouchy at hand to support this attack, and that the whole of Lobau's corps was in the field, fully prepared for active operations.

The consequences resulting from the absence of energetic measures on the part of the French emperor, in following up the defeat of the Prussians, on the evening of the 16th and morning of the 17th, will be fully developed in a subsequent chapter.

CHAPTER 7

The Prussians at Tilly

The bivouac on the field of Quatre Bras, during the night of the 16th, continued undisturbed until about an hour before daylight, when a cavalry patrol having accidentally got between the adverse picquets near Piermont, caused an alarm in that quarter that was quickly communicated to both armies by a rattling fire of musketry, which, rapidly augmenting, extended itself along the line of the advanced posts. Among the first who hastened to ascertain the origin and nature of the engagement was Picton, who, together with other staff officers, as they arrived in succession, on discovering that no advance had been attempted or intended on either side, soon succeeded in restoring confidence. Similar exertions were successfully made on the part of the French officers, and as day began to break upon the scene, both parties resumed their previous tranquillity. In this untoward affair, the picquets furnished by Kielmansegge's Hanoverian Brigade, and by the 3rd Brunswick Light Battalion were sharply engaged, and a picquet of the Field Battalion Bremen suffered considerably.

It was not long before Wellington, who had slept at Genappe, arrived at Quatre Bras, where he found Major General Sir Hussey Vivian, whose brigade of Light Cavalry, consisting of the 10th British Hussars (under Colonel Quentin), of the 18th British Hussars (under Lieutenant Colonel the Hon. Henry Murray), and of the 1st Hussars of the King's German Legion (under Lieutenant Colonel von Wissell), was posted on the left of that point with two strong picquets thrown out; one, of the 18th Hussars, under Captain Croker, on the Namur road, and the other, of the 10th Hussars, under Major the Hon. Frederick Howard, in front—with a picquet from the latter, under Lieutenant Arnold, on the right of the Namur road.

Vivian, on being asked what account he could give of the enemy, communicated to the duke the result of his observations, which were necessarily very limited, as, with the exception of the firing that had taken place, as before mentioned, along the line of picquets, the French had continued perfectly quiet, and had as yet given no indication of any offensive movement.

The duke then took a general survey of the field, and while sweeping the horizon with his telescope, he discovered a French vedette on some rising ground, in the direction of Fleurus, and a little to the right of the high road leading to Namur, apparently belonging to some picquet thrown out from Ney's extreme right on the previous night, after the battle had ceased; or to some detached corps placed in that quarter for the purpose of observation, and for the maintenance of the communication between Napoleon and Ney. The duke had received no intelligence of Blücher; and, probably, judging from the advanced position of the vedette in question that whatever might have been the result of the Battle of Ligny, the Prussians could not have made any forward movement likely to endanger Ney's right, he came to the conclusion that it was quite possible that, on the other hand. Napoleon might have crossed the Namur road, and cut off his communication with Blücher, with the design of manoeuvring upon his left and rear, and causing him to be simultaneously attacked by Ney. His Grace therefore desired Vivian to send a strong patrol along the Namur road to gain intelligence respecting the Prussian Army.

A troop of the 10th Hussars, under Captain Grey, was accordingly despatched on this duty, accompanied by Lieutenant Colonel the Hon. Sir Alexander Gordon, one of the duke's *aides de camp*. As the patrol advanced along the road, the vedette before mentioned began to circle, evidently to give notice of the approach of an enemy, and then retired. This induced the patrol to move forward with great caution, so as to guard against the possibility of being cut off. Nevertheless it continued, but with all due precaution, advancing along the road, until after passing a few scattered cottages, comprising a hamlet called Petit Marbais, it reached, about a mile and a half further on, some rising ground, about five miles from Quatre Bras, and beyond which was another height. A vedette was observed posted upon the latter, but who had evidently not yet discovered the approach of Captain Grey's troop. Down in the intervening hollow was an isolated house, at the door of which stood a dismounted sentry, and some horses were standing in an adjoining yard.

Captain Grey directed Lieutenant Bacon to patrol towards the house, while he remained with the remainder of the troop, concealed from the enemy's view, a disposition favoured by the nature of the ground, and the trees in the hedges, on both sides of the road. When Lieutenant Bacon's party moved forward, it was discovered by the vedette, who began circling, and fired his carabine. The French picquet posted in the house instantly rushed out; several of the men had their jackets and accoutrements off; and the post could easily have been captured, had the special duty on which the British patrol was engaged admitted of an attack. The French turned out very quickly and galloped to the rear along the high road, while Bacon's party was recalled. A few French cavalry galloped up to the vedette on the heights, but evinced no disposition to advance.

It had now become sufficiently evident that, commencing from this point, the French were in possession of the Namur road; but the principal object which Sir Alexander Gordon had in view was yet to be attained. The patrol now retired a little until it reached a cross road, which a peasant pointed out as the Prussian line of retreat. Pursuing this track, the patrol, within an hour, reached Tilly; where General Zieten, who had been placed in temporary command of the cavalry, was covering the retreat of the Prussian Army.

After remaining here about a quarter of an hour, during which Sir Alexander Gordon obtained from General Zieten the most ample information respecting the movements of the Prussians, the Patrol commenced its return, at a quick pace, striking into a cross road, which joined the high road at a point nearer to Quatre Bras than the one whence it had quitted it. The patrol reached Quatre Bras at about half past seven o'clock; and Sir Alexander Gordon immediately reported to the duke that the Prussians had retreated towards Wavre, that the French occupied the ground on which the battle had been fought; but that they had not crossed the high road, along which the patrol had proceeded almost into the immediate vicinity of their advanced posts.

This latter circumstance was very remarkable, and served to satisfy Wellington that, either Napoleon's victory had not been followed up with a vigour and an effect, by which the safety of his own army would have been periled, or, that it had not been of a character sufficiently decisive to have enabled the French emperor to avail himself of such a vantage ground.

Having ascertained that the contingency for which, as has already been explained, he was fully prepared, had actually taken place; he instantly decided upon retrograding his troops to a position in front of the point of junction of the roads leading from Charleroi and Nivelles upon Brussels, in which he might rely upon the co-operation of a sufficient portion of Blücher's forces from Wavre with his own, by which he would be enabled to confront Napoleon and his main army with ample means, and thus attain that great aim and end of all strategy, of "operating with the greatest mass in a combined effort upon a decisive point."

Hence, a change in the direction of the previously ordered movements became necessary, and the following instructions were issued:—

To General Lord Hill.

17th June 1815.

The Second Division of British Infantry to march from Nivelles on Waterloo, at 10 o'clock.

The brigades of the Fourth Division, now at Nivelles, to march from that place on Waterloo, at 10 o'clock. Those brigades of the Fourth Division at Braine le Comte, and on the road from Braine le Comte to Nivelles, to collect and halt at Braine le Comte this day.

All the baggage on the road from Braine le Comte to Nivelles to return immediately to Braine le Comte, and to proceed immediately from thence to Hal and Bruxelles.

The spare musket ammunition to be immediately parked behind Genappe.

The corps under the command of Prince Frederick of Orange will move from Enghien this evening, and take up a position in front of Hal, occupying Braine le Château with two battalions. Colonel Estorff will fall back with his brigade on Hal, and place himself under the orders of Prince Frederick.

Shortly after the departure of the before mentioned patrol of the 10th Hussars, along the Namur road, the duke received some despatches from England, to which he gave his attention; and now that he had satisfied himself as to the real state of things, and issued his orders for the movements of his distant troops, as also for the retreat of those present in the field, he laid himself down on the ground near Quatre Bras, covered his head with one of the newspapers he had been reading, which had accompanied those despatches, and appeared to fall asleep.

After remaining some time in this state, he again rose, mounted his horse, and rode a little distance down the field in front of Quatre Bras. He then looked about through his telescope, and expressed to those about him his astonishment at the perfect stillness of the enemy, remarking at the same time, "What if they should be also retiring? It is not at all impossible."

A second officer, Lieutenant Massow, had been despatched from the Prussian to the Anglo-Allied Headquarters; and it was about this time that he reached the duke, with a verbal communication respecting the retreat upon Wavre, and the position intended to be assumed in that quarter. It was of a nature which, taken altogether, was so far satisfactory, that Wellington immediately sent a verbal message by this officer to Blücher, acquainting him with his intended retrograde movements, and proposing to accept a battle, on the following day, in the position in front of Waterloo, provided the prince would detach two corps to his assistance.

The following is the manner in which the retreat of the Anglo-Allied infantry, then in full operation, was executed. It was an important matter to mask the retreat as much as possible, so as to gain time for the free and unimpeded movement of the army along the high road leading to the position in front of Waterloo. For this purpose, the Light Troops continued to maintain the line of outposts, until their respective supports, which had remained stationary sufficiently long to conceal the retreat of the troops in their rear, began also to retire.

The First and Fifth British Divisions, and the Second Dutch-Belgian Division, as also the Brunswick Corps, effected their retreat in excellent order, notwithstanding the delay that was created by the narrowness of the bridge and street of Genappe. Their retreat was covered by Alten's division, to which were added for this purpose, the 1st Battalion of the 95th British Panes, the 2nd and 3rd Brunswick Light Battalions, the Brunswick Advanced Guard Battalion, and the Light Companies of Byng's Brigade of Guards.

The main body of Alten's division commenced its retreat about eleven o'clock. Ompteda's Brigade of the King's German Legion was withdrawn to Sart à Mavelines, which it immediately occupied, as also the wood of Les Censes in its front. Halkett's British Brigade then retired secretly until it reached some favourable ground, a little distance in rear of Ompteda's Brigade, upon which it was immediately drawn up. Kielmansegge's Hanoverian Brigade was withdrawn still further to the rear, and occupied a third position. Thus posted, the division was ordered, in the event of being attacked, to retire by brigades alternately.

It was a little before midday when the Light Troops of Alten's division began to retire. They occupied the advanced line, commencing from the southern extremity of the wood of Bossu on the right, extending along Gemioncourt and the enclosures of Piermont, and crossing the Namur road on the left: from which line they gradually and slowly fell back upon Ompteda's Brigade, in a manner evincing admirable skill, steadiness, and regularity.

In order more effectually to mask the movements on the Allied side of the Namur road, the whole of the cavalry was drawn up in two lines immediately contiguous to, and in rear of, that road; the Heavy Cavalry forming the Second Line, and picquets being thrown out from the First Line, to relieve those of the retiring Infantry.

The main body of Alten's division now commenced its further retreat; but not by alternate brigades, this mode having been directed only in the event of an attack; the latter retired successively in the order in which they stood, preserving their relative distances, so that they might commence the alternate system of retreat, if attacked. To facilitate the passage of other portions of the army through the narrow defile of the bridge and town of Genappe, this division retired by Bezy, and crossed the Genappe, lower down the stream, by the bridge of Wais le Hutte.

In the early part of the morning, Ney had, like his opponent, been ignorant of the result of the Battle of Ligny: but he was aware that the Anglo-Allied Army had been considerably reinforced during the night, principally by the arrival of its cavalry.

The marshal calculated that if Napoleon had gained a victory, and crossed the Namur road, the longer Wellington remained in the position of Quatre Bras, the greater the danger he incurred of having not only his communication with Blücher effectually cut off, but also his main line of retreat upon Brussels intercepted; and that in such a case it was wiser not to advance against the British general, as the latter might then retire, and thus elude the effect of a combined operation between Napoleon's and his own forces. He also judged that if, on the other hand, the French emperor had been defeated, an attack made on his own part, upon the Anglo-Allied Army, might subject himself to the risk of having to contend against a combined operation between Wellington and Blücher; and thus expose both his own and Napoleon's forces to the probability of being defeated in detail.

In this uncertainty, Ney sent a message by General Count Flahaut, who happened to be still with him, and who was returning to rejoin the Emperor wherever he might be found, expressive of his anxiety to learn the result of the action of the preceding day. In the mean time, he kept his troops in a state of perfect quietude; his main body was posted in reserve on the heights of Frasne, between which and the outposts there were intermediate columns of support; but no movement whatever was attempted.

Ney at length received the information he had solicited, in a despatch from Soult, wherein the result of the Battle of Ligny was briefly described. It also stated that Napoleon was proceeding, with the principal portion of his forces, to the mill of Bry, close to which the high road leads from Namur to Quatre Bras, and that therefore it would not be practicable for the Anglo-Allied Army to act against him (Ney); but that, should such a case happen, the emperor would march directly upon it by that road, while Ney should attack it in front, and in this manner that army would at once be destroyed. The despatch required from Ney a report of the exact position of his forces, and an account of all that was going on in his front.

Hence it is evident that Ney's opinion, that a victory at Ligny ought to be followed up by a combined attack upon Wellington, perfectly coincided with Napoleon's views; but while Ney was thus justified in remaining inactive during the early part of the day, the fact of the emperor's not moving directly upon Genappe with the morning's dawn, and his excessive delay in breaking up his bivouac at Ligny, are inexplicable. A glorious opportunity had presented itself for the attainment of his original design of defeating both armies in detail, but which was completely lost by a most extraordinary and fatal want of energy and vigour in seizing upon the advantages which the victory of Ligny had placed within his reach.

Ney, having ascertained that Napoleon's forces were in motion, had commenced the advance of his own troops, when a second despatch reached him, dated, "in front of Ligny, at noon," intimating that the emperor had just posted a corps of infantry and the Imperial Guard in advance of Marbais, that he wished him to attack the enemy at Quatre Bras, and force him from his position; and that his operations would be seconded by the corps at Marbais, to which point His Majesty was proceeding in person.

Upon discovering that the Anglo-Allied Infantry had retired, and that the troops around, and in rear of, Quatre Bras, consisted of cavalry covering the retreat, Ney brought forward his own cavalry in advance, and appeared to regulate its movements so that its attack might be directed against the front of the British simultaneously with that of the cavalry which he now perceived advancing along the Namur road against its flank.

About this time, the 10th Hussars were moved across the Namur road, and down the slope in front where they were halted, in *echelon* of squadrons: and while they were thus posted, Wellington and his staff came to the front of the regiment. From this spot the duke was attentively watching, through his telescope, the dispositions and movements of the French, whom he could discover as soon as they reached the Quatre Bras side of Little Marbais; when all at once at a distance of about two miles, masses were seen forming on the side of the Namur road, conspicuously glittering in the sun's rays; by which the duke was at first induced to believe that they were infantry, whose bayonets were so brilliantly reflected; but it was soon discovered that they were *cuirassiers*.

After a short time, these were observed to advance, preceded by lancers, and it was not long before the picquet of the 18th British Hussars, posted on that road, began skirmishing, as did also the picquet of the 10th British Hussars, more in the front of the position, and likewise, still further to the right, in front of Quatre Bras, a picquet consisting of a squadron of the 11th British Light Dragoons, detached from Major General Vandeleur's Brigade, which comprised the 11th Light Dragoons (under Lieutenant Colonel Sleigh), the 12th Light Dragoons (under Colonel the Hon. Frederick Ponsonby), and the 16th Light Dragoons (under Lieutenant Colonel Hay). The 10th Hussars then fell back again into their proper place in the line. Vivian now took up a new alignment, throwing back his left so as to present a front to the enemy's advance, and to protect the left of the position. Vandeleur's Brigade was then in right rear of Vivian's and close to Quatre Bras.

The Anglo-Allied infantry having, some time previously, entirely crossed the Genappe, with the exception of the Light Companies of the Second Brigade of Guards on the right, and of the 1st Battalion 95th British Regiment (Rifles), on the left, which troops had been directed to remain until the last moment, and were now retiring to Genappe (where they were subsequently drawn up at the entrance of the town), and the duke having satisfied himself that a formidable body of the French cavalry was endeavouring to fall upon him and to molest his retreat, it became a question with His Grace, at that moment, how far it might be advisable to offer any serious resistance to the advance of the enemy; but Lieutenant General the Earl of Uxbridge, the commander of the Anglo-Allied cavalry, having remarked that, considering the defiles in the rear, and the distance to which the great mass of the infantry had already retired and from which it could offer no immediate support, he did not think the cavalry was favourably situated for making such an attempt, the duke assented to the correctness of this view, and requested His Lordship at once to carry into effect the retreat of the cavalry.

Uxbridge immediately made the following dispositions for this purpose. The First or Household Brigade of Heavy Cavalry commanded by Major General Lord Edward Somerset, and consisting of the 1st Life Guards (under Lieutenant Colonel Ferrior), of the 2nd Life Guards (under Lieutenant Colonel the Hon. Edward P. Lygon), of the Royal Horse Guards, or Blues (under Lieutenant Colonel Sir Robert Chambre Hill), and of the 1st (or King's) Dragoon Guards (under Colonel Fuller), together with the Second Brigade of Heavy Cavalry, commanded by Major General the Honourable Sir William Ponsonby, consisting of the 1st, or Royal Dragoons (under Lieutenant Colonel Clifton), of the 2nd Royal North British Dragoons, or Scots Greys (under Colonel Hamilton), and of the 6th, or Inniskilling Dragoons (under Colonel Muter), formed the centre column, which was to retire by the Brussels high road.

Vandeleur's and Vivian's Brigades constituted the left column, which was to effect its retreat by a bridge over the Genappe at Thuy, still lower down the stream than that by which Alten's infantry division had crossed.

The right column was formed of part of the Third Light Cavalry Brigade, commanded by Major General Sir William Dörnberg, the 1st and 2nd Light Dragoons of the King's German Legion (under Lieutenant Colonels Bülow and de Jonquières), while the remaining regiment, which was the 23rd British Light Dragoons (under Colonel the Earl of Portarlington), was employed as a portion of the rear guard of the centre column. The 15th British Hussars (under Lieutenant Colonel Dalrymple), belonging to the Fifth Cavalry Brigade, under Major General Sir Colquhoun Grant, was also attached to the right column; while of the two remaining regiments of the brigade, the 2nd Hussars of the King's German Legion (under Lieutenant Colonel Linsingen), and the 7th British Hussars (under Colonel Sir Edward

Kerrison), the former had been left in occupation of a line of posts on the French frontier, extending from Courtrai, through Menin, Ypres, Loo, and Fürnes, to the North Sea, and the latter formed a part of the rear guard of the centre column. This right column was to pass the Genappe by a ford higher up the stream than the town of Genappe.

These skilful dispositions had scarcely been arranged, when the picquet of the 18th Hussars, on the left, came in at a good round trot, followed by two or three squadrons of French cavalry, upon which Vivian's Battery of Horse Artillery, opened a fire whereby their advance was checked. The enemy, however, was observed to be very active in bringing up his artillery, which soon opened upon the Hussar Brigade. Vivian, having received the Earl of Uxbridge's instructions to retire, accompanied with an intimation that he would be supported by Vandeleur's Brigade, then in his rear, and observing that the French cavalry was pressing forward in great numbers, not only in his front, but also on his flank, he put his brigade about, and retired in line, covered by the skirmishers. The French followed, with loud cries of "*Vive l'Empereur!*" and just as the brigade reached a sort of hollow, their guns again opened, throwing shells, which mostly flew over the heads of the 18th Hussars, against which regiment they appeared to be principally directed.

In the meantime, Vandeleur's Brigade had been drawn up in support, on rather a commanding position, and Vivian approached it in the full expectation that it would open out for the passing through of his own men, and take the rear guard in its turn; but on the Hussars arriving within fifty or sixty yards of the Fourth Brigade, Vandeleur put it about, and retired—Vivian not being aware that Vandeleur had previously received orders to retire and leave the road clear for the retreat of the cavalry in his front. Vivian immediately occupied the ground thus vacated, and, with a view to check the enemy's advance more effectually, ordered the 18th Hussars to charge, as soon as the French approached within favourable reach.

The weather, during the morning, had become oppressively hot; it was now a dead calm; not a leaf was stirring; and the atmosphere was close to an intolerable degree; while a dark, heavy, dense cloud impended over the combatants. The 18th Hussars were fully prepared, and awaited but the command to charge, when the brigade guns on the right commenced firing, for the purpose of previously disturbing and breaking the order of the enemy's advance. The concussion seemed instantly to rebound through the still atmosphere, and communicate, as an electric spark, with the heavily charged mass above. A most awfully loud thunder clap burst forth, immediately succeeded by a particularly heavy fall of rain.

In a very few minutes the ground became perfectly saturated; so much so that it was quite impracticable for any rapid movement of the cavalry. The enemy's lancers, opposed to the Sixth British Brigade, began to relax in their advance, and to limit it to skirmishing; but they seemed more intent upon endeavouring to envelope, and intercept the retreat of the Hussars. Vivian now replaced the 18th Hussars by the 1st Hussars of the King's German Legion, as rear guard, with orders to cover well the left flank and left front of the brigade. He had already sent off his battery of Horse Artillery, to cross the Genappe by the bridge of Thuy, and despatched an *aide de camp* to Vandeleur, to request he would move his brigade as quickly as possible across that bridge, so that he might meet with no interruption in his retreat, in the event of his being hard pressed.

Of the centre column, the Heavy Brigades of Lord Edward Somerset and Sir William Ponsonby had retired along the Charleroi road, and were taking up a position on some high ground, a little in rear of Genappe, on either side of that road. The detached Squadron of the 11th Light Dragoons (under Captain Schreiber), was withdrawn and directed to retire through the above town. The 23rd Light Dragoons were also withdrawn, and posted upon the ascent between Genappe and the position occupied by the two Heavy Brigades. The 7th Hussars continued on the south side of Genappe, as rear guard.

Neither the centre, nor the right, column experienced any serious molestation in its retreat while on the French side of the Genappe: large bodies of cavalry were seen in motion, but their advanced guards limited their attacks to skirmishing.

At length the 7th Hussars retired through Genappe, after having thrown out their right squadron, commanded by Major Hodge, as rear guard, to cover the retreat of the centre column, regulating its proceedings in conformity with such orders as it might receive from Major General Sir William Dörnberg, who had been desired to superintend the movements of the skirmishers. Major Hodge led out the right troop, under Captain Elphinstone, to skirmish, while Lieutenant Standish O'Grady, who commanded the left troop, held the high road, from which he had occasionally to send assistance to the former, and frequently to advance, to enable the skirmishers to hold their ground, as their movements were difficult, through ploughed fields so soft that the horses always sank up to their knees, and sometimes to their girths. In this manner, every inch of ground was disputed, until within a short distance of Genappe.

Here Dörnberg informed Lieutenant O'Grady that he must leave him; that it was of the utmost importance to face the enemy boldly at this spot, as the Bridge in the town of Genappe was so narrow that the squadron would have to pass it in file; that he was to endeavour as much as possible to obtain time for drawing off the skirmishers, but not to compromise his troop too much. Lieutenant O'Grady then called in his skirmishers, and advanced with his own troop boldly up the road at a trot. The cavalry immediately opposed to him, went about, followed by him for some distance; and he thus continued alternately advancing and retiring, until he saw all the right troop safe on the road in his rear. He then began to retire at a walk, occasionally halting and fronting, until he turned the corner of the town of Genappe: when he filed the men from the left, and passed through the place at a gallop. Upon the arrival of the squadron at the opposite entrance of Genappe, it was posted between this point and the main body of the 7th Hussars, which had been drawn up on the road in a column of divisions, prepared to check the advance of the enemy on his debouching from the town.

The British left cavalry column continued its retreat, which was towards the little bridge of Thuy, by deep narrow lanes, converted by the tremendous pour of rain into perfect streams. Vivian withdrew the 10th and 18th Hussars from the position he last occupied, but on their approaching the Genappe an interruption occurred in consequence of Vandeleur's Brigade not having effected its passage across the bridge; and the delay became so great that he was induced to put about the 18th Hussars, with a view to their affording a support to the 1st German Hussars, should they require it. In a short time after this, Vandeleur's Brigade resumed its progress: the 10th Hussars followed; and, as the 1st Hussars, with which regiment Vivian himself was at the moment, continued to maintain a vigorous and effective skirmish, he ordered the 18th to resume its retrograde movement; having previously directed that some men of the 10th Hussars should be dismounted on reaching the opposite bank of the Genappe, and be prepared with their carbines to defend the passage, should the retreat of the remainder of the brigade be severely pressed.

After skirmishing some time, Vivian despatched a squadron of the 1st German Hussars to the bridge, and the moment he began to do so, the French cavalry again pushed forward with so much boldness and rapidity as to interpose between the left squadron and the main body of the regiment, and to compel that squadron to pass the Genappe lower down than the bridge over which the brigade passed the little stream. Having ascertained that all was ready, Vivian galloped down the road to the bridge with the remainder of the 1st German Hussars. The French followed them, loudly cheering, but as soon as the hussars cleared the bridge, and the enemy's dragoons reached it, some of the dismounted men that had been formed along the top of the opposite bank, in rear of a hedge, overlooking the bridge and a hollow way, through which the road led from it up the ascent, opened a fire upon the foremost of the French lancers that had come up to the other end of the bridge, while the remainder of the 10th, and the whole of the 18th Hussars, were drawn up along the rising ground or bank. The good countenance here shown by Vivian's Brigade, combined with the soft and miry state of the ground after the thunderstorm had set in, completely checked the pursuit by the enemy's cavalry, which now turned towards the high road.

The left cavalry column, after Vivian's Brigade had remained in its position for some little time, continued its retreat without further molestation (the enemy having contented himself with merely detaching a patrol to watch its movements) along a narrow cross road, running nearly parallel with the Charleroi high road, and leading through the villages of Glabbaix, Maransart, Aywiers, Frischermont, Smohain, and Verd Cocou. Here Vivian's brigade arrived in the evening, in the vicinity of the forest of Soignies, and bivouacked; while Vandeleur's Brigade passed the nighl somewhat nearer to the ground which had been selected for the position to be taken up by the Anglo-Allied Army.

The right cavalry column, consisting only, as previously stated, of the 1st and 2nd Light Dragoons of the King's German Legion, and of the 15th British Hussars, effected its retreat in good order, protected by its skirmishers, as far as the ford, which it crossed above Genappe. At this point, the French cavalry suspended its pursuit, and proceeded, in like manner as that on the right had done, to join the main body on the high road; while the British right cavalry column continued its retreat unmolested towards the position of Waterloo, in rear of which it bivouacked.

A large body of French cavalry, consisting of from sixteen to eighteen squadrons, was now entering Genappe by the Charleroi road, followed by the main body of the French Army under Napoleon.

The Earl of Uxbridge, who was desirous of checking the enemy's advance, so as to gain sufficient time for the orderly retreat of the Anglo-Allied Army, and to prevent a compromise of any portion of the rearmost troops, decided upon embracing the advantage which the narrow defile of Genappe seemed to present in aid of his design. The town consists mainly of houses lining the high road, on the Brussels' side of the bridge. The road then ascends a ridge, the brow of which is about six or seven hundred yards distant, and here Lord Uxbridge had halted the Heavy Brigades of Lord Edward Somerset and of Sir William Ponsonby, and posted them so as to cover the retirement of the Light Cavalry.

At first, he formed them in line; Somerset's on the right, and Ponsonby's on the left, of the high road; but observing by the enemy's formidable advance, that the Light Cavalry would soon be compelled to fall back, His Lordship drew up Somerset's Brigade in a column of half squadrons upon, but close to, the right of the road itself, so as to admit of troops retiring by its left; and formed Ponsonby's Brigade into a column of half squadrons upon the left of the high road, and somewhat to the rear. The 7th Hussars were formed at some little distance in the rear of Genappe, and the 23rd Light Dragoons were drawn up in support of that regiment, and about midway between it and the Heavy Cavalry on the height. The squadron of the 7th Hussars, under Major Hodge, it will be recollected, was halted between the main body of that regiment and the town of Genappe.

Thus posted, the centre retiring cavalry column remained about twenty minutes, when loud shouts announced that the French had entered the town. Presently a few horsemen appeared galloping out of the street, and dashed at speed into Major Hodge's squadron. They were found, on being taken, to be quite inebriated. In a few moments afterwards, the French column showed its head within the town; the leading troop consisted of lancers, all very young men, mounted on very small horses, and commanded by a fine looking, and, as it subsequently appeared, a very brave man. The column remained about fifteen minutes within the town, its head halted at the outlet facing the British rear guard, and its flanks protected by the houses. The street not being straight, and the rear of the column not being aware that the front had halted, continued pressing forward, until the whole mass became so jammed that it was impossible for the foremost ranks to go about, should such a movement become necessary.

Their apparent hesitation and indecision induced Lord Uxbridge, who stood upon some elevated ground adjoining the right of the road, to order the 7th Hussars to charge. The latter, animated by the presence of the commander of the cavalry, who was also their own colonel, rushed forward with the most determined spirit and intrepidity; while the French, awaiting the onslaught, opposed to them a close, compact, and impenetrable *phalanx* of lances; which, being securely flanked by the houses, and backed by a solid mass of horsemen, presented a complete *chevaux de frise*. Hence, it is not surprising that the charge should have made no impression upon the enemy; nevertheless, the contest was maintained for some considerable time; the hussars cutting at their opponents, and the latter parrying and thrusting, neither party giving way a single inch of ground; both the commanding officer of the lancers, and Major Hodge, commanding the leading squadron of the hussars, were killed, gallantly fighting to the last.

The French had by this time established a battery of Horse Artillery on the left of Genappe and upon the opposite bank of the river, from which they opened a brisk fire upon the British Cavalry in support, and several shot struck the main body of the 7th Hussars, upsetting men and horses, and causing great impediments in their rear. The French lancers now advanced, and drove the 7th Hussars upon their reserve; but here the 7th rallied, renewed their attack, and forced back the lancers upon the town. The latter having been reinforced, rallied, in their turn, and drove back the hussars. These, however, again rallied, and resolutely faced their opponents, with whom they gallantly continued a fierce encounter for some time longer, when to terminate a conflict which was most obstinate and sanguinary without being productive of any favourable result, but in which the bravery of the 7th Hussars shone most conspicuously, and became the theme of admiration of all who witnessed it,

Lord Uxbridge decided upon withdrawing that regiment and charging with the 1st Life Guards. As soon as the hussars went about, in pursuance of the orders received, the lancers followed them. In the *mêlée* which ensued, the French lost quite as many men as did the hussars; and when at length the latter were able to disengage themselves, the former did not attempt to follow thorn. The 7th retired through the 23rd Light Dragoons, took the first favourable turn off the road and reformed in the adjoining field.

During this contest, the French, having become sensible of the evil that might arise from the closely wedged state of the cavalry in the town, began to clear the rear of the most advanced portions of the column, so as to admit of more freedom of movement in case of disaster. A battery of British Horse Artillery had taken post close to a house on the height occupied by the Heavy Cavalry, and on the left of the road; and it was now replying to the French battery on the opposite bank of the river.

So exceedingly elated were the French with having repulsed the 7th Hussars in this their first serious encounter with the British cavalry, that immediately on that regiment retiring, the whole column that was in Genappe raised the war cry, and rent the air with shouts of "*En avant!—En avant!*" evincing the greatest impatience to follow up this momentary advantage, and to attack the supports; for which, indeed, the opportunity appeared very favourable, as the ranks of the latter were suffering considerable annoyance from the well directed and effective fire of the French guns on the opposite bank of the river.

They now abandoned the secure cover to which they had been indebted for their temporary success, and were advancing up the ascent with all the confidence of a fancied superiority, when the Earl of Uxbridge, seizing upon the advantage presented for attacking them while moving up hill, with their flanks unsupported, and a narrow defile in their rear, and being also desirous of affording the 1st Life Guards an opportunity of charging, brought forward that regiment through the 23rd Light Dragoons, who opened out for its passage to the front.

The Life Guards now made their charge, most gallantly headed by Colonel Sir John Elley, deputy adjutant general, who, at the moment of contact with the enemy, began by cutting down two men right and left. It was truly a splendid charge; its rapid rush down into the enemy's mass, was as terrific in appearance as it was destructive in its effect; for although the French met the attack with firmness, they were utterly unable to hold their ground a single moment, were overthrown with great slaughter, and literally ridden down in such a manner that the road was instantaneously covered with men and horses, scattered in all directions. The Life Guards, pursuing their victorious course, dashed into Genappe, and drove all before them as far as the opposite outlet of the town.

This brilliant and eminently successful charge made a deep impression upon the enemy, who now conducted his pursuit with extreme caution. The 23rd Light Dragoons, which had supported the 1st Life Guards in their charge, became again the last regiment in the rear guard, and continued so during the remainder of the retreat. Ponsonby's Brigade had deployed to the right of the high road, and the guns were so disposed as to take advantageous positions, retiring *en échiquier.*

The enemy, after quitting Genappe, tried to get upon the flanks of the centre retiring column, chiefly upon the right flank; but the Royals, Greys, and Inniskillings, manoeuvred beautifully; retiring by alternate squadrons, and covered by their own Skirmishers, who completely beat the French Light Cavalry in that kind of warfare. Finding that from the deep state of the ground, there was not the least danger of his being turned by the enemy, Lord Uxbridge gradually withdrew Ponsonby's Brigade to the high road. He kept the Light Cavalry, protected by the Household Brigade, as the rear guard, and slowly retired into the chosen position m front of Waterloo, the guns and rockets constantly plying the enemy's advance, which, although it pressed forward twice or thrice, and made preparations to attack, never ventured to come to close quarters with its opponents; and the column received from it no further molestation.

On arriving at the foot of the Anglo-Allied position, the 23rd Light Dragoons moved off to the (Allied) right of the high road, and into the hollow in which lies the orchard of the Farm of La Haye Sainte. Here they were drawn up, prepared to meet the French advanced guard, should it follow them, or to fall upon its Flank, should it venture to continue its march along the road. The latter, however, halted upon the height which intervenes between La Haye Sainte and La Belle Alliance, and opened a fire upon the centre of the Duke of Wellington's line, above the former farm, from two batteries of Horse Artillery.

Picton, who was then upon the rising ground in rear of La Haye Sainte, and who was intently watching the enemy's advance along the high road, perceived columns of infantry advancing from La Belle Alliance. He immediately took upon himself to unite the two batteries nearest at hand, which were those under Major Lloyd of the British artillery, and Major Cleeves of the King's German Legion (although not belonging to his own division), and to place them in position on the high ground close to the Charleroi road. The guns immediately opened a brisk cannonade upon the French columns, of which they had obtained a most accurate range just as their leading divisions had entered the enclosed space between the high banks which line the high road where it is cut through the height before mentioned as intervening between La Belle Alliance and La Haye Sainte. This mass of the enemy's infantry suffered severely from the fire, to which it stood exposed about half an hour: for the head of the column having been unable to retrograde, in consequence of the pressure from its rear, and prevented by the high bank on either side of the road from filing off to a flank, could not readily extricate itself from so embarrassing a situation.

During the whole of this fire, the Allied batteries were replied to, though very ineffectually, by the two batteries of French Horse Artillery posted on the height in question.

It was now twilight: the approaching darkness was greatly accelerated by the lowering aspect of the sky. Picquets were hastily thrown forward by both armies, and to so great a height had the mutual spirit of defiance arisen, that the near approach of opposing parties, advancing to take up their ground for the night, led to little cavalry affairs, which, though unproductive of any useful result to either side, were distinguished, on different points of the lines, by a chivalrous bravery which seemed to require a prudent restraint.

In one of these affairs, Captain Heyliger of the 7th Hussars, made a very brilliant charge with his troop; and when the Duke of Wellington sent to check him, His Grace desired to be made acquainted with the name of an officer who had displayed so much gallantry. A very spirited charge was also made by the right troop of the 2nd Light Dragoons of the King's German Legion, under Lieutenant Hugo; who was allowed by his commanding officer to volunteer for that service, and who, from the vicinity of Hougomont, boldly rushed up the height intervening between that point and Mon Plaisir, and gallantly drove back a portion of the French advanced guard of cavalry; recapturing at the same time three carriages filled with British sick and wounded.

The manner in which the Duke of Wellington withdrew his army from the position of Quatre Bras to the one of Waterloo, must ever render that retreat a perfect model of operations of this nature, performed in the immediate presence of a powerful enemy. Those dispositions which have been described as having been made by him for the purpose of masking the retirement of the main body, of affording perfect security to the passage of the defile in his rear, and of ensuring the orderly and regular assembly of the several corps on the ground respectively allotted to them in the new position, evince altogether a degree of skill which has never been surpassed.

In such operations, the covering of the army by its cavalry and Light Troops necessarily forms an important feature; and a glance at the manner in which this duty was fulfilled by the Earl of Uxbridge, with the cavalry, Horse Artillery, and a few Light Battalions, at his disposal, is sufficient to show that the exemplification of such feature on this occasion was exceedingly beautiful. Indeed, so orderly and so perfect were all the arrangements connected with this retreat, from its commencement to its close, that the movements partook more of the appearance of a Field Day upon a large scale, than of an operation executed in the actual presence of an enemy; and this was particularly observable as regarded the protection afforded by the cavalry and Horse Artillery, which manoeuvred to admiration, and in a style that, combined with the brilliant charge by the 1st Life Guards at Genappe, evidently impressed the enemy with a due sense of the efficiency of the gallant troops immediately in his front.

In the course of the evening, the duke received from Prince Blücher a reply to the request he had made for his support in the position he was now occupying. It was highly characteristic of the old man, who had written it, in the following terms, without previously conferring with, or addressing himself to, anyone:—

I shall not come with two corps only, but with my whole army; upon this understanding, however, that should the French not attack us on the 18th, we shall attack them on the 19th.

The duke, who, as has already been explained, had, from the commencement of the campaign, considered it very possible that Napoleon would advance by the Mons road, still entertained apprehensions of an attempt on the part of his opponent to turn him by Hal, and seize Brussels by a *coup de main*. For this, however, he was fully prepared, having made his dispositions for the security of that flank, in the manner pointed out in the following instructions, which he issued to Major General the Hon. Sir Charles Colville:—

17th June 1815.
The army retired this day from its position at Quatre Bras to its present position in front of Waterloo.
The brigades of the Fourth Division, at Braine le Comte, are to retire at daylight tomorrow morning upon Hal.
Major General Colville must be guided by the intelligence he receives of the enemy's movements in his march to Hal, whether he moves by the direct route or by Enghien.
Prince Frederick of Orange is to occupy with his corps the position between Hal and Enghien, and is to defend it as long

as possible.

The army will probably continue in its position in front of Waterloo tomorrow.

Lieutenant Colonel Torrens will inform Lieutenant General Sir Charles Colville of the position and situation of the armies.

The respective lines of picquets and vedettes had scarcely been taken up along the low ground that skirted the front of the Anglo-Allied position, and the last gun had just boomed from the heights, when "heaven's artillery," accompanied by vivid flashes of lightning, again peeled forth in solemn and awful grandeur; while the rain, pouring down in torrents, imparted the utmost gloom and discomfort to the bivouacs, which the opposing armies had established for the night, upon the ground destined to become one of the most celebrated in history.

CHAPTER 8

Preparations of Troops

It was not until the night of the 16th, after Zieten's and Pirch's *corps d'armée* had retired to Tilly and Gentinnes, that it was decided the Prussian Army should retreat upon Wavre. This decision was communicated in the orders then transmitted from the Prussian Headquarters to the First and Second *Corps d'Armée* (Zieten's and Pirch's) directing them to bivouac at Bierge and St Anne, in the vicinity of Wavre; as also in the orders forwarded, on the next morning, to the bivouacs of the Third and Fourth Corps (Thielemann's and Bülow's), at Gembloux and Basse Bodecée, directing them to fall back, and bivouac at La Bavette and Dion le Mont near Wavre.

Zieten's and Pirch's corps retired by Mont St Guibert, in rear of which defile the latter corps remained a considerable time as rear guard, while the former marched on to Wavre, where it arrived about midday, crossed the Dyle, and took up its position at Bierge. Pirch followed the same route, but took post on the right bank of the Dyle, between St Anne and Aisemont.

With the first glimmering of daylight the troops, which, under the command of General Jagow, had continued in full possession of Bry and its immediate vicinity during the night, began to retire, firstly, in the direction of Sombref, and thence to Gembloux, which they reached before the arrival of Thielemann's corps. After the receipt of the order pointing out the direction of the retreat, Jagow conducted these troops, in the course of the 17th, towards their respective brigades.

Lieutenant Colonel Sohr, whose cavalry brigade with half a horse battery, formed the rear guard of the line of retreat of Zieten's and Pierch's corps, received orders to take up a concealed position between Tilly and Gentinnes, thence to watch the movements of the enemy; and, as soon as he found himself pressed by the latter, to fall back upon the defile of Mont St Guibert.

Thielemann, who, it will he recollected, had received a message from Gneisenau, leaving it optional with him to retire by Tilly or Gembloux, according to circumstances, decided on falling back upon the latter point; being well aware that the enemy was in possession of the villages of St. Amand and Ligny, and of the field of battle to within a very short distance from Sombref.

He had collected together his widely disseminated brigades, and drawn in his advanced posts; an operation which, executed in the darkness of the night, retarded his departure so much that it was two o'clock in the morning before the reserve artillery, which formed the head of the column, struck into the road which at Point du Jour, leads from the Namur *chaussée* to Gembloux. The rear guard of this line of retreat, which consisted of the Ninth Infantry Brigade, under Major General Borcke, and the reserve cavalry, under General Hobe, and was drawn up along the Namur road, having in its front the Fleurus *chaussée*. Leading directly towards the enemy, did not commence its march until after four o'clock, when the sun had risen. The main body of the corps reached Gembloux at six o'clock in the morning.

On approaching this place, Thielemann learned that Bülow had posted the Fourth Corps about three miles in rear of Gembloux, upon the old Eoman road; whereupon Major Weyrach, *aide de camp* to Prince Blücher, who had continued with Thielemann during the night of the 16th, set off to seek out the field marshal, and to report to him the position and attendant circumstances of the Third and Fourth *Corps d'Armée*. He soon succeeded in discovering the Prussian Headquarters at Mélioreux, and communicated the above important information to Count Gneisenau.

Thielemann gave his own corps a halt on the other side of the town, in order that his troops might obtain rest and refreshment.

The advance of Bülow's corps had reached Basse Bodecée, upon the old Roman road, at nightfall of the 16th of June. Here that general became acquainted with the loss of the Battle of Ligny: whereupon he ordered the brigades of his corps to be posted at intervals along this road, with the exception of the Thirteenth (under Lieutenant General Hake), which was directed to bivouac more to the rear, near Hotto-ment, where the same road is intersected by that which conducts from Namur to Louvain.

Both corps remained for some hours in a state of uncertainty as to the direction to be taken for forming a junction with the First and Second Corps. Thielemann wrote to Bülow that he had received no orders from Prince Blücher, but that he presumed the retreat was upon St Trond. He also stated that he had not been followed by the enemy, but that he had heard distant firing on the right, which he concluded was connected with the Duke of Wellington's Army.

At length, about half past nine o'clock, Prince Blücher's *aide de camp*, Major Weyrach, arrived at Bülow's Headquarters, and brought the orders for the retreat of the Fourth Corps to Dion le Mont, near Wavre, by Walhain and Corbaix. The orders also required that Bülow should post the main body of his rear guard (which consisted of the Fourteenth Brigade) at Vieux Sart; as also that he should send a detachment, consisting of one regiment of cavalry, two battalions of infantry, and two guns of Horse Artillery, to the defile of Mont St, Guibert, to act, in the first instance as a support to Lieutenant Colonel Sohr, who was at Tilly, and then, upon the latter falling back, to act as rear guard in this direction. Lieutenant Colonel Ledebur was accordingly detached upon this duty with the 10th Hussars, the Fusilier battalions of the 11th Regiment of Infantry and 1st Regiment of Pomeranian Landwehr, together with two guns from the Horse Battery No. 12. The corps itself moved directly upon Dion le Mont, and on reaching: the height near that town, on which is situated the public house of *A tous vents*, took up a position close to the intersection of the roads leading to Louvain, Wavre and Gembloux.

At two o'clock in the afternoon, Thielemann commenced his march upon Wavre; where the corps arrived late in the evening, and took up its position at La Bavette, leaving the Ninth Infantry Brigade (General Borcke) and the cavalry brigade of Colonel Count Lottum, on the right bank of the Dyle. In this position the corps was now rejoined by Colonel Marwitz' Cavalry Brigade, which had retired by Tilly; as also by the 2nd Battalion of the 3rd Kurmark Landwehr, and the two squadrons of the 6th Kurmark Landwehr Cavalry, which troops had been left at Dinant. The squadron of the 7th Uhlans that had been detached to Onoz, also joined, but having fallen in with a superior force of the enemy's cavalry, had experienced a great loss. The two squadrons of the 9th Hussars, belonging to this corps, had not yet arrived from Ciney.

The Prussian Headquarters were established, early on the 17th, at Wavre. The veteran field marshal, who was still suffering considerably in consequence of his fall, was obliged to seek rest the moment he arrived there, and did not quit his bed during the remainder of the day.

In the course of the forenoon, Lieutenant Massow, who had been despatched with a message to the Duke of Wellington, returned with the one from His Grace, communicating the intention of the latter to fall back upon Waterloo and accept a battle there, provided he received the support of two Prussian corps. (See chapter 7.) There was every disposition to enter into this proposal, but some degree of uncertainty existed as to whether Bülow's corps would join the army on the 17th, as also a certain misgiving respecting the park of ammunition of both Zieten's and Pirch's corps, which had been directed upon Gembloux, a circumstance that excited apprehensions as to the possibility of furnishing the much needed supply of ammunition to these corps which were at hand. In this state of uncertainty, no other resolution could be adopted than that of holding the position in front and in rear of the Dyle (with the advanced guard of the Fourth Corps as far forward as Mont St Guibert), until the required ammunition should be obtained; and Blücher deferred replying to Wellington's communication, in the hope that his army would very soon be relieved from the unpleasant circumstances above mentioned.

While the Prussians were thus effecting their retreat in good order, along the cross roads of that part of the country (high road there was none), no corresponding activity manifested itself on the part of the French, whom the morning's dawn found still lying in their bivouac. Their vedettes stood within half a mile of the columns of Thielemann's rear guard; the retreat of which, not having commenced until after sunrise, might have been easily remarked: and had the French detached but the smallest patrol, they could not have failed to discover the direction of that retreat—whether towards Namur or Gembloux.

It was not until after Thielemann had retired a sufficient distance to escape further notice that any disposition for movement occurred to disturb the perfect quietude of their repose. Then, Pajol with a division of his Light Cavalry Corps, under Lieutenant General Baron Soult, consisting of the 1st, 4th, and 5th Hussars, was detached in pursuit of the Prussians. He struck into the Namur road, and shortly afterwards Lieutenant General Baron Teste's infantry division of Lobau's corps (the Sixth), followed in support, and took up a position on the heights of Mazy.

Pajol had not proceeded very far when he perceived a Prussian battery retiring upon Namur, which he lost no time in capturing and forwarding to headquarters; where the circumstance strengthened the belief that Blücher had retreated by that road. It was the Prussian Horse Battery No. 14, belonging to the Second Corps, which, having towards the end of the battle expended every shot, had driven off the field to procure a fresh supply of ammunition, but had not succeeded in falling in with the Reserve ammunition waggons. The battery neither returned to its own corps, nor did it comply with Thielemann's express order to march upon Gembloux, but consumed much time in uselessly driving first in one direction, and then in another. It was accompanied at this moment by a squadron of the 7th Prussian Uhlans, which the Third Corps had neglected to recall from Onoz. The squadron retired on the approach of the French cavalry, and escaped with a loss of 30 men; but all the guns fell into the hands of the enemy.

Pajol, feeling at last some reason to doubt that Namur was a point in the Prussian retreat, diverged from the high road, and proceeded to St Denis, where he was joined by Teste's division. A brigade of Excelmans' Cavalry Corps had been detached to offer support to Pajol, should the latter require it; but in consequence of certain information, gained upon the road, it was subsequently directed to proceed towards Gembloux, on approaching which it discovered traces of the Prussian retreat.

Grouchy, who commanded the right wing of the French Army in Napoleon's absence, repaired early in the morning to the emperor's quarters at Fleurus, for instructions, according to an order he had received to that effect on the previous evening. He was desired to wait and accompany the Emperor, who was going to visit the field of battle. The latter, however, did not start from Fleurus until between eight and nine o'clock, and on reaching St Amand, he examined the approaches by which this village had been attacked the day before; then, he rode about the field, gave directions for the care of the wounded; and, as he passed in front of different regiments, that were falling in without arms on the ground where they were bivouacked, he was received with loud cheers. He addressed himself to nearly all the corps, and assured them of the lively satisfaction he had felt on witnessing their conduct in the battle. Having dismounted, he conversed freely, and at great length, with Grouchy and Gérard, on the state of public opinion in Paris, the different political parties, and on various other subjects quite unconnected with those military operations upon the successful issue of which depended the stability of his present power.

That Napoleon should have neglected to follow up the advantages which fortune had thrown in his way on the morning of the 17th of June, is quite incomprehensible. With the exception of a Prussian picquet at Gentinnes, his whole front as far as Gembloux, was perfectly clear of an enemy. Wellington was still in position at Quatre Bras, where his left had become exposed by the retreat of the Prussians, and in rear of which point was the defile of Genappe. There was nothing to prevent Napoleon from marching directly upon that defile; and supporting, by a vigorous attack upon the Anglo-Allied left and rear, a simultaneous movement against the front by the force under Ney. Whither had fled the mighty spirit which had shone forth with such dazzling brilliancy in former wars, and which had never displayed the energy of its powers of combination, and activity in following up successes, more eminently than in the campaign of the previous year?

When before did he omit pressing every advantage to the utmost, or neglect to seize that moment of time, in which, having defeated one portion of his enemies, he was enabled to fall with combined force upon another? His army was not more fatigued than was that of Wellington, which had arrived at Quatre Bras by forced marches. The troops which he subsequently did lead upon that point, when it was too late, consisting chiefly of the Imperial Guard and the Sixth Corps, were comparatively fresh. The former had not been engaged at Ligny until towards the termination of the action, when they suffered scarcely any loss; the latter, which arrived later, had remained intact. The idea of forming a junction with Ney, with a view of attacking Wellington, was certainly entertained; but its execution was most unaccountably and unnecessarily delayed until its intended effect could not but fall powerless upon a vigilant enemy, fully prepared, by having improved the precious moments of time, thus lost, to detect the purpose of the movement, and to ward off the intended blow.

With an army greatly inferior in numbers to the united forces of his adversaries, Napoleon's prospects of success rested exclusively upon his utmost skill and address, not only in preventing that union of force, but also in so planning, arranging, and executing his combinations, that having succeeded in defeating one opponent with a superior mass, he might then precipitate himself in like manner upon another, at the very moment when the latter might be occupied or engaged with one of his marshals. This would have exacted of him the most untiring energy, the application of all his great resources in strategical science, a lightning-swift decision, and a daring resolution both in adopting and in executing all his movements.

It was by the exercise of such powerful mental resources as these, that, unaided by a sufficiently corresponding amount of physical force, he had conducted the Campaign of 1814; but the spirit by which they were conceived, and the genius which instinctively seized the means of their execution, seemed to have abandoned him in this, his last campaign: a faint gleam of the old spirit was visible in its opening movements, but it was now rather a wildfire, dazzling him for a moment, on the downward path to his destiny, than the star which had so often led him to victory. The last flash of his genius was brief, and, on the memorable plains of Fleurus, seemed to disappear, and leave him in utter darkness.

The same fatal inactivity which had marked the French emperor's proceedings on the evening of the 15th, and during the morning of the 16th, again manifested itself upon the 17th of June: and it was not until nearly noon of this day, upon receiving a report of a reconnaissance, made in the direction of Quatre Bras, and upon learning that a considerable body of Prussians had been discovered at Gembloux, that he made any disposition for the movement of his troops, beyond the previous detaching of Pajol's Light Cavalry in pursuit of the Prussians along the Namur road.

He now ordered the following troops to proceed to occupy a position in advance of Marbais, across the Namur road, facing Quatre Bras:—

Lobau's Infantry Corps (the Sixth), with the exception of the Twenty First Division, under Lieutenant General Teste, which had already been detached in support of Pajol;

Milhaud's Corps of Heavy Cavalry (*Cuirassiers*),

Lieutenant General Baron Subervie's Light Cavalry Brigade, from Pajol's Corps;

the Third Light Cavalry Division (belonging to the Third Corps), under Lieutenant General Baron Domon:

and the Imperial Guard, both cavalry and infantry.

To Marshal Grouchy he confided the pursuit of the Prussians, and for this purpose he placed at his disposal as great an extent of force as his limited means would admit: a force, certainly not sufficient to enable that marshal to confront the whole Prussian Army, should the latter, after having rallied and concentrated its strength, make a stand against him, but quite so to enable him to watch its movements, and to manoeuvre so as to maintain his communication with the main army, and, if pressed by superior numbers, to effect a junction with Napoleon.

The following were the troops thus detached under Grouchy:—

	Infantry.	Cavalry.	Artillery.	Guns.
Third Corps, General Count Vandamme	14,508	...	936	32
Fourth Corps, General Count Gérard	12,589	2,366	1,538	38
Twenty first Division (Sixth Corps), Lieutenant General Baron Teste	2,316	...	161	8
Fourth Division (First Cavalry Corps), Lieutenant General Count Pajol	...	1,234	154	6
Second Cavalry Corps, Lieutenant General Count Excelmans	...	2,817	246	12
	29,413	6,417	3,035	96
Deduct loss on 16th, ...	3,900	800	400	...
Total . .	25,513	5,617	2,635	96

33,765 men and 96 guns.

The Seventh Infantry Division, under Lieutenant General Girard (belonging to the Second Corps) having suffered very severely in the battle, was left upon the field.

Napoleon's instructions to Grouchy were extremely simple and concise:

> Pursue the Prussians, complete their defeat by attacking them as soon as you come up with them, and never let them out of your sight. I am going to unite the remainder of this portion of the army with Marshal Ney's corps, to march against the English, and to fight them if they should hold their ground between this and the Forest of Soignies. You will communicate with me by the paved road which leads to Quatre Bras.

No particular direction was prescribed, because the emperor was totally ignorant of the real line of the Prussian retreat. At the same time he was strongly impressed with the idea that Blücher had retired upon Namur and Liege, with a view to occupy the line of the Meuse, whence he might seriously endanger right of the French Army, as also its main line of operation, should it advance upon Brussels.

Grouchy did not hesitate to remark to the emperor, that the Prussians, having commenced their retreat at ten o'clock the previous night, had gained several hours' start of the troops with which he was to follow them; that although the reports received from the advanced

218

cavalry conveyed no positive information as to the direction in which the great mass of the Prussian Army had effected its retreat, appearances as yet seemed to justify the supposition that Blücher had fallen back upon Namur; and that as he would thus have to pursue in a direction contrary to that which Napoleon was himself going to take, with very little chance of being able to prevent the execution of any dispositions the Prussians might have resolved upon when quitting the field of battle, he begged to be allowed to follow the emperor in his projected movement upon Quatre Bras.

Napoleon declined to entertain this proposition, repeated the order he had already given to him, adding that it rested with him (Grouchy) to discover the route taken by the Prussians, whose defeat he was to complete by attacking them the moment he came up with them; while he himself would proceed to fight the English.

The order was immediately given for the advance of the troops previously assembled near Marbais, preceded by Subervie's division of Light Cavalry, as advanced guard. By the time they reached Quatre Bras, which was about two o'clock, the whole of Wellington's infantry had crossed the Genappe, and was retiring along the high road to Brussels, protected by the Cavalry, which was now pressed by the French, in the manner described in the preceding chapter.

The march of the French troops through Bry, in the direction of Quatre Bras, became known to the Prussians through Lieutenant Colonel Sohr, who still held his cavalry brigade, even at this time, posted in rear of Tilly. Shortly afterwards, some of the French cavalry having approached, he began to retire slowly towards Mont St Guibert, and, as he frequently formed up, in wait for the enemy, he did not reach that point until the evening of the 17th. Here he found Lieutenant Colonel Ledebur, who had arrived with his detachment, and had received orders to maintain the defile.

Upon the departure of Napoleon, Grouchy ordered Vandamme and Gérard to get their corps under arms, and to move them, in the first instance, to the junction of the Gembloux road with that to Namur; and having subsequently received intelligence that a considerable body of Prussians had passed through the former town, he desired that those two corps should continue their movement upon that point. In the meantime, he repaired to the advanced posts of Excelmans' Dragoons, which were by this time beyond Gembloux. It was part of this cavalry which followed Lieutenant Colonel Sohr, on the left. They merely threw out skirmishers against him; and, as night set in, they abandoned the pursuit in this direction.

The corps of Vandamme and Gérard did not reach Gembloux until very late in the evening. The former was posted in advance, the latter, in rear, of the town; near which also, and on the right bank of the Ormeau, was stationed the Sixth Light Cavalry Division, under General Vallin, who succeeded to the command, upon Lieutenant General Maurin being wounded at the Battle of Ligny. The First Brigade of Lieutenant General Chastel's Tenth Cavalry Division, consisting of the 4th and 12th Dragoons, under General Bonnemain, was pushed on to Sart à Wallain, and the 15th Dragoons (from General Vincent's Brigade of the Ninth Cavalry Division, under Lieutenant General Baron Soult), were detached to Perwès. From both these points, reports were sent into Gembloux that the Prussians had retired upon Wavre.

Pajol, with his Light Cavalry and Teste's infantry division, had returned from St Denis, between Namur and Gembloux, to the original position occupied by the latter in the morning, at Mazy, in the immediate vicinity of the field of Ligny; a movement for which no satisfactory cause has ever been assigned.

The extent of information obtained by Grouchy concerning the Prussian retreat, and the nature of the dispositions which he adopted in consequence, will be best explained by the following despatch which he addressed to the emperor:—

> *Gembloux, le 17 Juin,*
> *à dix heures du soir.*
>
> *Sire,— J'ai l'honneur de vous rendre compte que j'occupe Gembloux et que ma cavalerie est à Sauveniéres. L'ennemi, fort d'environ trente mille hommes, continue son mouvement de retraite; on lui a saisi ici un pare de 400 bétes a cornes, des magasins et des bagages.*
>
> *Il paraît d'après tous les rapports, qu'arrivés a Sauvenières, le Prussiens se sunt divisés en deux colonnes: l'une a dû prendre la route de Wavre, en passant par Sart à Wallain, l'autre colonne parraît s'être dirigée sur Perwès.*
>
> *On peut peutêtre en inférer qu'une portion va joindre Wellington, et que le centre, qui est l'armée de Blücher, se retire sur Liége: une autre colonne avec de l'artillerie ayant fait son mouvement de retraite par Namur, le Général Excelmans a ordre de pousser ce soir six escadrons sur Sart à Wallain et trois escadrons sur Perwès. D'aprés leur rapport, si la masse des Prussiens se retire sur Wavre, je la suivrai dans cette direction, afin qu'ils ne puissent pas gagner Bruxelles, et de les séparer*

de Wellington.

Si, au contraire, mes renseignemens prouvent que la principale force Prussienne a marché sur Perwès, je me dirigerai par cette ville à la poursuite de l'ennemi.

Les Généraux Thielman et Borstell faisaient partie de l'armée que Votre Majesté a battue hier; ils étaient encore ce matin à 10 heures ici, et ont annoncé que vingt mille hommes des leurs avaient été mis hors de combat. Ils ont demandé en partant les distances de Wavre, Perwès et Hannut. Blücher a été blessé légèrement au bras, ce qui ne l'a pas èmpêché de continuer à commander après s'être fait panser. Il n'a point passé par Gembloux.

    Je suis avec respect, de Votre Majesté,
        Sire, le fidèle sujet,
                  Le Márechal Comte de Grouchy.

TRANSLATION

                  Gembloux, 17th June,
                at ten o'clock in the evening.

Sire,—I have the honour to report to you that I occupy Gembloux, and that my cavalry is at Sauvenières. The enemy, about thirty thousand men strong, continues his movement of retreat. We have seized here of his, a pen of 400 horned cattle, magazines and baggage.

It would appear according to all the reports, that, on arrival at Sauvenières, the Prussians divided themselves into two columns: one of which took the road to Wavre, passing by Sart à Wallain; the other column would appear to have been directed on Perwès.

It may perhaps be inferred from this that one portion is going to join Wellington; and that the centre, which is the army of Blücher, is retiring on Liége. Another column with artillery having made its retreat by Namur, General Excelmans has the order to push this evening six squadrons on to Sart à Wallain, and three squadrons on to Perwès. According to their report, if the mass of the Prussians is retiring on Wavre, I shall follow them in that direction, so as to prevent them from reaching Brussels, and to keep them separated from Wellington.

If, on the contrary, my enquiries prove that the principal Prussian force has marched on Perwès, I shall proceed by that town in pursuit of the enemy.

Generals Thielemann and Borstel formed part of the army that Your Majesty defeated yesterday. They were still here at 10 o'clock this morning, and have announced that twenty thousand of their men have been disabled. They asked, in leaving, the distances of Wavre, Perwès, and Hannut. Blücher has been slightly wounded in the arm; which, however, has not hindered him from continuing to command after having his wound dressed. He has not passed by Gembloux.

I am with respect,
Sire,
The faithful subject of
Your Majesty,
Marshal Count de Grouchy.

Although the information conveyed in this despatch was incorrect on some points, and imperfect on others, inasmuch as it represented that Prussian columns had retired upon Namur and Perwès, which was not the case, and gave no account of the columns (First and Second Corps) which had retreated by Tilly and Gentinnes, still it was well calculated to satisfy Napoleon, that at least the spirit of his instructions had been understood by the marshal. The latter had stated that he suspected a portion of the Prussian troops was proceeding to join Wellington, and that, should he ascertain, through his cavalry detached to Sart à Wallain and Perwès, that the great mass of the Prussians was retiring upon Wavre, it was his intention to pursue them in that direction, "so as to prevent them from reaching Brussels, and to keep them separated from Wellington."

Four hours afterwards (that is, at two o'clock on the morning of the 18th) he sent off another despatch to the emperor, reporting that he had decided on marching upon either Corbaix or Wavre.

The retreat of the Prussian Army, after its defeat at Ligny on the 16th of June, was conducted with great skill, and executed in very good order. By detaining Thielemann's corps upon the field of battle until the morning of the 17th, ample security was afforded to the line of retreat by Gembloux; and by not withdrawing Bülow's corps from that town until Thielemann drew near to it, the distance between the main bodies of these two corps became so limited as to present the ready means of opposing their combined force to a vigorous pursuit should such be attempted.

By the evening of the 17th, the entire Prussian Army (with the exception of the Ninth and Thirteenth Brigades, and the Reserve Cavalry of the Third Corps, which arrived by six o'clock on the following morning) had assembled in the immediate vicinity of Wavre—two corps on the right, and the remaining two corps on the left, bank of the Dyle—in perfect order, and fully prepared to resume the offensive. Upon the two lines of retreat, the rear guards were well disposed at Vieux Sart and Mont St Guibert; where they continued during that night, and whence they retired leisurely on the following day.

On the Prussian left, patrols were despatched towards the main road leading from Namur to Louvain. On the right, a detachment was sent from Zieten's corps to Limale, on the left bank of the Dyle, to cover the flank, and patrols were pushed higher up the river, to communicate with the post of Mont St Guibert. Major Falkenhausen had been detached, during the day, to Seroulx for the purpose of reconnoitring the country in the vicinity of Genappe. and of the high road to Brussels; and he succeeded in discovering, from the wooded tracts beyond Seroulx, the advance of the French Army along the *chaussée*. Patrols were also detached towards Lasne, Couture, and Aywiers, to observe the defiles along the rivulet of the Lasne.

Such were the dispositions of the defeated Prussians on the evening of the 17th, while the victorious French had not advanced beyond Gembloux. The former had fallen back, in good order, upon a line with, and a short distance from, the Anglo-Allied Army on their right; while their opponents, though encountering no obstacle of importance, had made but little progress, and were widely diverging from, instead of closely co-operating with, the main army from which they had been detached. These dispositions, so ably planned and so efficiently performed, were well calculated to facilitate the grand operation of the morrow, namely, Blücher's flank movement to the right, to effect a junction with Wellington.

The retreat to Wavre did not in any way incapacitate the Prussian Army for the resumption of actively offensive operations. With respect to its material, it so happened that the Park of Reserve Ammunition Waggons had, in the first instance, been directed upon Gembloux; and Colonel Röhl, who superintended the Ordnance Department of the army, sent his *aide de camp* during the night of the 16th to conduct this reserve to Wavre; whilst he himself hastened to the latter town, for the purpose of putting the whole of the artillery, accordingly as it arrived there, again in a fit state for action. The supply of ammunition, however, was necessarily incomplete; but in order to prevent any failure in this respect, should some mishap occur to the Park of Reserve Ammunition Waggons, a courier was despatched to Maestricht, with directions for the speedy transport of a supply of ammunition from thence to the Army, by means of the common waggons of the country. Similar orders were conveyed to Cologne, Wesel, and Münster: and, by way of precaution, an express was sent to Liege for the removal of the Battering Train to Maestricht; as also for the destruction, in case of danger, of the iron foundry in the arsenal of the former place.

Fortunately, however, the Reserve Ammunition Waggons reached Wavre safely at five o'clock in the afternoon of the 17th. The corps and batteries were furnished with a complete supply of ammunition, and the army was thus placed in a perfectly efficient state for commencing another battle. This turn of affairs was most encouraging, and Blücher delayed not another moment in despatching to Wellington the reply to which allusion has already been made.

As regards the influence which the defeat at Ligny exercised over the morale of the Prussian Army, its injurious effects were made manifest amongst the newly raised drafts from the Rhenish and Westphalian Provinces, and from the Duchy of Berg. Of these troops, 8,000 men betook themselves to a flight which admitted of no check until they reached Liege and Aix la Chapelle. Among the Rhenish troops, particularly those from Provinces which had formerly belonged to France, there were many old French soldiers; and although several of them fought with great bravery, others evinced a bad disposition, and there were instances in which they passed over to their former companions in arms. Such, however, was not the case with the troops from the other western districts of the Prussian State: there was scarcely a single man amongst the missing, who belonged to any of the old Westphalian Provinces, Mark, Cleve, Minden, and Ravensberg, whilst several came from that of Münster.

But the morale of the great mass of the Prussian Army continued unshaken. The spirit of the troops was neither tamed nor broken; and their enthusiasm, though damped, had not been subdued. Unbounded confidence was placed in the firm decision and restless energy of their aged and venerated chief; who, though suffering from the effects of his fall, by which his whole frame had sustained a severe shock, evinced not the slightest apprehension of fatal consequences to the campaign resulting from this defeat. His unbending nature led him to cast aside for the moment those purely political interests and theoretically strategical principles, by which a more cautious and less enterprising commander might have been induced to secure the line of the Meuse, and to preserve his direct communications with the Prussian States, and thus afford but a doubtful and an inefficient support to his ally. Placing full reliance on the resources of his own mind, and on the stern, warlike character of his troops; he devoted his whole energies to the attainment of the one grand object—that of crushing Napoleon by combining with Wellington. This confidence in himself and in his soldiers was strikingly and characteristically manifested in the concluding words of a general order which he issued to the army on the morning of the 17th.

I shall immediately lead you against the enemy;—we shall beat him, because it is our duty to do so.

Towards midnight of the 17th, a communication reached Blücher from General Muffling (already mentioned as having been attached to the British Headquarters) to the following effect.

The Anglo-Allied Army is posted with its right upon Braine l'Alleud, its centre upon Mont St Jean, and its left near La Haye; having the enemy in its front. The duke awaits the attack, but calculates upon Prussian support.

As the last minute of the last hour of the 17th passed to the first minutes of June 18th, 1815 all knew the great day of reckoning was finally upon them.

With the coming day a great battle would be fought to decide the future of the First Empire of the French, Europe and of the emperor himself.

LEONAUR

ALSO FROM LEONAUR
AVAILABLE IN SOFTCOVER OR HARDCOVER WITH DUST JACKET

THE FALL OF THE MOGHUL EMPIRE OF HINDUSTAN *by H. G. Keene*—By the beginning of the nineteenth century, as British and Indian armies under Lake and Wellesley dominated the scene, a little over half a century of conflict brought the Moghul Empire to its knees.

LADY SALE'S AFGHANISTAN *by Florentia Sale*—An Indomitable Victorian Lady's Account of the Retreat from Kabul During the First Afghan War.

THE CAMPAIGN OF MAGENTA AND SOLFERINO 1859 *by Harold Carmichael Wylly*—The Decisive Conflict for the Unification of Italy.

FRENCH'S CAVALRY CAMPAIGN *by J. G. Maydon*—A Special Correspondent's View of British Army Mounted Troops During the Boer War.

CAVALRY AT WATERLOO *by Sir Evelyn Wood*—British Mounted Troops During the Campaign of 1815.

THE SUBALTERN *by George Robert Gleig*—The Experiences of an Officer of the 85th Light Infantry During the Peninsular War.

NAPOLEON AT BAY, 1814 *by F. Loraine Petre*—The Campaigns to the Fall of the First Empire.

NAPOLEON AND THE CAMPAIGN OF 1806 *by Colonel Vachée*—The Napoleonic Method of Organisation and Command to the Battles of Jena & Auerstädt.

THE COMPLETE ADVENTURES IN THE CONNAUGHT RANGERS *by William Grattan*—The 88th Regiment during the Napoleonic Wars by a Serving Officer.

BUGLER AND OFFICER OF THE RIFLES *by William Green & Harry Smith*—With the 95th (Rifles) during the Peninsular & Waterloo Campaigns of the Napoleonic Wars.

NAPOLEONIC WAR STORIES *by Sir Arthur Quiller-Couch*—Tales of soldiers, spies, battles & sieges from the Peninsular & Waterloo campaigns.

CAPTAIN OF THE 95TH (RIFLES) *by Jonathan Leach*—An officer of Wellington's sharpshooters during the Peninsular, South of France and Waterloo campaigns of the Napoleonic wars.

RIFLEMAN COSTELLO *by Edward Costello*—The adventures of a soldier of the 95th (Rifles) in the Peninsular & Waterloo Campaigns of the Napoleonic wars.